3D Creature Workshop

3D Creature Workshop

Bill Fleming

CHARLES RIVER MEDIA
Rockland, Massachusetts

Publisher: David F. Pallai
Executive Editor: Jenifer Niles
Production: Benchmark Productions, Inc.
Cover Design: Printed Image and Komodo Studios
Printer: InterCity Press

CHARLES RIVER MEDIA, INC.
P.O. Box 417
403 VFW Drive
Rockland, Massachusetts 02370
781-871-4184
781-871-4376 (FAX)
chrivmedia@aol.com
http://www.charlesriver.com

This book is printed on acid-free paper.

3D Creature Workshop
Bill Fleming
ISBN 1-886801-78-9
Printed in the United States of America

  99 00 01 02 7 6 5 4

CHARLES RIVER MEDIA titles are available for site license or bulk purchase by institutions, user groups, corporations, etc. For additional information, please contact the Special Sales Department at (781) 871-4184.

Contents

Introduction

No single aspect of 3D creation has been more elusive than creature design. The 3D industry is very young — in fact, it is in its infancy. This presents us with a rather unique and somewhat awkward situation. With the industry being so young, yet growing at such a feverish pace, we are left with very few adequate resources for acquiring knowledge, particularly when it comes to creating realistic 3D creatures.

In spite of the growing number of creatures appearing in film and on TV, very few are truly exceptional. It's not due to lack of talent on the part of the 3D artists, but rather to a need for a better understanding of the 3D creature development process. Countless steps are involved in creating 3D creatures. Most are relatively simple, yet if skipped, they can completely undermine the creature's believability. Of course, not all creatures need to be realistic. In fact, there is great demand for animated creatures as well. Although they are certainly easier to surface than realistic creatures, we still have to invest a great deal of time to ensure the model looks good.

To make a long story short, this book was created to shed light on the process of creating advanced 3D creatures and characters. Although it's certainly not the end-all of 3D creature design, it is a great start on your journey to creating extraordinary 3D creatures. You will explore the critical steps in creating a creature design, model the creature with high detail, and surface it to blow the viewer's mind. There are certainly more topics than we could possibly cover in a mere 450 pages — or 4,500 pages for that matter. This book hits on the key points to ensure that you'll gain a solid foothold for creating 3D creatures. You should find a great deal of the information in this book both informative and thought provoking.

One thing you'll find unique to this book is the fact that it covers both the pros and cons of 3D creature modeling. Tutorials that seem to go from beginning to end without a hitch are annoying, since this never occurs in reality. This book covers reality, both the good and the bad. Creature modeling isn't a matter of simply following a few steps that result in a perfect creature. There is a great deal of tweaking involved and plenty of problem solving along the way. Creature modeling is a love-hate relationship for even the most seasoned creature guru. It requires a great deal of patience and determination to create awe-inspiring creature creations. So if you're up to the challenge of creating eye-popping 3D creatures, this book is just the ticket.

OVERVIEW OF THE BOOK AND TECHNOLOGY

Technology that expands the capabilities of 3D products is steadily being developed. Even the most basic 3D programs now possess many of the essential tools for creating photo-realistic creatures. Though the capabilities of 3D programs will continue to grow, the principles of 3D creature design will always remain constant. This book covers many different approaches to modeling 3D creatures in LightWave 5.5, 3D Studio MAX 2.0, and Animation Master 5. These techniques, although covered for specific programs, are not fixed to just these programs. Basically, polygon, patch, and spline modeling are very similar regardless of the program you are using.

This book covers both a general overview of 3D creature design as well as very specific tutorials for LightWave 5.5, 3D Studio MAX 2.0, and Animation Master 5. If you have older versions of the programs don't worry, most of the techniques can be used in earlier versions of the programs.

HOW THIS BOOK IS ORGANIZED

This book is divided into five parts that will take you logically through the process of developing realistic creatures. Each part is a complete concept, allowing you to reach closure at the end. You don't have to read one part to understand another. If you are interested in modeling creatures only in LightWave you can read Part II and skip the other parts of the book. I do recommend that you read Chapter 9, which covers photorealistic creature surfacing, regardless of which program you actually use. In fact, you'll benefit from the entire book, even the parts that refer to a program you may not have, since the principles of polygon, patch, and spline modeling are common to most programs. Let's take a quick glance at the content of the book.

PART I: CREATURE DESIGN

This part has two chapters that cover the foundation of creating 3D creatures. Every realistic creature begins with a comprehensive design based on a wide variety of factors. These chapters will provide you with a in-depth look at the process of creating realistic creature designs that are ready for animation.

Chapter 1: Realistic Creature Design

Here is where you lay the foundation of 3D creature design. In this chapter you'll learn the major elements of creature design and how to create a creature biography to guide you through the development process. You'll also discover the value of source material and the role it plays in creature design.

Chapter 2: Single Mesh Creature Modeling

Creature animation has come a long way in the past couple years, from jointed creatures that showed obvious seams, to single-mesh creatures that look totally seamless and organic. Of course, this also forced us to redefine the way we model our creatures. In this chapter you'll learn how to model your character for bones animation. You'll also explore the issues regarding creature clothing, such as where to put the wrinkles and how far to inset the ends of the clothes.

PART II: LIGHTWAVE CREATURE MODELING

Although LightWave has been around for many years it really hasn't received much credibility for being a powerful creature animation tool. That's all about to change. LightWave actually has some of the most powerful modeling tools for creating highly detailed creatures. In this part we will cover the principles of creature modeling in LightWave.

Chapter 3: Getting to Know Metaform

Although LightWave is most well known for its MetaNurbs technology, there happens to be a little creature-modeling gem buried within the program that is by far one of the best tools in the industry for creating highly detailed creatures. In this chapter we'll cover the basics of modeling creatures with Metaform. After we get comfortable with the techniques, we'll model a moderately detailed creature using Metaform.

Chapter 4: Advanced Creature Modeling with Metaform

Here's where the fun begins. In Chapter 3 you got your feet wet, modeling with Metaform. Now you dive head-on into modeling a highly detailed creature using the same techniques, but this time with more detail. By the time you have completed this chapter you'll be able to model any creature that comes your way.

PART III: 3D STUDIO MAX CREATURE MODELING

3D Studio MAX gained a quick reputation for being a powerful character animation tool, but very little was said about its creature modeling capabilities. It seemed that all of the creatures animated in MAX were modeled in another program. This part focuses on changing this so that all of the creatures are actually modeled in MAX. You'll be exploring several modeling techniques in MAX that include patches and splines.

Chapter 5: Getting to Know Patches in MAX

Patch modeling is a new and untapped method of creature modeling. It allows you to literally draw a cage that makes up the volume of the character and then to surface the cage with a mesh. Though it's a great technique for creature modeling, it does have some pitfalls you need to avoid. In this chapter we'll cover the pros and cons of patch modeling and then we'll put the technique to the test by modeling an intermediate level creature.

Chapter 6: Breaking Knuckles—Creature Creation with Surfacetools

Although the patch modeling technique covered in Chapter 5 is great for creature modeling, another more flexible method, called *spline modeling*, lets you create highly detailed creatures. In this chapter we'll cover spline modeling with Surfacetools, a modeling plug-in for MAX. You'll be modeling the most unique character with splines. By the time you're done with this chapter the only thing that will limit your modeling is your imagination.

PART IV: ANIMATION MASTER CREATURE MODELING

Animation Master is the low price leader of the 3D industry, but don't let that fool you! Animation Master is a very sophisticated character modeling and animation tool. In this part we'll cover creature modeling using splines in Animation Master.

Chapter 7: Getting to Know Spline Patches

The main modeling method of Animation Master is spline patches. Of course, you need to have a thorough understanding of patches before you can create truly dazzling 3D creatures. Fortunately, this chapter focuses on understanding the types of patches and where they are best used to create highly detailed creatures. You'll learn the pros and cons of spline patch modeling in Animation Master and you'll put the theories to the test by modeling an intermediate-level 3D creature.

Chapter 8: Forging Steele—Creating an Action Hero

Now that you've spent some time working with spline patches, you're ready for something more advanced. In this chapter you'll be modeling an advanced-level superhero character from head to toe with spline patches. Once you've created this character you'll be able to model any creature with Animation Master.

PART V: SURFACING YOUR CREATURES

Nothing has a greater impact on the believability of your creature than its surface. The modeling is important, but the surfaces are crucial. Of course, creature surfacing is also the most difficult aspect of the creature development process. To make this process easier to manage, this part focuses on shedding light on the specific steps of creating realistic, seamless creature surfaces.

Chapter 9: Photorealistic Creature Surfacing

How many creatures have you seen with seams or image map stretching? All too often. Nothing undermines the credibility of a creature like seams and stretching. These won't be problems that you have to endure any longer. This chapter focuses on how to create seamless surfaces that don't show any signs of image map stretching. Of course, we don't stop there. We'll also show you how to create unparalleled detail in your creature surfaces so they literally pop off the screen!

WHO SHOULD READ THIS BOOK

This book is for any 3D artists who desire to take their creature creations to the next level. If you are truly dedicated to making inspirational 3D creatures you should read this book. If you want to create 3D creatures with unprecedented levels of detail then this book is for you.

If you fall into any of the following categories, you should read this book:

Seeking a Career in 3D. If you are seeking a career in 3D graphics this book is a must. Though there are literally thousands of 3D artists seeking work, only a handful are capable of generating 3D creatures. A proficiency in creating highly detailed creatures puts you at the top of the stack of resumes in the major studios. You should read the book cover-to-cover because it will give you a distinct advantage in the job market.

Multimedia/Games. If you are in the multimedia or game industry you are well acquainted with 3D creatures because they have permeated every aspect of your industry. Where it was once acceptable to use 2D or low quality 3D creatures, you are now required to create high-end creatures that may even rival the ones we see in film. Competition is fierce, forcing you to keep improving the quality of your 3D creatures. In this book you'll discover hundreds of techniques for wowing your customers and clients with realistic 3D creatures.

Film/Broadcast. No industry is more particular about the quality of 3D work than yours. Every form of visual media is being saturated with 3D graphics, whether it's needed or not. From virtual sets to animated stunt characters, 3D effects have become a part of nearly every film and broadcast production. Traditional techniques of using animatronics are being replaced with the more flexible methods of digital creature effects. This book will provide you with the knowledge to create realistic and highly detailed creatures for your next project or production.

Print Media. Computer graphics have taken your industry by storm. More 3D creatures are popping up in print media every day. Your industry is probably the most challenging when it comes to 3D creatures. Unlike the film industry where most things move by you too fast to get a really good look, your work lies there motionless so even the smallest flaw can stand out like a beacon. This book will show you countless techniques for creating eye-popping creatures that will keep your viewers glued to the page.

Creature Modelers. You are the foundation of every creature animation. It all starts with modeling. If you want to know the secrets of making highly detailed creature models you should dive right into the modeling chapters of this book. You'll discover dozens of proven techniques for adding detail to your creature models.

3D Texture Artists. There is no more important element of photorealistic 3D creatures than the textures. You are saddled with the responsibility of creating the eye candy. It's up to you to create realistic textures that make the creature photorealistic. You've mastered the painting technique but now you want to learn the elements that make a creature texture realistic. You should skip ahead to Part V where you'll learn how to add subtle nuances to your texture to make them undeniably realistic.

Hobbyists. You've been experimenting with 3D creatures and you really want to do something spectacular. Let's face it, you *want* to show the world what you're capable of doing. You want to leave them dumfounded when they look at your 3D creatures. Well, you're only 450 pages away from doing just that! Remember — 3D creatures are more attention to detail than artistic talent. Let everyone else be artistic, you'll be the creature creator!

Whether you are an amateur or a professional you will benefit from reading this book. In short, if you are a 3D artist who's interested in creating awesome 3D creatures, read this book!

TOOLS YOU WILL NEED

You will, of course, need one of three 3D programs to take advantage of the information this book has to offer. You'll need LightWave 5.5, 3D Studio MAX 2, or Animation Master 5. You can use older versions of the programs, but some features will be available only in the most recent release. You'll also need Photoshop 3.0 or greater to take advantage of Chapter 9, which covers photorealistic creature surfacing. You can use other painting programs if you don't have Photoshop, but some items will be different.

A working knowledge of the modeling and surfacing aspects of your 3D program are required to grasp the concepts in this book. The main focus of this book is to illustrate the intermediate and advanced principles and techniques of 3D creature modeling; it doesn't cover the basics. If you are just beginning to explore 3D, you should become more acquainted with your program before starting this book.

The last item you need is dedication. You have to be dedicated to creating 3D creatures. It doesn't happen overnight. It takes practice and experimentation. In time, it will become second nature. You won't even have to think about doing it.

WHAT'S ON THE COMPANION CD

The companion CD contains a variety of support materials for creating 3D creatures. You'll find support files for each of the modeling chapters as well as color JPG versions of all the figures in this book. As you read through the chapters you'll come across references made to the CD for support files. All of the files on the CD are organized by chapter for easy reference.

GETTING STARTED

3D creature creation can be the hardest thing you'll ever accomplish if you don't understand the techniques and principles. Fortunately, you currently have these techniques and principles at your fingertips. After reading this book you'll find 3D creature creation to be one of the easiest endeavors you've undertaken. You are only 450 pages away from knowing everything you'll need to create stunning 3D creatures. What are you waiting for, dive in!

Creature Design

The first step in creating realistic creatures is to start with a detailed design. This means that you need to gather a great deal of background information on the creature. You could just simply sketch a random creature as your source material, but that won't guarantee that it will be realistic. It's one thing to create a cool creature, but it's an entirely different story when it comes to creating realistic creature designs.

If you want to sell the viewer on the realism of your creature you'll have to invest some time in the design phase. You can't count the number of creatures on TV, in films, and even comic books that are anything but realistic. Although the developers of the creatures may have invested a great deal of time in the production, they obviously didn't invest enough time in the design. There is some degree of flexibility with fantasy creatures, but you still have rules to follow. For example, the creature would still need to conform to the laws of physics. There are actually high-profile creatures in Hollywood that would be completely incapable of locomotion because they were so poorly designed. They looked cool on the big screen — until they moved. Then they looked completely unnatural, which undermined their realistic credibility.

There is much to consider when you create realistic creatures. For this reason, two full chapters are dedicated to the subject to ensure that you get off to a good start with creature modeling. Part I takes a look at the principles behind realistic creature design and how you can apply them to your creature creations.

Let's not waste another moment. Let's take a look at how we design realistic creatures.

1

Realistic Creature Design

What makes a creature realistic? There are many things to consider when designing your creatures, such as the environment it inhabits, what it eats, whether it's predator or prey, its intelligence, the time of day it's active, how it moves, and so on. There are literally thousands of things to consider. Fortunately, most of them are common sense. Luckily there is an accessible supply of awesome source material in the world around us. Creatures are everywhere we look. Sure, a cat is rather boring but its eyes are awesome. A horse is very common but have you ever stopped to examine the powerful muscularity in its legs? How about those rats and mice that inhabit broken-down warehouses and dumps? They have those great tails and that cool little nose. Let's not forget those pesky roaches that plague our homes. They are loaded with killer creature details that strike fear into the hearts of man. Well, they would if they were ten feet tall!

As you can see, creature design source material is all around us, waiting to be used. If you've taken a close look at the Hollywood creatures lately, you'll notice they are composed of very recognizable parts. This is what makes them realistic. If they were created with details you had never seen before, they would appear unrealistic. If you are a science fiction fan, you've noticed that nearly every gruesome creature in film has been a biped. Yep, they almost always have two arms and two legs. This is done so that the creature appears more acceptable to the viewer. Let's face it, we're very comfortable with the biped design since we live it every day of our lives. Here again, the creature designers borrowed the details of creatures in reality. In this case, humans were the source of inspiration.

There is an abundance of source material in the world around us, so why is the design so important? That's a great question. If you want to sell the viewers on the reality of your creature you'll need to put some energy into the design. While the viewers may not be authorities on creature design they definitely are capable of spotting design blunders, whether they realize it or not. We're all accustomed to seeing certain attributes in creatures around us so we tend to expect those attributes in the 3D creatures we view. That's why Hollywood typically falls back on the safety of the biped creature design — the viewer is accustomed to seeing it.

Of course, you can't simply start with a foundation of arms and legs and throw anything you'd like on the creature. Every element on the creature needs to have a purpose. The beauty of nature is that every detail you'll find on creatures is 100 percent justified. They all have a purpose. They may seem pointless at first, but a little exploration soon reveals their justification. For example, the hatchling American alligator is born with the coloration of a bumblebee, with yellow and black stripes. What kind of sense does this make? Why would they be so colorful? It's actually rather ingenious — they are covered in bright colors so they are visible to predators. At first glance this may seem an error in design judgment, but it actually makes perfect sense when you consider that the American alligator lays a large number of eggs. Only a few of the hatchlings are intended to survive; otherwise there would be too many adult alligators, throwing the ecosystem out of balance. To prevent the alligators from overpopulating, the babies are brightly colored little snacks for predators such as raccoons, birds, foxes, etc. Now you're thinking the alligators should just lay fewer eggs to balance the ecosystem. That might work, but the hatchlings are a valuable food source for many of the other creatures in the environment. You see, every detail of real-world creatures has a logical purpose.

To become a realistic creature designer you'll need to invest a great deal of time exploring the creatures of our world — not simply borrowing body parts from them for design but actually taking the time to understand the reason they appear as they do. This is a crucial step in the process of creating realistic creatures. You'll need to have a firm handle on the types of body parts that are required for certain functions. For example, an elephant has a trunk that serves as its hands. If you were designing a fictional pachyderm, which happened to be a biped, you'd want to remove the trunk. Why, you ask? Simply because a biped has hands and would no longer have a use for the trunk. Mother Nature doesn't add pointless features to her creatures; therefore, neither should you.

So how do you go about designing a creature? It requires a deep exploration of the world the creature inhabits. Basically, a creature's environment determines its features. This brings you to the foundation of creature design, the *biography*. Let's take a look at the role biographies play in the design of realistic creatures.

CREATING A CREATURE BIOGRAPHY

The very first step in designing a creature is to create its biography, which tells you everything you need to know in order to design the creature properly. All too often the tendency is to dive headfirst into modeling creatures without stopping to consider its background. For example, if the creature were capable of flight you would assume it would have wings, but this isn't always the case. Not all things that fly are birds. There are flying fish, squirrels, lizards, and even snakes. Yes, snakes can fly too. Well, they don't actually fly but there are several species in the rain forest that will hurl themselves from one tree to another, over great distances. For a moment in time, they are actually flying.

As you can see, there are many possibilities for flight that don't always require wings. If your creature were capable of climbing trees, you would have to rule out standard wings and go with something less conventional like a baggy flap of skin that catches the wind, as seen on the flying squirrel or lizard. This way you can have wings for flight and four legs for climbing. This, of course, is just one example of why you need a complete character biography before you start building the creature. The last thing you want to do is get halfway through the modeling process and realize that the design doesn't make sense.

ALWAYS START YOUR CREATURE WITH A COMPREHENSIVE BIOGRAPHY.

You cannot design a realistic creature effectively until you've spent a day in its shoes. You need to explore the creature's habitat, food, and predators before you can make it convincingly realistic. Always start your design with a comprehensive creature biography.

So what should the creature biography include? Basically, it includes everything about the character that's relevant to its design. Though there are literally thousands of possibilities, you'll find it's easiest merely to spend a day in your character's shoes. Basically, live its life for a day. This will tell you everything you need to know in order to design the character. In fact, why don't you step out and take a walk in a creature's shoes to see just what you'll encounter. Take a look at the test character in Figure 1.1.

Our test character is a rather unique creature called a Komodosaurus, which we will be using as the basis of discussion during this chapter. This is a bit of a reverse-engineering approach since the creature is already modeled, but it will make the discussion a great deal easier to grasp. Slip on this creature's shoes and go for a walk.

The Komodosaurus is a prehistoric creature found on a distant M-Class planet that's in its Jurassic period. This, of course, leaves many possibilities for the creature's design. It could take on hundreds of different forms. To make the design process easier, we need to narrow the description of our character, starting with the creature's habitat.

WHAT IS THE CREATURE'S HABITAT?

Where does your creature live? This is the first question you need to ask yourself when designing your character since it will have the largest impact on the creature's build. For example, if the creature lived in the desert it likely would be reptilian. On the other hand, if it lived in the rain forest it would lean toward amphibian or insect. If it lived in the water it would likely have fins and gills. Of course, it if lived in the forest it's likely to be a furry creature. These aren't steadfast rules, but they do help narrow down the design of the creature.

The environment has a great deal to do with the physical attributes of the creature. To properly design your creature you'll need to explore the environment it inhabits. Take a look at the world of our Komodosaurus in Figure 1.2.

FIGURE **1.1** *Creating a creature biography.*

FIGURE **1.2** *The Komodosaurus habitat.*

As you can see, the Komodosaurus habitat is an arid environment, something along the lines of an Arabian desert, which is filled with palm trees and plenty of sand. This gives you a good idea of how to begin the creature design. The creature would need to be something that has tough skin to protect it from the harsh sun. It would also need a foot with relatively long toes to allow for digging and stability in the loose sand. Also, since there isn't an abundance of water it will have to require little water to survive. In fact, it will need to be creative about getting the little water that it does need.

Basically this is the description of a camel. Of course, you can't forget the period in which the creature lives. Since this is a Jurassic period there wouldn't be mammals such as camels so you need to go in another direction. The next obvious choice is something reptilian like a dinosaur. This would provide the creature with a rugged, scaly skin to protect it from the harsh sun. In fact, desert-dwelling reptiles like to spend time in the sun to elevate their body temperature so they can digest their food effectively. Since they are cold blooded, the environment controls their body temperature.

How about the need for long toes and claws? Reptiles typically have long toes and claws to allow for climbing and digging, and to provide better traction in the loose sand. Since you're working with a reptile, you'll also need to incorporate a few other reptilian features to make the creature believable. For example, reptiles have a unique ear. It's basically a hole in the side of their head with a thin layer of skin over it, which vibrates much the way your eardrum does. Take a look at Figure 1.3 to see the reptilian ear that was added to the Komodosaurus.

While looking at the Komodosaurus' head, examine the eyes. The sun is rather harsh in this environment so you'll need to add some sort of protection for the eyes. Most reptiles have a pronounced ridge over their eyes, which shades them from the sun. As you can see in Figure 1.3, a ridge over the eye was added, as well as a second eyelid that serves to block the sunlight. This heavy moveable eyelid is common on many desert-dwelling reptiles such as the Uromastyx lizard from Egypt. It allows them to block out the light completely so they can sleep in broad daylight.

Consider the nose; since you're making a reptilian creature you'll need to add a couple of holes at the end of the nose on either side for the sinuses. Although reptiles actually sense things with their tongue rather than smelling them, they still need their sinuses to breathe.

How about its need for water? Desert-dwelling reptiles get all the water they need from vegetation or the prey that they eat, whether it's an insect or animal. As long as we're on the subject of food, let's take a look at the next step in the development of a creature biography: What does the creature eat?

WHAT DOES THE CREATURE EAT?

What the creature eats has a major impact on its entire physical structure from head to tail — if it has a tail. There are four categories for creature diets: herbivore, carnivore,

FIGURE 1.3 *The Komodosaurus' head.*

insectivore, and omnivore. Herbivores eat vegetation, carnivores eat meat, insectivores eat insects, and omnivores eat everything. The diet of the creature is a critical part of the biography that determines a number of its features such as the type of teeth, eye placement, snout length, and limb structure. Let's first take a look at the impact the diet has on a creature's teeth.

Creature Teeth

There are countless ways of representing a creature's teeth but it's very easy to determine the right approach by first examining the creature's diet. Before we look at the impact the diet has on the dental structure of a creature, let's take a look at the four types of creature teeth, as shown in Figure 1.4.

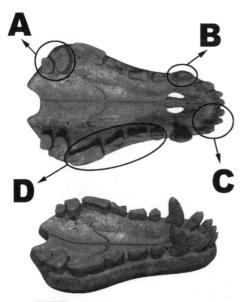

FIGURE **1.4** *Creature teeth.*

Figure 1.4 shows a rendered jawbone of a canine (dog). Let's take a look at each tooth and the role each plays in eating food.

A) **Molars.** These teeth are used to grind the food to aid digestion. These teeth have the most power since they are located closest to the hinge of the jawbone, giving them a great deal of leverage.

B) **Premolars.** These teeth also are used to grind the food. These teeth are typically sharper since they are used to break up the food before the molars grind it into digestible pulp.

C) **Canines.** These are the most popular teeth featured on fantasy creatures. Canines have little to do with eating — they actually serve as weapons for subduing the prey. Typically they are rather long and come to a point, though the point is rarely sharp since the creature would end up constantly hurting itself.

D) **Incisors.** These teeth are used as cutting tools for tearing flesh off the prey. In the case of omnivores and herbivores they are more blunt and used to cut vegetation.

Now take a look at the four classifications of creature diet, and the types of teeth you can expect to see.

Herbivore. Since these are vegetarians they have little need for large incisors for killing prey or tearing flesh. Instead, they have an abundance of premolars and molars for grinding up their food. They will often have a row of relatively blunt incisors in the front of their mouth for cutting the vegetation. Of course, not all herbivores actually chew their food. Many simply swallow it so they have no need for molars. Instead, they simply have a rough bony ridge for cutting the vegetation, like one continuous incisor. This type of dental structure is most commonly found in reptiles.

Carnivore. This is the most common type of creature that's created in 3D, typically because they are more menacing. Obviously, the most prominent features of the carnivore jawbone are the canine teeth, which are used to kill the prey. The number of canines can vary widely depending on the creature. For example, alligators are pretty much all canines. They have no need for molars since they don't chew their food. They don't chew at all so they don't have incisors either. They just violently whip their head from side to side to dismember prey.

Insectivore. You rarely see these creatures represented in 3D since they are typically very small creatures, which makes them far less intimidating than a carnivore. Insectivores have an abundance of molars and incisors since many of them chew their food. They rarely have canines since the insects are too small to require being killed or subdued. You'll also find insectivores that have a singular bony ridge in place of teeth as found in reptiles and amphibians. They swallow their food whole so they have no need for molars, which are used to grind food.

Omnivore. Here we have the jack-of-all-trades. The omnivore typically has an equal balance of all teeth. They eat insects and vegetation so they require molars to grind their food, canines to subdue their animal prey, and incisors to tear flesh off the prey. These teeth are very similar to those found in humans, though we have very small canines since we use our hands to kill prey. Of course, there is always the exception to the rule so you also must consider the reptile omnivores, which simply have a bony ridge for teeth. They swallow their prey whole so they don't need canines or molars.

Now you have a good understanding of the types of teeth, their use, and where they will be found in a creature based on its diet. Now you can determine the proper dental structure for our Komodosaurus effectively. Figure 1.5 shows the teeth of the Komodosaurus.

As you can see, the Komodosaurus clearly has the teeth of an omnivore. Incisors are in the front for tearing flesh, canines behind them for subduing prey, and premolars/molars in the back for grinding food. There is more to determining the dental structure of the Komodosaurus than simply determining that it was an omnivore — you also have to consider how it finds its prey. Not all flesh-eating creatures hunt live prey. For example, a typical monitor lizard feeds off the carcasses of prekilled prey much the way a vulture does so it has no need for large canines. It lets the larger predators with canines kill the prey, and then feeds off what they leave behind.

When creating your creature you'll need to determine how it kills its prey as well as what it eats. This will have a major impact on the dental structure of the creature. Since we're on the subject of how a creature finds its prey, let's take a look at the placement of a creature's eyes.

Creature Eye Placement

The creature's diet has a great deal to do with its eye placement. In fact, if you place the eyes improperly you'll completely undermine the creature's design. To consider eye placement, first examine the food chain. There are three types of creatures in the food chain: predator, prey, and scavenger.

FIGURE **1.5** *A Komodosaurus' teeth.*

The predator hunts its food so it needs to have good eyesight. It also needs to have the eyes mounted on the front of its skull so it can track the prey. If the eyes were mounted on the side of the head it would be very difficult to track the prey. Of course, there are several exceptions to the predator eye placement, such as amphibians and reptiles. These peculiar creatures usually have the eyes mounted on the sides of their heads. Why, you ask? Well, it actually makes sense — reptiles and amphibians don't tend to run down prey, so frontal eye placement isn't necessary. Instead, they typically wait for the prey to come to them. Yes, they are lazy, but aggressive eaters nonetheless.

Things get a little trickier when you consider prey. These creatures can be both predator and prey so they will have varying eye placement. To simplify things follow this simple rule: Herbivores and insectivores have side-mounted eyes, whereas carnivores have front-mounted eyes. The omnivore can vary depending on whether it tracks prey or not. Most creatures that track prey have front-mounted eyes.

Now you just have the scavenger to consider. These lazy hunters don't track their prey so they have no need for front-mounted eyes. They are mounted on the side, regardless if they're carnivores or not.

Are you confused yet? It can be tough to determine the proper eye placement considering the number of possible variations. To make it easier, take a look at a few simple guidelines for determining eye placement.

Carnivores. Front-mounted eyes unless it's a scavenger or reptile, then they are side mounted as seen in dinosaurs and monitor lizards.

Reptiles and Amphibians. Side-mounted eyes.

Marsupials. Side-mounted eyes, but rotated slightly forward as with a kangaroo or koala bear.

Primates. Front-mounted eyes.

Pachyderms. Side-mounted eyes.

Rodents. Side-mounted eyes.

Birds. Side-mounted eyes unless it's a tracking predator such as an eagle or owl, which have front-mounted eyes.

Insects. Side-mounted eyes for all insects except spiders, which have front-mounted eyes.

Hopefully these guidelines will add clarity to the chaos of determining creature eye placement. Before you determine your eye placement you should consider these guidelines to ensure you have placed them properly.

Let's take another look at Komodosaurus in Figure 1.5 to see where its eyes were placed. As you can see, the eyes are clearly mounted on the side of the head, which is the case with reptiles. Even though he does eat meat, he is a scavenger so he doesn't track down his prey, leaving him with little need for front-mounted eyes.

Now that you have a handle on the eye placement, let's take a look at how the creature diet determines the limb structure.

Creature Limb Structure

A creature's limb structure is primarily determined by its specific dietary needs. The guidelines for creature limb structure are relatively easy. The fist thing you need to do is determine the dietary classification of the creature; that is, whether it's a carnivore, herbivore, insectivore, or amphibian. This will give you a general indication of the limb structure. Then you'll need to narrow down the specific diet to determine the exact limb structure. Basically, all animals have four limbs and walk on all of them. Of course, there are exceptions, which are dictated by the creature's diet.

For example, primates walk on four limbs but can also walk on two, like man. This exception has a great deal to do with their diet. A great deal of primate food is located in the trees so they need to be able to climb. Therefore they need to have articulated fingers on their hands to allow them to grasp branches. If your creature is a tree climber, it is going to need more flexible limbs and articulated hands.

Actually, the guidelines for creature limb design are very simple. If it's a tree dweller it will have articulated hands and digits and the capability to walk on two legs. If it doesn't climb trees, then it will likely walk on all four legs. Naturally, there are exceptions to the rule such as tree frogs, which walk on all four legs and spend all of their time in trees. Squirrels and chipmunks also walk on all four legs but they do have articulated hands because of their diet. They have the need to handle their food so they have flexible hands. Raccoons also climb trees and have articulated hands but they walk on all four legs. There certainly is much to consider when developing creatures! Just keep in mind that your creature typically should have four limbs. They would have articulated hands if they handle their food or climb trees. They would walk on two legs if they have evolved significantly.

Of course, many dinosaurs walked on two legs, but that's because they were closely related to birds. Raptors and T-Rex creatures were very similar to birds in skeletal structure. They had powerful hind legs, rather small front legs, and big heads. In fact, this would be a great time to take a look at how the limb structure determines the snout length.

Creature Snout Length

The snout length of the creature is determined by its limb structure, which is defined by the creature's diet. It all has to do with the front limbs of the creature and how it eats. If the creature walks on all four legs, it typically has a longer snout since the mouth is pretty much used as the creature's hands. On the other hand, if it's a tree climber with articulated hands such as a primate, or a marsupial like the koala bear, it will have a short snout since it has flexible hands. Creatures that feed themselves with their hands have shorter snouts since they don't treat the mouth as a tool or weapon. This brings us to another aspect of the creature's diet that affects the snout length — whether it uses the mouth as a weapon.

Carnivores have longer snouts because they use them as weapons, and herbivores have short snouts because they don't subdue prey with their mouths. The snout length will be long on a quadruped herbivore because it doesn't have articulated hands, but the mouth will be short because it doesn't kill prey with it. Of course, there are the extraordinary exceptions to the rule such as elephants and anteaters but these are well justified. An elephant gets most of its food from trees so it needs a long trunk to act as its arm and hand, making it possible to reach up into the tree and pull down the food. An anteater has a long snout for digging into anthills to find its food.

You need to consider the diet and limb structure of your creature carefully before you determine its snout length. Let's take yet another, final, look at Figure 1.5 to see the justification behind the snout length of the Komodosaurus.

You can see that the snout is very long because he is a quadruped herbivore. He also has a long mouth because he uses it as a weapon for protection. It also functions as his arms so he needs a long mouth to grasp things.

As you can see, the diet has a major impact on the creature's design. Be sure that you spend the time to research the creature's diet before you finalize its design.

Now let's move on to another critical element of the creature's biography: What are the creature's predators?

WHAT ARE THE CREATURE'S PREDATOR DEFENSES?

The creature's predators have a large impact on its design. The creature will need to have some level of defense against its predators if it is to survive. It's important to note that a creature's defensive features aren't always aggressive, like teeth and horns. Quite often they are more evasive, like the ability to run quickly or hide in small places. For example, mice are basically a food source for most of the smaller carnivores. Therefore they don't have any major defenses. The only protection they have from predators is to run and hide in small places.

Of course, there are a variety of more aggressive defensive features found in creatures such as prickly spines on a porcupine, heavy plating as seen on the armadillo, and even poison, which you'll find in many reptiles and amphibians. You need to consider the exact predators of your creature before you can properly design its defenses. If the predator can run fast, you'll need to provide your creature with a defense against the predator's speed. If the predator has powerful jaws you'll need to incorporate some level of armoring in your creature design to protect it. You get the idea.

Creature design requires far more than simply creating your creature's design. You also need to design the environment, food, predators, prey, etc. There is much to consider when creating your creature. Let's take a look at the Komodosaurus' defenses against predators as shown in Figure 1.6.

Figure 1.6 shows the Komodosaurus' considerable defenses. What, you don't see anything? Well, it's actually not all that obvious, but very effective in its purpose. The Komodosaurus' predators are creatures much like the T-Rex and Allosaurus. These creatures have very large heads and powerful jaws, which can do significant damage to a Komodosaurus. To protect itself, the Komodosaurus has a very heavy bone plate on the top of its head and shoulders, which you can see in the image. This bone plate is about six inches thick and completely impervious to the predator's teeth, protecting the vital organs of the Komodosaurus. If you take a look just behind the shoulder girdle you'll see an abundance of thick, bay skin which also served to protect the Komodosaurus from the predator's powerful bite.

What about offensive measures? How does the Komodosaurus convince the predator to go away and leave him alone? The Komodosaurus uses its weight and power to its advantage, because it actually outweighs the predator and has considerable power and speed. It can reach speeds of 60 mph over a very short distance — moving its weight at this speed makes quite a weapon! The Komodosaurus uses its power and speed to ram the

FIGURE **1.6** *The Komodosaurus' predator defenses.*

belly of the predator, literally exploding its internal organs. It's a bit gruesome but it beats being eaten!

Now you're wondering how the Komodosaurus itself survives the impact. Take a close look at Figure 1.6 and you'll see that it has a very large and heavy head. In fact, it has a considerable block of thick bone on the tip of its nose, which acts effectively as its battering ram. This thick bone protects the skull on impact and increases the damage to the predator. Now you're wondering how its spine holds up under the impact. Take a look at the Komodosaurus and you'll see that the head is in perfect alignment with the spine. This supports the spine so it can handle the impact. If the head were out of alignment with the spine, like that of a horse, it would easily break its neck.

The front of the Komodosaurus is well protected, but what happens when he is attacked from the rear? That's where its powerful tail comes in handy — take a look at the backside of the Komodosaurus in Figure 1.7.

As you can see, the tail is quite considerable in size and can easily shatter the leg bones of the predator, giving the Komodosaurus enough time to turn around and ram it. The tail is lined with very large muscles that give it a serious amount of power. You can also see that the tail has a rather large and prominent bone structure that gives it strength.

FIGURE **1.7** *The Komodosaurus' powerful tail.*

Since we're looking at the tail let's examine the legs and the next step in the creature's biography — its mode of locomotion.

HOW DOES YOUR CREATURE MOVE?

This, of course, is a rather important element of the creature design. It determines a great deal of the creature's appearance. It's also a relatively simple aspect in creature design. Basically, you need to consider how your creature moves about. Does it walk, crawl, climb, swim, slither, or fly?

Once you have an idea of the locomotion, you can determine the proper limb structure based on its movement. Of course, don't forget to consider the diet when creating the limb structure. Although determining the general limb structure is relatively straightforward, you will need to go a little deeper into the creature design to determine the specific attributes of the limbs. For example, if the creature is a fast runner it will need powerful hind legs. If it's a jumper it will need big feet and long toes to give it leverage. If it's a climber it will need rather lean limbs so it's more agile in the trees.

Take another look at Figure 1.7 to see the detail that was added to the hind legs of the Komodosaurus. As you can see, the hind legs are very muscular and powerful. This was necessary to allow the creature to achieve speeds of up to 60 mph when running. With the immense mass of the creature it needed very strong legs to move quickly. You probably also noticed that the hips are mounted rather high, which gives the legs a greater degree of leverage to move the ponderous mass of the Komodosaurus.

As you can see, it requires some thought to design the limbs accurately for proper locomotion. You should spend a great deal of time studying the creatures of our world before you attempt to create creatures of another world. It will give you a solid understanding of how they move. In fact, you should probably dedicate some time to watching nature channels on TV to get a detailed understanding of how particular creatures move.

Well, that about does it for the physical attributes based on a creature biography. You can see how the creature probably would have looked entirely different if we didn't take the time to spend a day in its shoes. Now, of course, there is still one element of creature design that we have yet to discuss — creature surfacing. Let's take a look at how we determine the surfacing of creatures.

DETERMINING THE CREATURE SURFACING

You can spend countless hours modeling the perfect creature, but if you surface it improperly you'll undermine all of your modeling efforts. Surfacing is the bridge between 3D and reality. It can turn your creature into a living, breathing entity. We'll be discussing the process of creating creature surfacing in Chapter 9. For now, let's take a look at how we determine the elements to include in our creature surfacing.

When designing your creature's surfaces you'll need to consider the environment and its predators carefully. If the environment is harsh like the desert you'll probably want to go with something scaly. On the other hand, it it's humid like the rain forest you might want something more like an amphibian skin. Of course, in a forest you would probably lean toward fur, particularly if it's cold. There are simple guidelines for creating creature surfaces.

Cold Environment. Long fur unless it spends a great deal of time in the water.

Warm Environment. Short fur and scales.

Humid Environment. Short fur and skin.

Of course, as always, there are some exceptions to the rules. You might find a creature like a polar bear that spends a great deal of time in the water but still has fur. The same would apply for a beaver. Naturally these creatures have very thick fur so the water doesn't actually touch their skin.

That's the very general look at creature surfacing, but what about the specifics? That all depends on the environment and the predators that might hunt your creature. You see, your creature may need camouflage to hide from predators, or it might need it to hide from the prey just like you'll see with a cheetah or leopard. In fact, host animals are fairly well camouflaged based on the colors and patterns in their environment. If the environment is rather dry and arid like a desert, you can expect the creature to have sandy brown colors like a camel or desert lizard. All animals have some form of camouflage.

In addition to surface colors, you must also consider how harsh the environment is on the creature. You'll find that snakes have very hard scales because they are constantly slithering across the ground, which can be very harsh on skin. On the other hand, lizard scales are usually not nearly as hard because they aren't in constant contact with the environment. If you take a close look at snake scales you'll find that some are rather smooth and shiny like that of the glossy snake. This is because they live in an environment with smooth sand, which isn't that harsh on the scales. Of course, there are species of snake with very rugged scales, such as gopher snakes and rattlers. They have tough scales because they live in rocky and rugged terrain, which is very hard on the scales.

As you can see, the environment will have an impact on the specific details of your creature's surfaces. Speaking of details, let's take a look at the surfaced Komodosaurus shown in Figure 1.8.

Since the Komodosaurus is basically a large reptile we chose to surface it with small scales. Of course, it also resembles a pachyderm so we created a leathery skin hybrid so it had the look and feel of both hide and scales. It has the perfect surfacing for a dry, arid

FIGURE **1.8** *The surfaced Komodosaurus.*

environment with harsh sunlight. Notice that the skin is a bit oily; this is to keep the dust from getting in the cracks of the scales and causing infections. It's a neurotic detail but one that really adds to the dynamics of the creature.

We could have added some irregular coloration like what you'll commonly see in reptiles, but since the creature is a reptile/pachyderm hybrid we decided it would make the creature appear less realistic. In fact, creature color is an important item to consider when creating your creatures. The coloration of a creature varies widely between the male and female of the species. In fact, as you learned earlier, the infants of a species can have extraordinary color. Let's take a look at the coloration of the sexes.

CREATURE SURFACING FOR DIFFERENT SEXES

You'll find that the male of any given species is typically more colorful than the female. This happens for a couple of reasons. First, it serves as an intimidation factor to ward off creatures that encroach on its territory. It's also used to attract the females during courtship. The female of the species is attracted to the brilliant colors.

Keeping this in mind, you'll want to incorporate the proper coloration into your creature's surfacing. The tendency is to make 3D creatures rather bland and neutral in coloration, but this typically isn't the case in reality. Don't be afraid to add a splash of color to your creature's surfaces. In fact, let's take a look at a male dinosaur to get an idea of how color works well with a creature design.

Figure 1.9 shows a rather colorful creature that looks very natural in its environment. If this were a female of the species it still might have the patterns on the head and back but they would be very subtle. On the other hand, if it were a hatchling of the same

FIGURE **1.9** *Male creature coloration.*

species it would likely be even more colorful. You should endeavor to give your creatures sexual identity by adding color to their surfaces.

Now let's take a look at the final element of creature surfaces — the eyes.

CREATURE EYE DETAILS

The appearance of creature eyes varies widely, giving you a broad range of freedom in creating your creature's eyes. You only need to follow a few simple guidelines when creating creature eyes. You need to determine whether the creature is diurnal or nocturnal. In short, diurnal creatures are active during the day and nocturnal creatures are active during the night hours.

The look of the eye will vary depending on when the creature is active. Actually, there are really only two possibilities and they involve a variation in the appearance of the iris. The iris is either round for diurnal creatures, or a vertical/horizontal slit for nocturnal creatures. It's really that simple.

Of course, there are some exceptions to the rule. You will find some diurnal creatures with narrow irises but that's because they hunt their food in the evening hours at sunset, which requires a narrow iris to capture more light for night vision.

Let's take a look at the eye we used for the Komodosaurus, shown in Figure 1.10. The Komodosaurus is a diurnal creature and a scavenger so it has a round iris. If it were a hunter in the evening hours it would tend to have a narrow iris, but our Komodosaurus typically is asleep long before sunset.

As you can see, there are many things to consider when surfacing your creatures. Be sure that you study real-world creatures to get an idea of how their surfacing corresponds to their environment. It will help you a lot when it comes to surfacing your creatures.

Let's close this chapter with a look at gathering source material.

FINDING CREATURE SOURCE MATERIAL

Creating realistic creatures requires an abundance of quality source material since it's difficult to create them from our imaginations. Although our imaginations are definitely

FIGURE **1.10** *Figure 1.10 The Komodosaurus' eye.*

unique, they rarely incorporate the elements that make a creature realistic. There are so many subtle nuances in creatures that it would be impossible for us to remember all of them. It's important to have the source material in front of you when you create your creature design.

I have a very comprehensive library of source material, which I draw upon daily to help me create realistic creatures. In fact, my desk is completely covered in source material. You can never have too much source material — it's almost as important as your computer.

There are many ways to acquire source material, but we're going to take look at only the most useful ones. We'll start with the most obvious one — books.

FINDING SOURCE MATERIAL AT THE BOOKSTORE, LIBRARY, AND ON THE INTERNET

There are a number of places you can get source material, like the library and even on the Internet, but if you are seeking really high-quality source material you are better off visiting your local bookstore, or maybe even the online mammoth bookstore: *www.amazon.com*. Bookstores always carry a wide variety of books that feature an abundance of color images, and they have those wonderful children's educational sections. I know it sounds bizarre but you'll likely find the best source material in this section. Children's educational books are always filled with an abundance of color photos, unlike the adult books, which are more words than pictures.

Another benefit of getting source material from a bookstore is that you own the book, so you can vandalize it without having a psychotic librarian stalking you. Sometimes it's necessary to remove the pages from the book to scan them and most libraries don't appreciate this...

> ## MAKE THE CHILDREN'S EDUCATIONAL SECTION YOUR FIRST STOP WHEN SEEKING SOURCE MATERIAL.
>
> When looking for source material in a bookstore, you should head directly to the children's educational section. You won't find a better source of high-quality color images than a children's educational book.

Of course, libraries aren't all bad. They can be another good place to find source material. I've spent hours in the library digging up great source material. I find that the magazines are probably the best source material in the library since the books have been handled by thousands of people, which can leave them a little worse for the wear. If you're planning to scan images to use in your surfacing you'll find that libraries aren't the best place to go, since you'll want a high-quality, untainted image for the scan. Another drawback of libraries is the lack of color images in the books. It's important that your source material is full color so you don't have to guess at the colors. If you're lucky enough to have a city library nearby, I'm sure you'll find some very nice source material.

Of course, the fastest way to obtain source material is through the Internet. Although the images may not be very large, they are easily obtainable, usually full color, and don't cost you anything. I occasionally browse the Internet for images I want to use as a reference for painting the image maps, since high-resolution images aren't necessary. On the other hand, if I need to scan the image I prefer bookstores since they have large, high-quality originals.

So you know the bookstore is a great place to find source material, but what books should you be looking for? I have found a few books that have outstanding color photographs, which make perfect source material. For example, I heartily recommend that you purchase any of the books in the Eyewitness Book Series. These books were created for children, but they feature literally thousands of high-quality color photographs of nearly everything under the sun. You might even learn something, too. Yesterday I found out that there is a giant water bug that actually eats tiny fish. Cool, isn't it?

You'll find a list of outstanding resources for source material in Appendix A.

You know that books are a great place to find source material, but where else can you look? The great thing is that good source material is all around you. You just need to be able to bring it back to your studio. For this, you'll need a camera.

GATHERING SOURCE MATERIAL WITH AN INSTANT CAMERA

Quite often you'll discover that the creatures you need can't be found in books or on the web. In these situations you'll need to go into the world and find the objects yourself. For this task, you should invest in an instant camera. The world is filled with an endless supply of awesome source material, which you can capture in an instant (no pun intended) with a Polaroid camera.

CARRY AN INSTANT CAMERA WITH YOU AT ALL TIMES.

You never know when you'll come across a perfect surface while you're out and about. It would be a shame to lose out on such great source material. Always carry an instant camera with you. You don't have to physically carry it everywhere; just leave one in your car so you can access it easily.

I carry a Polaroid camera with me everywhere I go because I never know when I'll come across an awesome creature. Now you're wondering just how many times I go on safaris to get source material. Actually, it's all around your house. It can be dogs, cats, mice, horses, birds, insects, etc. All of these creatures have great details that you can incorporate into your creature design. I like to take trips down to my local reptile store and take pictures of the creatures in their terrariums. It's an awesome place to get source material. Of course, there's always the zoo, which is filled with a plethora of source material.

I'm always on the search for creature source material. I've spent hours cruising the zoo and wild animal parks to find those perfect creature details I was seeking. The moral of the story is, don't get caught without your camera! You'll kick yourself for missing the opportunity to capture the perfect creature source material.

It's easy to see that creature design requires a bit of planning. Although it can be somewhat extensive, it's actually a great deal of fun. In fact, it's my favorite aspect of the creature development process.

WRAP-UP

That about does it for creature design. We could have explored it a lot deeper but we're really focusing on creature modeling in this book. Don't worry, we'll be covering very detailed creature design in another book soon.

For now, let's move on to the next step in the creature design process — planning for animation. In the next chapter we'll take a look at the principles behind *Single Mesh* creature modeling so we can use Bones for our character animation. Before we dive into Chapter 2, let's take a break and allow the information we covered in this chapter to sink in a bit. I'll see you in the next chapter.

CHAPTER
2
Single Mesh Creature Modeling

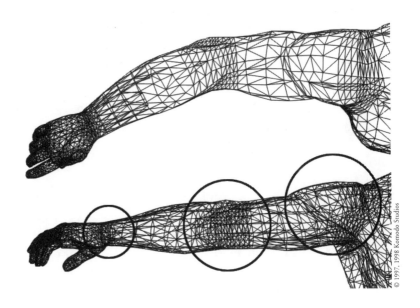

Creature animation has come a long way in the last couple of years, making the welcome transition from those obviously 3D jointed creatures to the now popular Single Mesh version. Although jointed characters were simple to animate using Inverse Kinematics, they posed the problem of obvious seams in the joint, which certainly made the creatures look artificial. In fact, insects are the only class of creatures that can be animated effectively using jointed body parts, since they have an exoskeleton (an external skeleton).

An insect has its bones on the outside rather than on the inside, which is the way all other creatures are composed. Since skeletons are naturally jointed, insects can be animated realistically with segmented body parts. Yes, there actually is another class of creature that can be animated realistically with jointed body parts. This, of course, would be the walking dead — those wonderful skeletons that were immortalized by the old Sinbad movies. Once again, in this case we have an exoskeleton. In fact, all we have is a skeleton.

What are the options for animating organic creatures with a single skin covering their skeleton? That's when we turn to Bones, which is a great name for the control objects since they serve the same function as our bones. To be exact, they actually serve the purpose of our tendons and muscles. These wonderful Bones are placed in the wireframe mesh much the same way our bones are. Then, when moved, they deform the mesh. In fact, why don't we take a look at the value of Bones, and why it's important to use them on organic creatures.

WHY USE BONES?

Bones are the most powerful means for creating realistic movement in your creatures. Nothing else even comes close. Although it may be easier to animate creatures using jointed models, you lose all of the visual benefits of using Bones. Bones will do more than rotate the mesh to accommodate a specific position. They also deform the mesh, giving the creatures skin and muscle movement.

When a creature moves, its muscles and skin move as well. If you use jointed models the parts simply rotate to their new position, leaving the mesh unaffected. They don't pinch and pull like real flesh does. For example, when you reach your arm over your head the pectoral (chest) muscle stretches upward because it's pulled by the joint. This effect cannot be achieved with jointed model animation since the mesh won't be deformed. On the other hand, when using Bones to animate your creatures you'll be able to create the muscle and skin movement since the model is a Single Mesh. The Bones will pull the chest upward when the arm is rotated.

Single Mesh modeling allows you to create a 3D creature with the same physical attributes as real-world creatures. Making single-skin models opens the door for cool creature movement effects like skin and muscle movement. Take a look at a Single Mesh creature that was animated using Bones, in Figure 2.1.

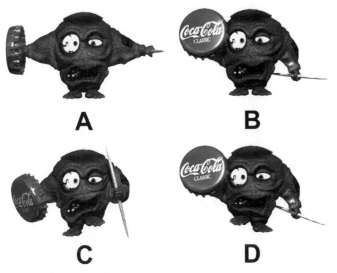

FIGURE **2.1**   *The effect of using Bones to animate your creatures.*

Figure 2.1 shows Sgt. Spore, a creature from an animated short film under production at Komodo Studio. Spore is a perfect example of how Bones cause the skin to move on your creatures. Take a look at image A, which shows Spore in his neutral position. The neutral position is simply the position given to the character when he was modeled. The next section takes a look at the guidelines for positioning your creature models. Right now, let's focus on the benefits of Bones animation.

Take a look at image B and you'll see Spore standing in his relaxed position. If you look closely you'll see that a fold of skin was created under his left arm when it was lowered. This is a very natural effect for a baggy-skinned creature such as Spore. It's also something that couldn't have been achieved with a jointed creature.

Now take a look at images C and B, which show Spore taking a step. Here you can see the wonderful benefits of Bones animation hard at work. Just take a look at his foot and the way it's lifting his jaw up. This is a very cool by-product of using bones. You see, the bones are deforming the mesh as they are moved. In this case it really helps to add personality to the creature. He really looks goofy, doesn't he? Well, that's just a part of his personality.

Take a look at the bottom of his left arm in image C. You can see that the skin under his arm is hanging down in a large bulge, which is the way it would naturally occur if a creature like Spore moved his arm forward. Actually, there was no tweaking done to create this deformation. All we did was rotate the arm forward and the Bones did the rest.

You can see how Bones can bring your creatures to life. In fact, to really see the impact of Bones, take a look at the *spore.qtm* file located in the *chapter 2* directory on the companion CD. This animation shows a simple walking cycle of Spore. It really shows the wonderful impact of Bones on the muscle and skin tissue.

By now you've probably surmised that Bones allows you to build a virtual skeleton in your creatures, which modifies the mesh when it's moved. You basically lay down a skeleton of individual Bones in the creature, then move the Bones to deform the model into the desired position. This is obviously oversimplifying the issue; using Bones requires a great deal of tweaking to insure that you don't completely mutilate the mesh when the bones are moved. It also requires plenty of planning so your model can actually be animated using Bones. In fact, let's take a moment to examine the rules of Single Mesh modeling, which ensure that we have properly modeled our creature for Bones animation.

THE RULES OF SINGLE MESH MODELING

As with most technical procedures there are rules to creating models for Bones animation. These rules serve as guidelines for modeling your creatures. The last thing you want to do is spend a ton of time modeling a 3D creature only to find out that it won't work with Bones animation. Believe me, it's not amusing. I did it several times when I first started modeling Single Mesh creatures.

Let's take a look at the guidelines:

1. **Spread out the body parts.** A Bone will affect the mesh in its immediate vicinity. For this reason, you need to keep the body parts from being too close together, or the Bones will end up fighting over the mesh between them. For example, when creating hands you'll want to leave a good deal of distance between the fingers so they can be boned individually. If they are too close the Bones will end up pulling the mesh of the finger that is too close. In fact, take a look at Figure 2.2, which shows a hand with fingers in two different positions.

    First, take a look at the hand in image A. This hand is in a position that is very commonly seen in 3D creatures. Unfortunately, the fingers are too close together to animate with Bones. If you applied Bones to these fingers they'd end up pulling each other apart. What we need to do is move the fingers apart as shown in image B. You can see that the fingers have been moved apart slightly so the Bones won't fight over their mesh. This also represents the midrange position of the fingers. What's the importance of a midrange position? That just happens to be the next rule.

2. **Position the limbs in their midrange.** One of the most common problems encountered with Bones animation is poor limb positioning. Quite often they are either too close together or in the extreme rotation of their movement. Either of these spells disaster for animating the creature. It's important that you position the limbs in their midrange position so the mesh won't be become corrupted. There's a limit to how far you can stretch a polygon before it looks unnatural. If you place your limbs in the midrange position you are guaranteed that you won't overstretch the mesh.

When you create a creature for Bones animation you are placing it in its neutral position. Basically this means that the body and limbs are positioned in their midrange so they can be properly animated with Bones. Figure 2.3 shows the typical neutral position for a biped creature.

Let's take a look at several limbs and explore their positioning. First, examine the arms. Notice how they are straight out to the side. This is the midrange position of the arm. Bipeds can rotate their arms over roughly 180 degrees of movement. They can reach straight up or straight down, making the midrange position straight out to the side. Now take a look at the arms from the top view and you'll notice that the forearm is bent slightly at the elbow. This is because the forearm can rotate from straight out to roughly 60 degrees inward, making the current position of the forearm the midrange.

Take a look at the hands. You can see how all of the fingers are bent slightly. This, of course, is the midrange position for the fingers. The tendency is to make the fingers straight out because it's easier to apply the bones, but this should be avoided because the mesh and textures will stretch horribly when you attempt to make a fist.

Finally, take a look at his legs. You can see that they are spread slightly, placing them in the middle of their range of motion. If you placed them closer together you would be unable to move the leg effectively to the side as in a karate sidekick. Sure, if you plan to have your creature only walk normally you could get away with rotating the legs inward but you should try to avoid doing this. It can be habit forming, and bad habits should be avoided. You should always place your creatures in the neutral position regardless of how they will be animated. Who knows; eventually you may want your creature to do a sidekick.

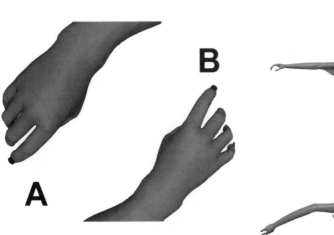

FIGURE **2.2** *Properly positioning body parts.*   FIGURE **2.3** *A biped neutral position.*

3. **Build mesh density around joints.** One of the most common mistakes made by 3D artists is that they never build enough mesh density into the joints. The joints are where you see the widest range of motion. Since they will be moving over a broad range, you'll need to provide more polygons; otherwise the polygons in the joints will stretch too far, causing them to flatten. The other problem created by low-detail joints is that the surface is anchored to each polygon on the model. Therefore, if you have a low polygon count in the joint, you'll end up stretching the surface dramatically, which looks awful. To avoid both polygon and surface stretching, always make the joints like elbows, knees, and knuckles at least twice the density of the body. Take a look at Figure 2.4, which shows the wrist, elbow, and shoulder joints of a properly modeled Single Mesh character. As you can see by the circled regions, the joints have been reinforced with a mesh that's double the volume of the body. This model can now be animated effectively using Bones. Be sure that you always add density to your creature joints if you plan to use Bones to animate it.

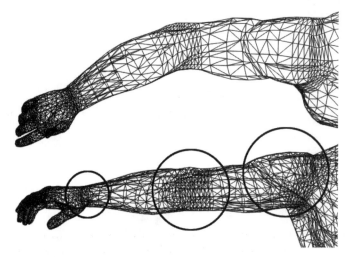

FIGURE **2.4** *Reinforcing the joints with a dense mesh.*

4. **Mirror your mesh.** When building Single Mesh creatures you can save yourself countless hours by mirroring your mesh. Basically, you build one half of the creature, then mirror the mesh and merge the points in the middle to create a Single Mesh as shown in Figure 2.5. As you can see, only half the creature was modeled; then it was mirrored to create the complete mesh. Of course, once you've mirrored your mesh you'll have perfect symmetry, which doesn't exist in real creatures. This is where you'll need to do a bit of tweaking. Actually it's relatively simple. All you need to do it pull one ear down slightly, shift a nostril over to the side a bit, or maybe even lower an eye slightly. Basically, you just need to make subtle changes so the model isn't perfectly symmetrical.

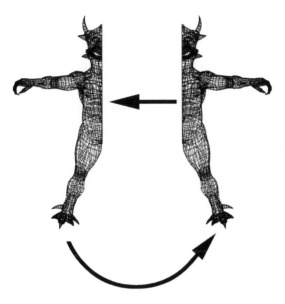

Figure **2.5** *Mirroring your mesh.*

Those are the rules of Single Mesh modeling. If you simply follow these rules religiously you'll avoid all of the drama and heartache of creating a model that doesn't work with Bones animation.

GETTING YOUR HANDS DIRTY

Now it's time to get your hands dirty modeling some very cool 3D creatures. Here is where you'll need to make a choice as to which tutorial you'd like to use. Three programs are covered in the modeling portion of this book. Part II deals with LightWave, Part III covers 3D Studio MAX, and Part IV explores Animation Master. Although you may possess only one of these programs, you should read through all the chapters. They will give you a variety of perspectives on creature modeling.

Of course, once you've mastered creature modeling with your specific program you should take advantage of Part V, which covers photorealistic creature surfacing. Nothing makes your creatures come alive like high-quality surfacing.

Now is a good time to take a short break before you dive in and get to work modeling the outrageous creatures in the tutorial chapters.

PART

II

LightWave Creature Modeling

This part covers modeling creatures with LightWave 5.5. LightWave has long been considered to have the best image output, but it hasn't gained much respect for its creature capabilities. Ironically, LightWave has some of the best tools for creature modeling and surfacing. In fact, it's one of only three programs on the market that can manage photorealistic creature surfacing. The other two products include SoftImage and Alias. LightWave is perfect for creature surfacing because it allows for multiple image map layers, which are a must for creating surface details, particularly bump maps. It's also one of the few products that has the ability to control surface diffusion with image maps. As you'll discover in Chapter 9, surface diffusion is the main component of photorealistic creature surfacing. In short, you'll soon see that LightWave is a very powerful tool for creating detailed organic creatures and characters.

VISIT THE COMPANION CD-ROM FOR COLOR IMAGES.

All of the figures shown in this book are mirrored, in color, on the CD-ROM. I recommend you open the CD and view the images while you read the book, or download the images for faster reference. There will be details in the figures that you can't see in the printed image.

In the following chapters we will be discussing the Metaform technology, which is the most flexible creature modeling tool in LightWave. I know many of you would consider MetaNurbs the best tool for organics, but that is only true in certain cases. MetaNurbs is great for creating molded organics such as organically shaped car bodies, telephones, furniture, or any other static object where the main detail is in the form of flowing lines. On the other hand, when creating organic creatures with tremendous detail such as muscles and wrinkles, you'll find MetaNurbs takes a backseat to Metaform.

We start by taking a look at the pros and cons of Metaform technology; when we have a handle on the technology, we'll model some creature parts to get the feel of the tools. Then we'll go on to modeling a highly detailed creature that should set the record straight as to the creature capabilities of LightWave. Of course, to get the most of this part you'll need a working knowledge of the basic functions of the LightWave Modeler. We'll be making reference to tools under the assumption that you know where they are located. If you aren't familiar with the tools in LightWave, take this opportunity to get to know them. If you already have a handle on where all of the tools are located you can dive right in. Let's get started.

3 Getting to Know Metaform

If you've been in the industry for the last couple of years you've probably seen a plethora of software developers claiming they had the perfect organic modeling tools. It's interesting that every product seems to have the same claim. Well, LightWave has had its time in the spotlight with MetaNurbs, which is certainly a major advance in organic modeling. But there is an even more practical and effective creature modeling tool that is rarely mentioned: Metaform.

What is Metaform, and why is it so great for modeling organic creatures? Metaform operates under the same principles as MetaNurbs, but with more control. Metaform is a smoothing feature, and a great deal more. Unlike the smoothing feature in the Subdivide Panel, which performs smoothing on the shape, Metaform performs smoothing on each individual polygon, which makes it better for shaping than smoothing.

Metaform works under the principle of tension between points on a polygon. Simply put, the farther apart the points, the more dramatic the smoothing effect. This is the main advantage of Metaform over MetaNurbs. MetaNurbs has a fixed tension control but Metaform gives you control over the tension of the smoothing by allowing you to change the Max Smoothing Angle.

The Max Smoothing Angle determines which polygons will actually be smoothed by the Metaform function. Any adjoining polygon with an angle greater than the Max Smoothing Angle will not be smoothed. Take a closer look at how this works.

Figure 3.1 shows an orthographic view of a simple cube object. You can see that the A selection is indicating two adjoining polygons, and the B selection is indicating the Adjoining Angle for the polygons. Since it's a cube, the Adjoining Angles are all 90 degrees. If you were to use a value less than 90 in the Max Smoothing Angle the cube would be divided but wouldn't change its shape. In fact, let's take a look at the example shown in Figure 3.2.

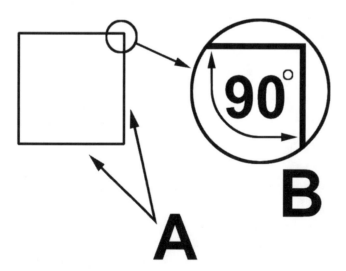

FIGURE **3.1** *How Metaform works.*

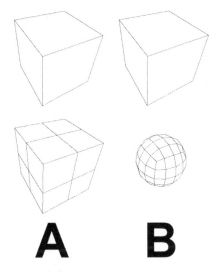

A   B

FIGURE **3.2**   *Using the Max Smoothing Angle to shape the mesh.*

Figure 3.2 shows the same simple cube, which has been Metaformed with two different Max Smoothing Angles. Image A represents a Max Smoothing Angle of less than 90, and Image B represents a value greater than 90. You can see that the object in Image A was divided by the Metaform action but didn't change its shape. On the other hand, the object in Image B became a ball because the Adjoining Angles of its polygons were less than the Max Smoothing Angle. As you can see, the difference is rather dramatic, which makes the Max Smoothing Angle a very useful tool for controlling the amount of detail added to your objects when you Metaform. Generally speaking, when creating organic creatures you'll want to keep the Max Smoothing Angle at 179.9 (its max value), to ensure that you create the most organic shape.

Speaking of organic shapes, let's take another look at how the Adjoining Angle of polygons affects the shaping of an object.

Figure 3.3 shows a box with three different mesh configurations that have all been Metaformed with a Max Smoothing Angle of 179.9. The top mesh in Image A shows a simple cube with one polygon on each of six sides. You'll notice that the cube was turned into a ball when Metaformed because all of the Adjoining Angles are 90 degrees, as indicated by the circled area on the model. Now take a look at Image B, which shows the same cube that has been faceted to create four polygons on each side. You can see that the cube retained most of its original shape when Metaformed. This is because it had Adjoining Angles greater than 179.9 degrees. Where? Well, take a look at the top, where the polygons meet in the center. You can see that the point where the polygons adjoin is completely flat, which makes the Adjoining Angle 180 degrees. This means that this portion of the model will not be smoothed because it exceeds the Max Smoothing Angle. Therefore, only the corners of the cube were smoothed when Metaform was applied.

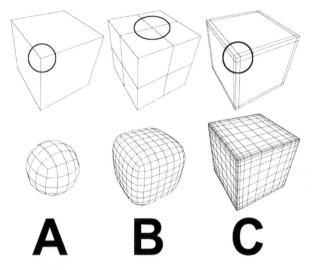

A B C

FIGURE **3.3** *The impact of polygon Adjoining Angles.*

Now take a look at Image C. Here you have a different approach to dividing the cube. Instead of simply faceting the cube, we've actually added a vertex that is very close to the edge on all sides, creating a single polygon in the middle. Since this polygon has an Adjoining Angle of 180 degrees with the adjacent polygons, it won't be smoothed by the Metaform function. Once again, only the corners have been smoothed. Since the middle polygon is so large we end up with a shape similar to a Las Vegas dice. Cool, isn't it?

As you can see, there are a variety of ways you can use the Max Smoothing Angle to your advantage when creating organic shapes. Of course, these have all been very simple examples. Why don't we take a look at the effects of Metaform on a more complicated object? In fact, let's see how it's actually used to shape a creature model.

As you can see, Figure 3.4 shows a couple of versions of an alien bat head. The image on the left is the basic model before Metaform was applied. The image on the right is the result of using Metaform with a Max Smoothing angle of 179.9. Big difference, isn't it? The mesh has been shaped into a very natural, organic object. Take a closer look at this little guy to see the impact of Metaform. Look at his nose in the image on the left and you'll see that it's very angular and unnatural; now take a look at the image on the right and you can see that it has a very soft, round, and natural shape. The same applies for his neck, mouth, eye sockets, and ears. Metaform has transformed these rough angles into smooth, organic lines.

Metaform is a great tool for organically smoothing out models, but what are the other benefits of this modeling technique? And how about the disadvantages; are there any, or is this the perfect modeling solution? Let's take a look at the pros and cons of Metaform modeling.

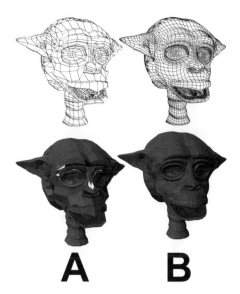

A   B

FIGURE **3.4** *Metaforming a creature model.*

THE PROS AND CONS OF METAFORM MODELING

The good news is that Metaform modeling is really one of the best possible organic modeling methods you can choose. It's certainly the best choice within LightWave. You've seen how the polygon smoothing function of Metaform can transform a simple, angular model into a very believable organic creature. This, of course is a major pro of Metaform modeling. Of course, this also opens the door to many other positive aspects like the fact that you can build a relatively low-detail mesh and simply Metaform it to create a highly detailed model.

Working with a low-detail mesh has many advantages. It's much easier to create details because the mesh isn't too dense to see anything. You also get a much faster refresh rate in OpenGL mode since the polygon count is low. One of the best aspects of Metaform modeling is that you can do less work to create the completed model since Metaform does a great deal of the work for you.

There are many advantages to using Metaform, what about disadvantages? There are actually no disadvantages to using Metaform. When it comes to polygon modeling, Metaform is a very clean and effective means for creating organic creatures. It's also very flexible because you can start the model any way you'd like. You can start with patches, basic shapes, or simply lying down points and manually creating polygons. You just need to make sure that you conform to the rules of Metaform modeling. Let's take a look at those rules.

THE RULES OF METAFORM MODELING

As with any technical process, there are guidelines to using Metaform modeling. These, of course, are designed to make your life easier by saving you the heartache of fixing problems late in the game.

1. **Always use four-point polygons whenever possible.** Although Metaform can actually smooth three-point polygons, you want to avoid this whenever possible. A four-point polygon provides the most accurate smoothing possible since it has even tension on four sides. A three-point polygon has tension on only three sides, which creates a weak spot on one side that can cause pinching problems with the mesh. Of course, you can't always use four-point polygons, so placement of three-point polygons becomes important. This brings us to rule number two.

2. **Always place three-point polygons away from small details.** Because three-point polygons cause pinching, you want to keep them away from small surface details that are elevated. Elevated details have a higher level of smoothing so the pinching caused by a three-point polygon will become more apparent. You should aim to keep three-point polygons on the areas of your model that are relatively flat since the smoothing tension in these areas is minimal, reducing the pinching effect of a three-point polygon. For example, when creating a head, you wouldn't want the three-point polygon to be around the high detail areas like the eyes, ears, and nose. On the other hand, the forehead and chin are perfect places since they don't have small details, and they spread the weight of the tension over a larger area. To get a better idea of the effects of three-point polygons, take a look at Figure 3.5.

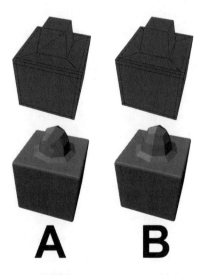

A   B

FIGURE ■ **3.5** *The disadvantage of three-point polygons.*

Here we have a simple bump created on the box. The front face of the bump in Image A is divided into two three-point polygons. You can see that after Metaform was applied the mesh on the front of the bump is irregular, causing it to look deformed. On the other hand, the bump on the object in Image B is very uniform. It's obvious that three-point polygons can cause problems with organic models. Although they are often unavoidable, they can be placed where they won't cause any problems.

Of course, don't confuse three-point polygons with tripled polygons. Although they are the same, tripled polygons are used only when you have completed the mesh. Four-point polygons can cause nonplanar errors in layout, particularly when bones are used. To avoid this problem, the mesh is tripled before being saved for animation use. This ensures that you will have no problems rendering it. Just be sure that you triple the mesh only after you are completely done modeling it. You never want to Metaform a tripled mesh. The results can be scary considering that most of the polygons will likely pinch.

3. **Avoid making your pre-Metaform mesh too dense.** If you make your mesh too dense you'll basically neutralize the effects of Metaform. When you have a dense mesh the smoothing effect is minimal because the polygons are too close together. Remember the boxes in Figure 3.2? The tighter mesh means that the smoothing effect is applied over a small area, which reduces the organic look of your model. Try to keep the mesh at the minimum number of polygons to get the most out of Metaform. Besides, if you have a dense mesh before the Metaform you'll end up with a really scary mesh afterward, which will probably exceed the point limit in LightWave (roughly 65,000 points).

4. **Avoid creating hard edges.** This rule applies to adding details to the model. For example, when creating the base of a horn you'll want to build a raised bump on the model and then make a depression in the bump for the horn. If you simply shift out the polygons and then shift them down to make the hole you'll have a sharp edge on the ridge of the hole. Since you have a severe Adjoining Angle, Metaform will try to smooth the polygons as best it can. Unfortunately this leads to a very sharp edge being created, which is very unnatural. What you want to do is add some thickness to the top of the bump so it smoothes properly. To see how this works, look at Figure 3.6.

Here we have a crude bump that has been created for the base of a horn. You can see that the edge of the bump in Image A is very harsh. Now take a look at the bump in Image B, which is very smooth at the top. This is because a layer of polygons was created to give thickness to the top of the bump. When Metaform was applied to the model it smoothed the edge to create a very organic ridge at the top of the horn. You can see how important it is to avoid hard edges.

As you can see, the rules of Metaform modeling are actually quite simple and easy to follow. If you apply these rules to your organic creature modeling efforts you'll save yourself a lot of time fixing problems, not to mention countless bottles of aspirin.

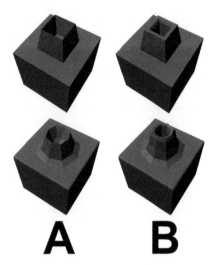

A   B

FIGURE **3.6** *The problem created by hard edges.*

Now that you understand Metaform and how to properly plan a model for its use, we are ready to take a look at the actual Metaform Modeling tools.

METAFORM MODELING TOOLS

How do you get the most out of Metaform modeling? It's actually quite simple — you merely need to become familiar with a few basic tools and how they are used. We won't be doing a deep exploration of the tools since you should already have a working knowledge of them before reading this book. What we will do is cover the most valuable tools in the Metaform modeling toolkit and where they are used. We'll use all of the tools to modify a simple cartoon hand so it has more detail. Let's take a look at the *Metaform Toolkit* in action.

First, load the *ToonArm.lwo* into the Modeler. You'll find the file in the Chapter 3 folder on the companion CD. Once you load the model, you're ready to explore the Metaform Toolkit.

SMOOTH SHIFT

This is the most important tool you'll be using. Smooth Shift is paramount to creating the details on organic creatures. It allows you to select groups of polygons and basically extrude them as a group. If you were to try the same action with extrude, the polygons would actually extrude individually, creating quite a mess. Although the Smooth Shift tool is paramount to Metaform modeling, it does have an inherent problem, which is easily avoided. If you attempt a Smooth Shift on polygons that are not parallel to one of the three axes, the polygons will cause errors. Most often they will arbitrarily divide themselves, creating serious problems. To avoid this problem, you should always set the Offset value to zero, and manually move the polygons. Let's see how the Smooth Shift feature is used to create creature details.

1. Figure 3.7 shows a relatively simple cartoon hand. What we are going to do is add a pad on the palm to make it the hand of a cartoon cat. To do this, first select the palm polygons as shown in Figure 3.8. To select the polygons, first hide the polygons on the back of the hand so the palm polygons are easier to see. Once you've selected the palm polygons you should unhide the back of the hand.

2. Now that the polygons are selected, **Smooth Shift** them with an Offset Value of 0 to create the palm pad. Then use the **Modify/Move** command to move the polygons back into the palm of the hand as shown in Figure 3.9.

3. Now you have the depression of the palm. You'll notice that the palm has a new surface at this point so that you can distinguish it from the hand. To do this, simply press the **Q key** and enter a new surface name, such as **Palm**, change the color to white, and press **Apply**. Getting back to the model, you can see how Smooth Shift has made it very simple to add detail to the palm. Of course, you're not done yet but since you just used the **Modify/Move** command, take a look at the role it plays in Metaform creature modeling.

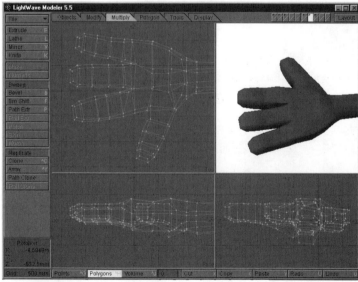

FIGURE **3.7** *A simple cartoon hand.*

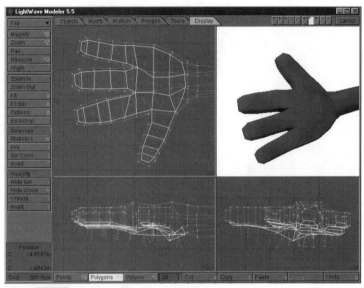

FIGURE **3.8** *Selecting the palm polygons.*

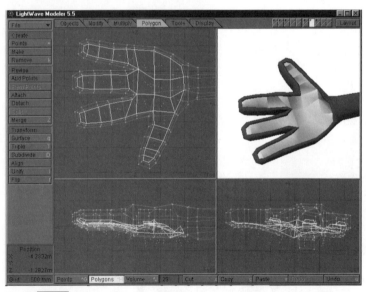

FIGURE **3.9** *Moving the palm polygons.*

MODIFY/MOVE

You'll find that this tool is invaluable when it comes to creating organic creatures. It's primarily used to move the Smooth Shifted polygons manually so you can avoid the division error discussed a minute ago. It's also used to move polygons around to create organic shapes, which you'll be doing in just a moment. Let's get back to the palm.

1. The next step in creating the palm is to **Smooth Shift** the polygons again and move them up so they are level with the rest of the hand polygons as shown in Figure 3.10.

2. You can't Metaform the hand yet because the palm polygons will be rounded too much. Remember the Adjoining Angles discussed earlier? Well, the palm is currently made of side and top polygons with an Adjoining Angle of 90 degrees. This will cause the polygons to smooth severely, which isn't the effect you're seeking. To prevent this, you need to create another set of polygons with an angle less than 90 degrees. To do this, use the **Smooth Shift** tool and a new tool called **Smooth Scale**. Let's look at what Smooth Scale does.

TOOLS/SMOOTH SCALE

This is a new tool found in LightWave 5.5. It's one of the best additions to the program, along with the *Knife* tool we'll be covering later. Smooth Scale is very similar to the Scale command except it doesn't scale from a control point but rather scales the polygons from their outside edge, ensuring that they maintain their proportions. Without this tool, you'd spend a lot of time tweaking points to make sure the newly scaled polygons were proportional. Let's put the Smooth Scale tool to work.

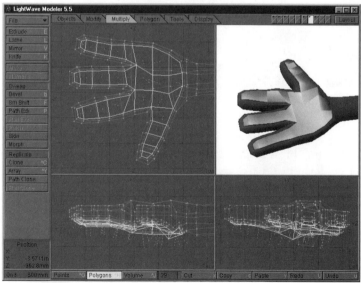

FIGURE **3.10** *Forming the palm pad.*

1. The first thing you need to do is create a new segment of polygons, so **Smooth Shift** the upper polygons on the palm and move them away from the palm slightly. It's important to note that Smooth Scale will not work unless the Smooth Shifted polygons are moved away from their parent polygons.

2. With the upper palm polygons still selected, click on the **Smooth Scale** button under the Tool menu and enter a value of –50 mm and press **OK**. You need to enter a negative value because we want the polygons to be scaled smaller. Once the polygons are scaled, you'll need to move them to a position just slightly above the parent polygons as shown in Figure 3.11.

3. To see what the new palm looks like, **Metaform** the hand by pressing **SHIFT-D**. Now click the **Metaform** button and enter a Max Smoothing Angle of 179 and press **OK**. You should have a hand that resembles the one in Figure 3.12.

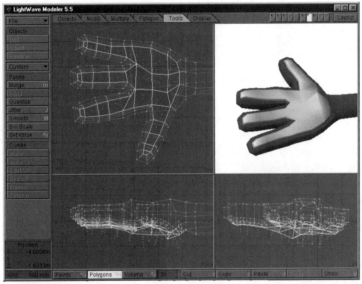

FIGURE **3.11** *Smooth Scaling polygons.*

You can see how the tool of the Metaform Toolkit can be very useful for creating creature details. Before continuing, press the **Undo** button to revert the model back to its pre-Metaform state. Now we have just a few more tools to examine. Let's look at the Knife tool first.

MULTIPLY/KNIFE

This is one of the new features added to LightWave 5.5. It's also a lifesaver! The principle behind Metaform modeling is to create a very simple mesh so you can create the basic

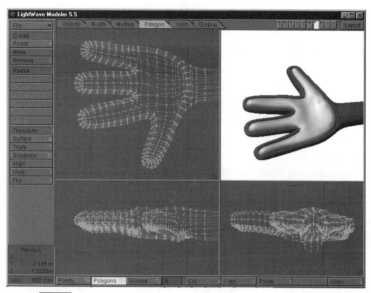

FIGURE **3.12** *The Metaformed hand.*

details and still be able to distinguish the details. A high-density mesh can be nearly impossible to edit. The knife tool allows you to add polygons to specific areas of the mesh, so you don't have to Metaform the whole thing to increase the density in a single area. Let's add some detail to the toon arm. Take a look at Figure 3.13.

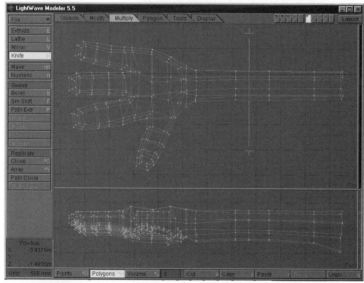

FIGURE **3.13** *Using the Knife tool to add polygons.*

1. Figure 3.13 contains the toon arm, which is too low in polygon count for you to add significant detail. To get around this problem you need to add segments to the elbow area. To do this, press **SHIFT-K**, which activates the knife tool. Then place the cursor above the area you want to divide, hold down the mouse button, and drag to the other side. Now release the mouse button and press **ENTER** to divide the polygons as shown in Figure 3.13. You could use the right mouse button, which will divide the polygons automatically when you release the mouse, but then you wouldn't be able to tweak the cutting area.

2. You need just one more division before moving on, so go ahead and use the Knife tool to add a division on the other side of the elbow area as shown in Figure 3.14.

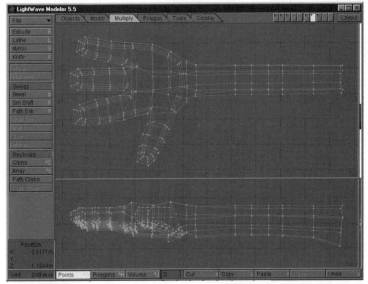

FIGURE **3.14** *Additional Knife divisions.*

Now we're ready to use the Stretch tool. Let's take a look at the value of the Stretch tool before we actually put it to use.

MODIFY/STRETCH

The Stretch tool is extremely useful for adding organic details to your creature models. It's typically used to stretch points and polygons to create bulges in the mesh. For example, you can select the points on either side of an arm and stretch them out to create the tricep and bicep simultaneously. In fact, let's do that to our toon arm.

1. Select the points on either side at the base of the toon arm, press the **H key** to activate the Stretch tool, and stretch the points out a bit as shown in Figure 3.15.

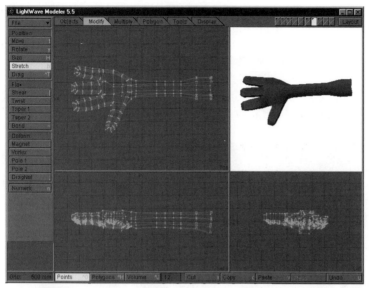

FIGURE **3.15** *Using the Stretch tool to create muscle details.*

Let's continue to explore the tools of the Metaform Toolkit. The next tool is *Drag*. It's relatively obvious what this tool does, but it warrants a look since it will be the most frequently used tool for creating creature models.

MODIFY/DRAG

This is your tweaking tool. Probably 75 percent of creature modeling is tweaking on the point level. You'd be surprised how dragging a simple point can add tremendous detail to your creature models. Let's put the tool to work by creating the tricep and forearm bulges on our toon arm.

1. Here's where the arm really starts to take shape. Start by selecting a few points on the top and bottom of the arm; then drag them individually until they resemble the image in Figure 3.16.
2. You're really getting somewhere now. The toon arm has started to take shape and resemble something more than a simple tube. Although you'll frequently find that cartoon characters have tubular limbs, I like to see more detail, particularly since it's so easy to add.

3. The last thing you need to add to the arm is an elbow. To do this, select the polygon at the back of the arm and drag it out a bit as shown in Figure 3.17.

Now we're finally to the last tool of the Metaform Toolkit, the *Magnet* tool. Let's take a look at where we use the magnet tool in creature creation.

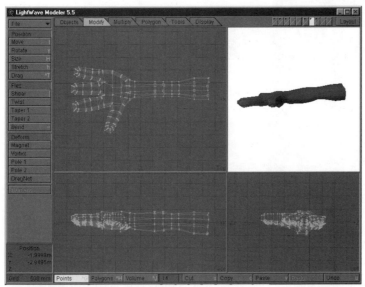

FIGURE **3.16** *Dragging points to add details.*

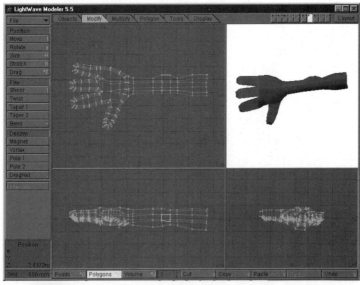

FIGURE **3.17** *Adding an elbow with the Drag tool.*

DEFORM/MAGNET

This is your finishing-touch tool. It's what you use to add chaotic details to your models to make them appear more organic and natural. You'll also need to use the Magnet tool to remove symmetry from the model. Real creatures don't have perfect symmetry; therefore you need to add some chaos to your creatures. This is easy to do with the Magnet tool. You can simply drag one ear down slightly, make one bicep larger than the other, move an eye a bit, you get the idea. This is a very useful tool for adding those finishing touches. Go ahead and add some detail to the cartoon arm with the Magnet tool.

1. First, press **SHIFT+:** to activate the Magnet tool. This brings up the tool in its default mode, which has an automatic range. This won't work since it will tend to deform the entire mesh. You need to set a Fixed Range. Do this by pressing the **N** key to bring up the numeric requester. Then click the **Fixed** button and press **Apply** to accept the change.
2. Press and hold the right mouse button to resize the Magnet tool bounding box until you have something that resembles Figure 3.18.

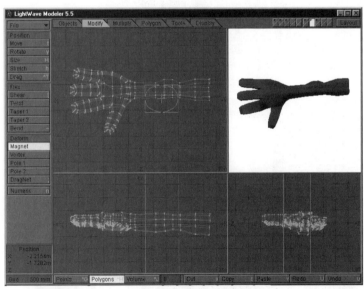

FIGURE **3.18** *Using the Magnet tool in Fixed Range mode.*

3. Position the bounding box as shown in Figure 3.18, hold down the left mouse button, and drag the mesh until you have something like Figure 3.19.
4. You've just added some detail to the forearm; do the same to the bicep. Position the Magnet bounding box as shown in Figure 3.19 and drag the bicep out so you have something similar to Figure 3.20.

5. Now you have something that looks more natural and organic. You simply need to add a bit of a bulge to the lower part of the arm under the bicep and you're done. Go ahead and resize the Magnet tool in the **Face View Window** and drag the lower arm down as shown in Figure 3.21.

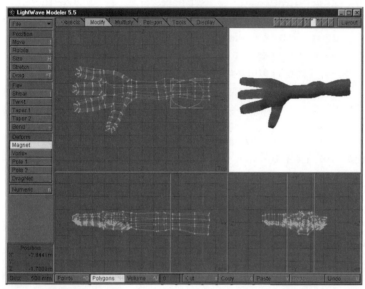

FIGURE **3.19** *Modifying the mesh with the Magnet tool.*

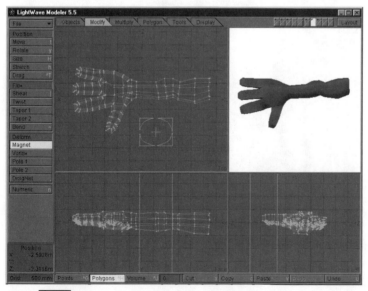

FIGURE **3.20** *Creating bicep mass with the Magnet tool*

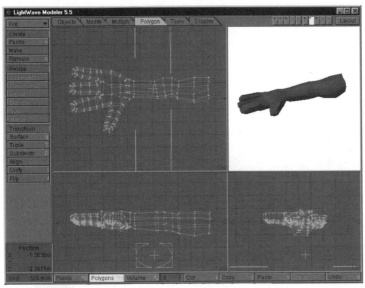

FIGURE **3.21** *Adding the finishing touch on the arm.*

You're done with the arm; Metaform the object to see the final results that are shown in Figure 3.22.

That about does it for the Metaform Toolkit tools and uses. You can see how these tools go a long way toward adding organic details to your creature models. With just a bit

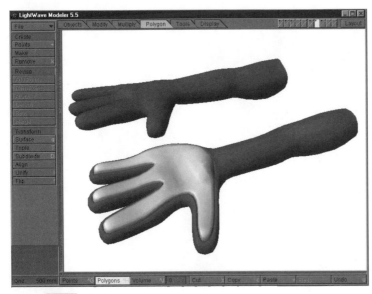

FIGURE **3.22** *The completed arm.*

of experimentation you'll find countless way to use these tools in your daily creature modeling regime.

Now that we have covered the tools of Metaform modeling, let's take a look at the approach; that is, how we plan our models to be modeled with Metaform.

METAFORM MODELING TECHNIQUES

One of the major benefits of Metaform modeling is that you can begin the model many different ways. There really isn't a right or wrong way to begin but there are cases where certain techniques are advantageous. Let's take a look at the two main ways you can begin your model and where they are best used.

THE BASIC CUBE

This is a very common method for Metaform modeling. Basically, you start with a simple cube, Metaform the object twice to increase the polygons count, and begin shaping the object. The shaping is done by Smooth Shifting polygons away from the mesh and then using the other tools in the Metaform Toolkit to shape the mesh. This is a great technique for modeling low detail creatures or static objects. In fact, let's take a look at a character that was created from a simple cube. Check out the Robby the Rabbit in Figure 3.23.

FIGURE **3.23** *Robby the Rabbit, modeled with the Basic Cube method.*

Robby the Rabbit was completely modeled from a simple cube. The process begins with the head, since it's more spherical. The cube is Metaformed twice to increase the density of polygons and to round it into a ball. Next, the ball is molded into a head by Smooth Shifting polygons and dragging points.

After the head is completed, the neck is created by Smooth Shifting the polygons at the base of the head. Then the body is created by Smooth Shifting polygons from the neck. Finally, the arms and legs are Smooth Shifted from the body. Though it sounds a bit complicated, it's actually very easy.

As you can see, this technique works very well for animated characters, but what happens when you want to make something that's realistic? Well, if you planned on making a highly detailed realistic creature you would need more, very specific, control over the mesh. In these cases, you'll want to use the *Flat Mesh technique*.

THE FLAT MESH

This is a highly recommended technique for complex creature design. It's also the most unusual in concept since you're starting the creature as a flat mesh. Although it takes a bit of getting used to, it's definitely worth the investment because it will greatly speed the modeling process. You start your model with a flat mesh of polygons, with the detail where it's necessary. For example, when creating a face you need specific mesh density around the eyes, mouth, and nose. With the Flat Mesh technique you simply draw a flat mesh, including the density where needed, and then extrude the mesh to add depth. This way you have the polygons where you need them. Let's take a look at the creature shown in Figure 3.24, which was created using the Flat Mesh method.

Figure 3.24 shows the original flat mesh and the final model side by side. Compare the two models to see how the Flat Mesh method was used to plan for the creature details.

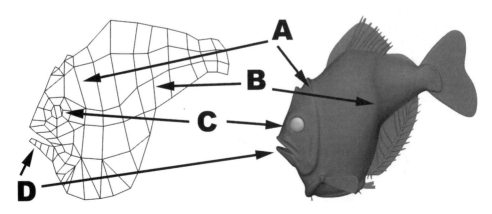

FIGURE **3.24** *Modeling a realistic fish with the Flat Mesh method.*

A) Here is the gill ridge that separates the head from the body. On the flat mesh we added the basic outline for the head/gill. When we created the head, we selected all of the head polygons and **Smooth Shifted** them away from the body to create the ridge that runs down the back of the head.

B) This segment represents the end of the body and the beginning of the tail. We created the line on the flat mesh so the polygons could be Smooth Shifted to add depth. Actually, first both the body and head were Smooth Shifted together, then the head was Smooth Shifted again to raise it above the body.

C) Naturally, we included some polygons for the eye. To create the eye socket, we merely Smooth Shifted the polygons inward. Then they were Smooth Shifted again to create the actual eyeball.

D) The shape of the mouth was laid down in the original flat mesh. This made it very simple to create the mouth details. If you take a look at the upper lip you'll see a row of polygons that runs down the lip and past the back of the jaw. This group of polygons was Smooth Shifted to create the upper jawbone. The polygons on the lower lip were Smooth Shifted to create the lower jawbone.

As you can see, the mesh didn't start off looking like much but it certainly ended up looking highly detailed. This model was created in roughly three hours, which is extraordinarily fast considering the high level of detail. This speed was made possible because the Flat Mesh provided the foundation of the main details in the model. The modeler first extruded the **Flat Mesh**, then used **Smooth Shift** to add depth to the main details. Next, the model was **Metaformed** to increase the mesh density so the fine details could be added. This process takes a bit of getting used to but once you get the hang of it you'll be cranking out incredibly detailed models in record time.

Before you begin your next model, you need to determine the level of detail you'll be adding so you can identify the best possible way to start your model. The last thing you want to do is invest a great deal of time on a model, only to find out that you should have used a different starting method.

CREATING A CREATURE WITH METAFORM

As you can see, Metaform modeling is very flexible and powerful. You can use it to add incredible detail to your models. Speaking of incredible detail, now that we understand the Metaform Toolkit and the methods of beginning a model, we're ready to put this information to work by creating a detailed model using Metaform.

In the next chapter we'll be using Metaform to create a creature that has an extraordinary amount of detail. The final creature may seem a bit daunting, but you'll be surprised at just how easy it is to create. Let's jump right in and get started on our Metaform creature.

4

Advanced Creature Modeling with Metaform

Metaform is one of the most wonderful tools for adding extraordinary detail to your creature models. Splines, patches, and Nurbs are great modeling methods but polygon modeling gives you incredible flexibility in creating outrageous creature details. You have access to thousands of small polygons that can be modified individually to create intricate details.

In the following tutorial we'll be taking full advantage of polygons and Metaform. Let's jump right in and get started on our advanced modeling tutorial.

CREATING THE METAFORM CREATURE

The first step in the modeling process is to gather your source material. As we discussed in Chapter 1, source material can make or break your model. You have to ensure that you thoroughly research your creature before you begin modeling it.

In our tutorial we'll be modeling a very familiar creature so we actually won't need any source material, but we do need a creature biography. What is this familiar creature? A 3D PAC-MAN, of course. Not just any old PAC-MAN, but a *Living Toon* PAC-MAN.

Living Toons are hybrids between cartoon characters and real creatures. Basically, they are the best of both worlds. The Living Toon concept was pioneered by the certifiable minds of Komodo Studio, a leading 3D studio based in San Diego, California. Tired of the same old 3D cartoon characters, and not seeing the need to replicate real creatures in 3D since they already exist, they decided to combine both into a totally new creature called a Living Toon. These little creatures combine the personality of a cartoon character with the physical attributes of real creatures. Just imagine a cartoon character with visible bones, tendons, teeth, gums, detailed ears, etc. What we have is a realistic-looking cartoon that can inhabit our world but doesn't fall under our laws of physics. You can throw Living Toons off the Empire State Building and they'll bounce. You can run them over with a steamroller and they'll inflate themselves like nothing had happened. You can see how these characters would be a great deal of fun to animate.

In this tutorial, we're going to be taking the classic PAC-MAN and adding 3D details that make it a Living Toon creature. Before we get started we need to get a little background on this familiar character. Even though we are all familiar with the basic look of PAC-MAN, we need to consider the changes we'll have to make so he becomes a Living Toon. Let's take a look at the creature biography for Munch, our Living Toon PAC-MAN.

MUNCH'S BIOGRAPHY

Munch is a peculiar creature that lives in the swamplands in Florida. He's a direct descendant of Jurassic Pac, a rather aggressive prehistoric version of Munch that lived during the Jurassic Period. You can see an image of Jurassic Pac in Figure 4.1.

FIGURE **4.1** *Jurassic Pac.*

As you can see, these creatures weren't always cute and friendly. Actually, Munch is a genetic fluke. You see, the Jurassic Pac creature eventually evolved into what we know today as the Argentine horned frog, which is commonly referred to as the PAC-MAN frog. Somewhere along the line, a subspecies of the Jurassic Pac evolved in an entirely different direction, eventually becoming creatures like Munch. This is probably attributed to the fact that they lived exclusively in the deepest parts of the swamplands and had no real need to evolve that much. There were no major predators and their food source was plentiful, so their evolution took a slower approach than the Argentine horned frog's.

Of course, today we have encroached on their habitat with our freeways and houses so these little guys were finally discovered. In fact, these hungry little critters were discovered one day, chewing on the tire of a bulldozer. You've probably surmised that they aren't exactly the most finicky eaters — they'll eat just about anything. Of course, they don't have the dining habits of their ancestors. The Jurassic Pac was more than six feet in diameter and ate absolutely anything that moved. It was a ferocious predator. Packs of them (no pun intended) were known to have taken down a T-Rex occasionally. The Jurassic Pac had large, individual teeth for subduing prey, but the evolved Munch creatures have the dental structure of a typical amphibian. They have a rough, bony ridge in place of individual teeth. They have little need for large teeth since they swallow their prey whole.

One of the most striking features of Munch is his rotund shape. In fact, he's darn near perfectly round. Normally this would present a motion problem but these little creatures are quite creative. To move they inhale swamp gases, which are lighter than air. This causes them literally to float like a balloon. They achieve forward motion by flapping flippers and tail. It's not the most accurate means of movement, but with a mouth as big as theirs they have little trouble finding a meal. When they want to stop they simply exhale and they are gently lowered to the ground. So, if they fly to find food, how do they normally get around? Well, they are amphibians so they swim to get from one place to another. They go airborne only when they have trouble finding food in the water.

Since they are amphibians, they have very large, bulging eyes that make it easier to see their prey in the murky waters. Another feature they possess, which is common to frogs, are poison sacs behind their eyes. Many amphibians have these poison sacs to ward off predators. The Munch creatures are capable of shooting a very pungent fluid up to five feet through little holes in the sacs.

So if Munch eats everything in sight, what eats him? His natural predators are alligators, snapping turtles, and raccoons. Munch is nowhere near the size of his ancestors, which were six feet in diameter. Munch is only six inches in diameter so his species falls prey to a number of swamp-dwelling creatures. Although the poison sacs work great on smaller predators like raccoons, they don't do much to ward off alligators. This is where his flight abilities come in handy. When danger approaches he simply blows up with gas and floats away.

That about does it for Munch's biography. We could continue to explore his details but we'd be here all day. We'll explore more of his specific details as we model him.

MODELING MUNCH

Munch is a rather complicated creature to model. Although PAC-MAN is a very simple character, Munch is a seriously advanced version, which incorporates a number of little details. In fact, we could probably have added even more detail but we are limited on space in this book. This brings up a good point. Adding detail is probably the most enjoyable aspect of modeling creatures. Of course, you have to balance the detail with the purpose of the model. If you are modeling it for a contract you'll want to limit the detail you add to that which is specified in the contract. If you add more detail it's basically coming out of your pocket. On the other hand, if you are modeling the creature for your portfolio or merely a hobby, I suggest you go all out and keep modeling until you reach the point limit! Don't limit your imagination if you don't have to!

To create Munch we will be using the cube method since he's basically a ball. We could have tried the Flat Mesh method but it wouldn't have made it any easier. In fact, it would probably have made it more complicated. Creating the body is very easy with a cube since we simply Metaform it a couple of times and we'll have a round ball. So why don't we just start with a sphere? Well, a sphere has a ring of three-point polygons around the axis at the top and bottom, which would make Metaform modeling a real nightmare. Remember the rules of Metaform Modeling? We want to avoid three-point polygons because they can cause pinching. They usually aren't a problem by themselves but if you wrap a bunch of them around a center point you'll have a real problem avoiding the pinching. For this reason we use a Metaformed cube because all of the polygons are quads.

What about starting with a creature sketch? We won't be using source material for this creature because it really isn't necessary. Why? I usually recommend you start with a sketch of the character first, and then use the sketch as a template in the background for modeling, but that wouldn't make much sense for a creature like Munch since he's basically a ball with a mouth. In this case, we can start with the basic model and shoot from the hip to add the details. I find it can be a lot of fun just to go a little nuts adding details while you're modeling. Occasionally it can be fun to break the rules. This book wouldn't be very honest if it focused only on the rigid method of always working from a source sketch. Besides, if you plan to do creature modeling for broadcast you'll need to get used to working without a source sketch. Advertising agencies are notorious for having no source material for their ideas.

MODELING MUNCH'S BODY

We're going to start Munch with a simple cube, Metaform it a couple times, and then begin developing the mouth. Let's get started with the body.

The first thing we need to do is create a simple cube and **Metaform** it twice to round it into a ball, adding enough polygons so we can start adding the details. You should have something similar to the object in Figure 4.2.

Next, cut the mesh in half so we can save time by building one side and then mirroring it to complete the model. Select all of the polygons on the right side of the center axis and delete them as shown in Figure 4.3.

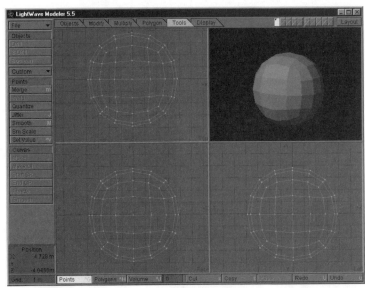

FIGURE **4.2** *Creating the foundation of the body.*

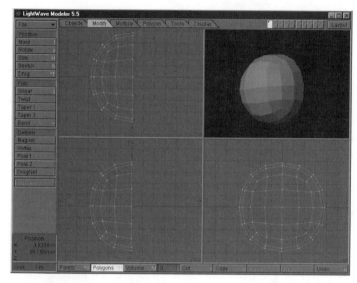

FIGURE **4.3** *Cutting the model in half.*

Now we need to start creating the mouth. We'll be creating the standard wedge mouth as seen on PAC-MAN but we need to modify the mesh to make this possible. This is where the Knife tool becomes necessary. Press **SHIFT-K**, then, in the **Side View Window**, drag the **Knife** tool from the center point out to just under the edge of the first polygon on the edge of the mesh as shown in Figure 4.4. Then press **Enter** and repeat the process on the lower side of the mesh to create the lower edge of the jaw.

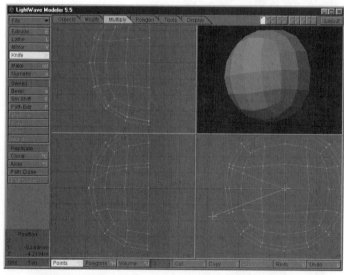

FIGURE **4.4** *Using the Knife tool to create the mouth outline.*

Next, weld the points created by the Knife tool in the center of the mesh by simply selecting all the points around the center point and pressing **CTRL+W** to weld them. Of course, now you probably have some undesirable one- or two-point polygons, so we'll need to delete them. Press **CTRL+H** to enter polygon edit mode, then press **W** to pop up the information window. If you have numbers in the data boxes next to the 1 or 2 vertices boxes, simply press the **PLUS** button to select them and then press your **Delete** key to remove them. Now we're ready to continue.

We need to create the mouth edge, which we will eventually Smooth Shift to create a sort of lip. Drag the points at the top of the polygons near the base of the mouth as shown in Figure 4.5.

Now we are ready to cut our mouth into the body. Before we do this, give the mesh a new surface name **Body** and make it yellow so it looks a little more like PAC-MAN. To create the mouth depth, select the eight polygons in the mouth wedge, then **Smooth Shift** them and scale them down a bit to create a small ledge as shown in Figure 4.6. Be sure to scale the polygons from the center point so they line up properly.

Now give these polygons a new surface name called **Mouth** so we can differentiate the mouth from the body. You should also give them a pink color so they are visibly different.

When Smooth Shifting polygons you'll be creating polygons on the axis (shown in Figure 4.7), which need to be deleted so you don't end up with a panel on the inside of the mouth. As you create these polygons, be sure to delete them so you don't end up with a confusing mess of polygons on the seam.

Now we have to do a bit of error correction. When we dragged the points to create the lip polygons we ended up dragging them inward as well. We now need to pull these

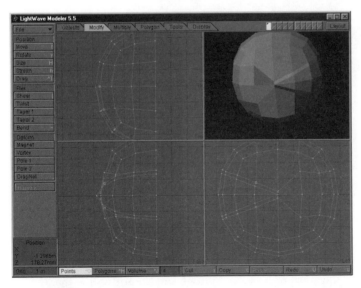

FIGURE **4.5** *Forming the polygons around the mouth edge.*

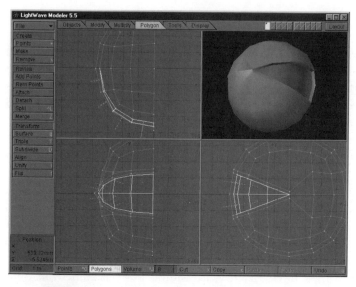

FIGURE **4.6** *Creating the mouth inset.*

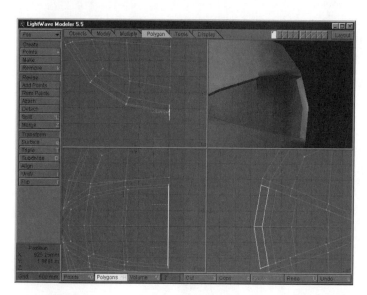

FIGURE **4.7** *Deleting polygons created by Smooth Shifting along the seam.*

out so the lips have thickness. Select the four points at the base of the mouth and drag them outward so they line up with the outer edge as shown in Figure 4.8.

To create the edge of the mouth that lies on the outside of the gums, which we'll be creating later, select the eight polygons in the mouth wedge and **Smooth Shift** them. Now stretch them vertically a bit to add some depth to the mouth edge as shown in Figure 4.9.

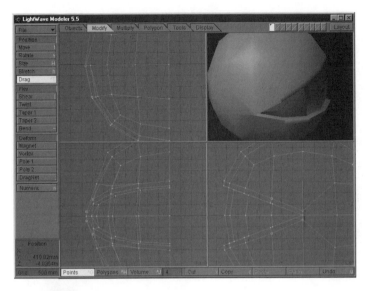

FIGURE **4.8** *Correcting the lip edge.*

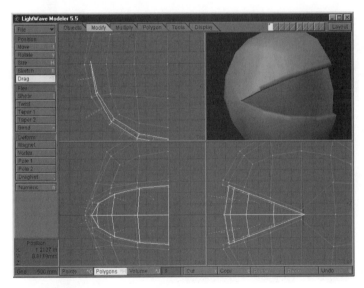

FIGURE **4.9** *Forming the edge of the mouth.*

This will reinforce the upper edge of the mouth edge so it doesn't round too much when we Metaform the object. Next, we need to create some depth to the mouth edge. **Smooth Shift** the polygons again and scale then slightly as shown in Figure 4.10.

To start building the gums where we'll be placing the teeth, start by **Smooth Shifting** the polygons again and then scale them slightly as shown in Figure 4.11. This will create the top edge of the gums.

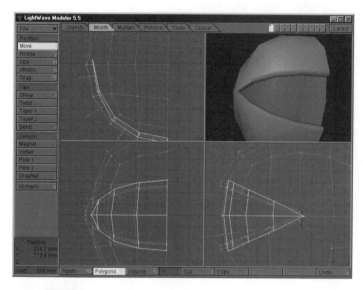

FIGURE **4.10** *Adding depth to the gums.*

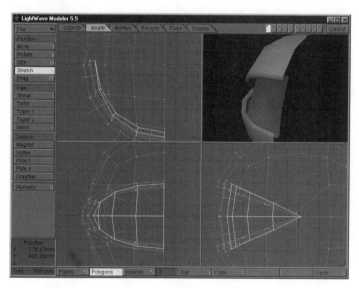

FIGURE **4.11** *Creating the top edge of the gums.*

To add depth to the gums, repeat the same process we did with the mouth edge. First **Smooth Shift** the polygons and scale them slightly, stretching them vertically a bit to create a subtle rounded edge on the gums. Then **Smooth Shift** the polygons again and stretch them vertically to complete the gums as shown in Figure 4.12.

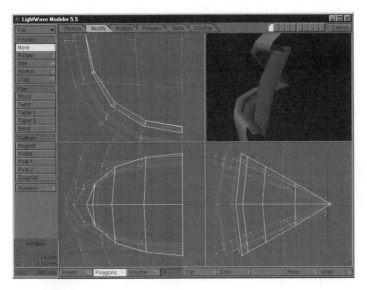

FIGURE **4.12** *Completing the gums.*

To create the actual mouth interior, **Smooth Shift** the polygons once, then scale them down about a quarter of the mouth's depth. Repeat the process so you have something like the model in Figure 4.13.

You've probably noticed that the mouth interior is fairly flat. Fix that problem by dragging the six polygons at the top and bottom of the mouth away from the gums as shown in Figure 4.14.

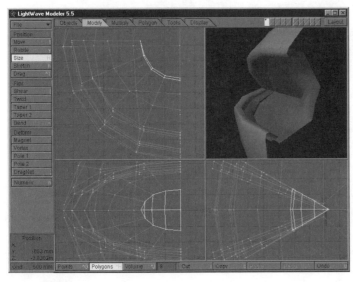

FIGURE **4.13** *Creating the mouth interior.*

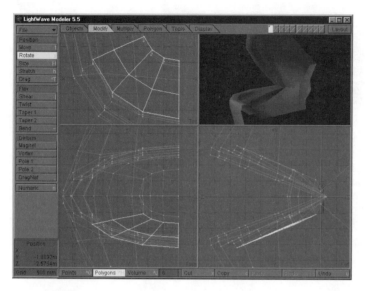

FIGURE **4.14** *Creating mouth depth.*

Now we need to create the fold of flesh at the corner of the jaw — you know, the kind you typically see on large dinosaurs like the T-Rex and Raptor. These are great for making the mouth look very organic and natural. First, select the Mouth polygons and **Hide Unselected** so we can isolate the mouth. Then select the two polygons at the corner of the mouth as shown in Figure 4.15, and **Hide Unselected**.

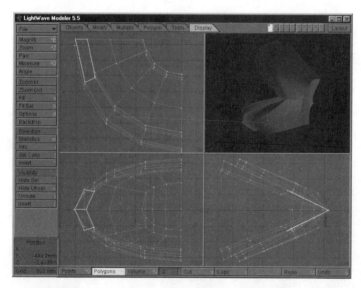

FIGURE **4.15** *Selecting the corner of the mouth.*

Start building the tissue in the corner of the mouth. This can be a bit tricky, so hang in there. First, **Smooth Shift** the upper polygon and move it down slightly, then drag the back points of the new polygon toward the front and align them to be parallel with the corner point. Repeat the same process with the lower polygon so you have something similar to Figure 4.16.

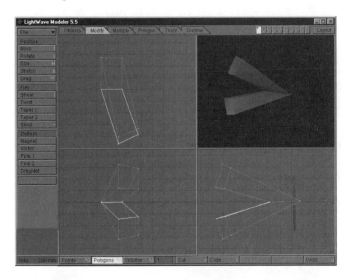

FIGURE **4.16** *Creating the corner mouth tissue.*

Next, weld the points at the base of the jaw tissue and delete the two polygons on the seam as shown in Figure 4.17.

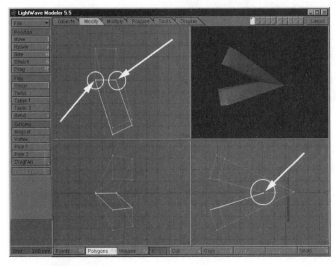

FIGURE **4.17** *Cleaning up the jaw tissue.*

We're just about done with the jaw tissue. To create the completed tissue, repeat the steps until your model looks like the one in Figure 4.18.

Be sure to line up the points in the **Top View Window** so you don't have bulges on the sides of the tissue. **Drag** the points at the wide end of the jaw tissue to create the curved surface shown in Figure 4.19.

To create the throat, **Unhide** the body, then select the polygons at the back of the mouth, stretch them flat, and widen them slightly as shown in Figure 4.20.

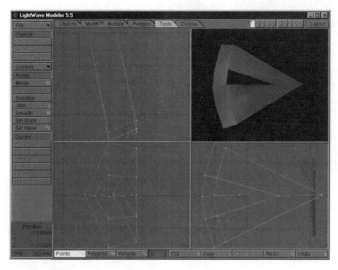

FIGURE **4.18** *The completed jaw tissue.*

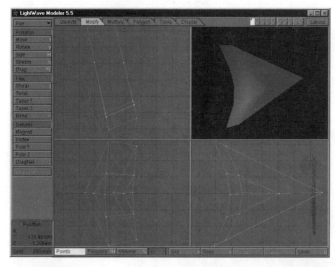

FIGURE **4.19** *Shaping the jaw tissue.*

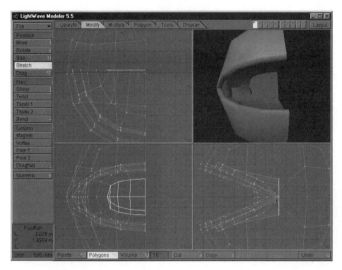

FIGURE **4.20** *Starting the throat.*

Smooth Shift several layers of polygons back into the body to create the throat. **Rotate** them slightly so the throat curves around under the jaw. **Smooth Shift** the throat of your model so it looks like the one in Figure 4.21.

Select the points on the inside edge of the gums and drag them inward to widen the gums so we can eventually place teeth in them. Figure 4.22 shows this process.

Since the top and bottom of the mouth appear somewhat flat, we'll need to shape them. Round the base of the gums by dragging the points at the base inward, then move the polygons inward to add depth to the gums as shown in Figure 4.23.

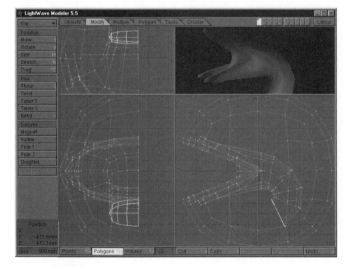

FIGURE **4.21** *Creating the throat.*

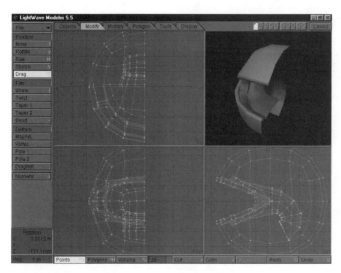

FIGURE **4.22** *Widening the gums.*

We can see some pinching at the back of the mouth where the gums meet the mouth interior. This is easily remedied by selecting these polygons and dragging the points downward to add height to the gums as shown in Figure 4.24.

You can see how we're adding plenty of detail for Munch's mouth. We'll be focusing a lot of effort on detailing the mouth since it's his most prominent feature. Most 3D artists neglect the mouth interior, which tends to make their models appear artificial. Detailed mouths will separate your creatures from the pack. Continue modeling by creating his tongue.

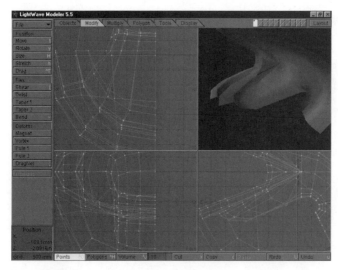

FIGURE **4.23** *Adding depth to the mouth.*

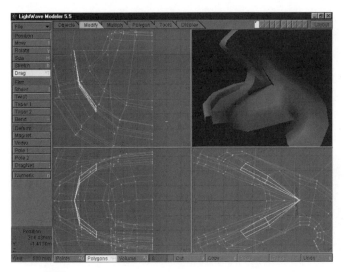

FIGURE **4.24** *Adding depth to the gums at the base of the jaw.*

Start by selecting the polygons at the base of the mouth and rotating them forward slightly. Then drag the outer points to shape the tongue as shown in Figure 4.25.

Before we continue with the tongue, we need to give it a surface name. Name the selected polygons **Tongue**. Now we can continue modeling the tongue. This is a fairly simple process; simply **Smooth Shift** several segments forward and scale the last couple of segments slightly to create a rounded tip as shown in Figure 4.26.

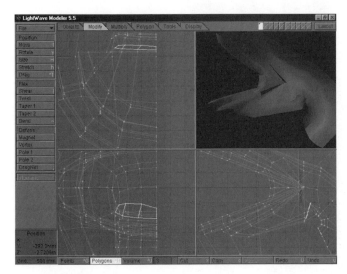

FIGURE **4.25** *Starting the tongue.*

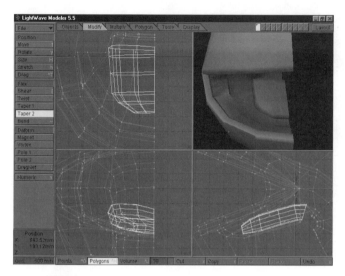

FIGURE **4.26** *Creating the tongue.*

Next, shape the inner portion of the tongue so it looks natural. Nothing looks worse than a flat tongue. We'll shape the tongue by selecting the upper points along the seam and dragging them into position as shown in Figure 4.27.

That was easy; now we need to shape the tip of the tongue so it isn't flat. Figure 4.28 shows where you should move the points at the tip of the tongue so that it's rounded.

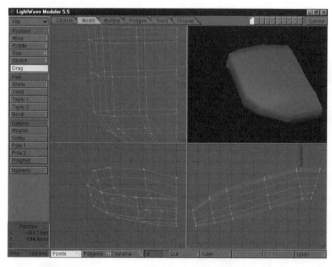

FIGURE **4.27** *Shaping the inner portion of the tongue.*

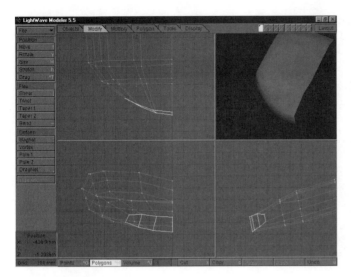

FIGURE **4.28** *Shaping the tip of the tongue.*

That completes the tongue — what else can we do to create detail in the mouth? A mouth wouldn't be complete without tendons — these are my favorite details in 3D creature mouths because nobody ever includes them. Nothing is quite as striking as tendons in the mouth and throat.

We'll need to add a couple of tendons on either side of the tongue and some muscular detail on the roof of the mouth to complete the mouth interior (except for the teeth, which we'll be adding in a moment). Making the tendons is very tricky because it involves a great deal of tweaking. You can't simply Smooth Shift and scale the polygons because of the odd angle of the gums. For this reason you'll need to examine the sample figure closely to match the position of the points.

Let's make some tendons, starting with the lower gums. Select the second row of polygons in front of the seam on the base of the mouth. Make sure you select the polygons that run up to the edge of the gums. Now **Smooth Shift** the polygons, scale them, and then tweak the point so you have something that resembles Figure 4.29.

It may take a bit of time to get it just right so take it slow. We need to make the details visible so let's rotate the tongue upward so it's flat. This will also make surfacing the tongue a great deal easier. To rotate the tongue, simply press the **W key** and select the Tongue surface, then rotate the polygons so they resemble Figure 4.30.

We have just one more detail to add to the mouth — the tendon detail on the roof of the mouth. First, select the **Mouth** polygons and **Hide Unselected**. Then deselect the lower polygons of the throat and **Hide Unselected**. Select the second row of points that are parallel to the seam and drag them downward as shown in Figure 4.31.

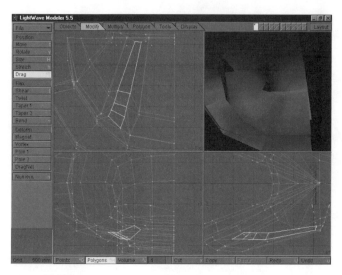

FIGURE **4.29** *Modeling the tendons in the lower jaw.*

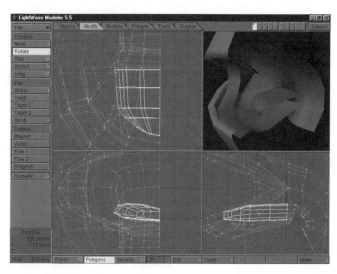

FIGURE **4.30** *Rotating the tongue.*

We need to accentuate the new ridge we created by moving the point on the left closer as shown in Figure 4.32.

That was a bit of work, wasn't it? We're almost done. Now we need to start adding details to the body of Munch. We'll come back later to add the teeth.

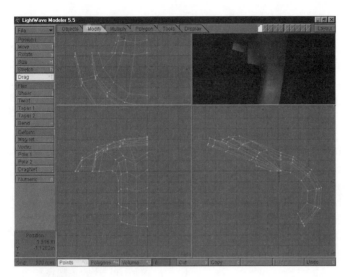

FIGURE **4.31**   *Adding the detail to the upper mouth.*

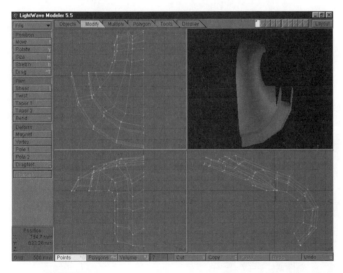

FIGURE **4.32**   *Accentuating the ridge on the roof of the mouth.*

Why don't you take a short break, get something to eat, take a nap, watch a movie, basically anything to take your mind off the modeling for a while, then come back refreshed and ready to finish Munch.

Ready to go? Let's start detailing Munch's body.

ADDING DETAILS TO MUNCH'S BODY

We'll be adding quite a bit of detail to Munch to make him appear as realistic as this cartoon character can look. Since he's a descendant of a prehistoric creature, we'll start by adding a nice ridge around the mouth, which is typical in dinosaurs.

First, select the **Body** surface and **Hide Unselected**. Then select the polygons around the edge of the mouth and drag the points to create an irregular shape as shown in Figure 4.33.

To continue the ridge around the back of the mouth, add some polygons by using the **Add Points** tool. First, select the two polygons at the base of the jaw, then use the **Add Point** tool to add a polygon just behind the back of the jaw. Then manually select the new point and the ones above and below it, then press the **CTRL+L** to split the polygons, creating two new polygons behind the jaw as shown in Figure 4.34.

This is a fine example of when you need to add polygons manually to create details on your model. You'll find this is quite common when creating detailed models.

To add some depth to the ridge, **Smooth Shift** the polygons around the ridge and then stretch them out a bit. Finally, **Smooth Scale** the polygons with an offset of roughly −200mm to round them off as shown in Figure 4.35.

To add some thickness to the ridge, select the points on the outside of the ridge and drag them outward. Then, for a final touch, drag the points on the front of the upper and lower jaw to create a bulge as shown in Figure 4.36.

Now add the socket for the eye. Since we're dealing with an amphibian, we should create a bulging eye like those of a frog or salamander. This will also help to add personality to

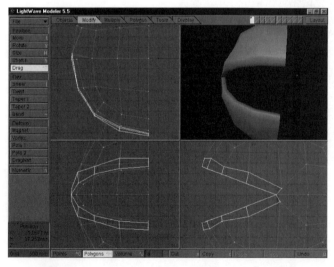

FIGURE **4.33** *Adding detail to the mouth ridge.*

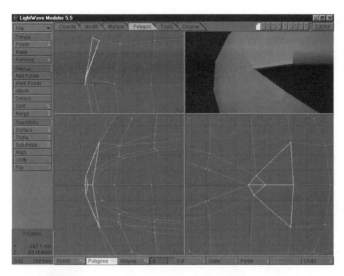

FIGURE **4.34** *Completing the jaw ridge polygons.*

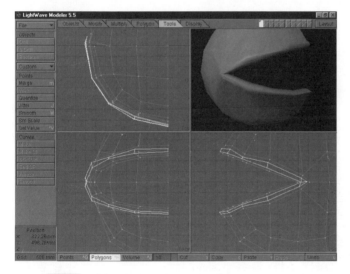

FIGURE **4.35** *Adding depth to the mouth ridge.*

our creature. Making the eye socket will require several **Smooth Shift** layers and a bit of tweaking.

First, select the four polygons on the front-left side of the head. Then drag them around until they form a round shape. Finally, **Smooth Shift** the polygons twice and position them as shown in Figure 4.37.

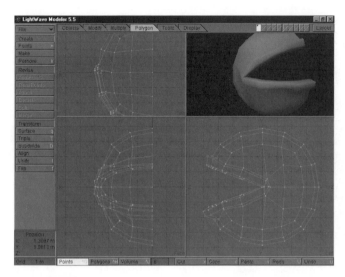

FIGURE **4.36** *Widening the ridge.*

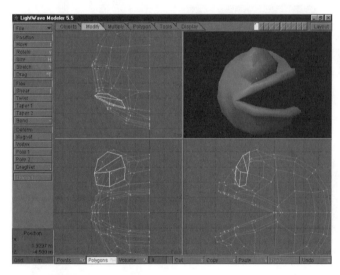

FIGURE **4.37** *Making the eye socket.*

Add the depression in the socket. This requires a couple **Smooth Shift** actions since we need to build a ridge around the front of the eye socket. **Smooth Shift** and scale the polygons three times and position them so they appear like the ones in Figure 4.38. Be sure to rotate the polygons backward a bit as shown in the image.

We need to do a bit of tweaking to the lower part of the eye socket. We want to make the lower portion smooth so we need to line up the points at the base of the eye socket as shown in Figure 4.39.

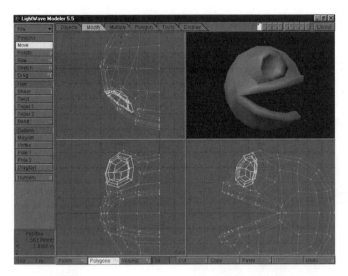

FIGURE **4.38** *Creating the depression in the eye socket.*

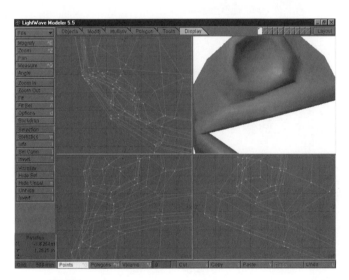

FIGURE **4.39** *Tweaking the lower eye socket points.*

That pretty much does it for the eye sockets. We might add a bit more detail later on but for now we'll move on to the tail. We need to create a rather thick and muscular tail since it's Munch's primary method of movement in both water and air.

To make the tail we simply need to **Smooth Shift** some polygons away from the lower back of the body. First, we need to hide some polygons so we can see what we're doing. Select the body surface and **Hide Unselected**. Now deselect the front of the body and **Hide Unselected** again. Now we have a clear view of the back. Next we need to select the two polygons at the base of the body and tweak the points to create the basic shape of the tail as shown in Figure 4.40.

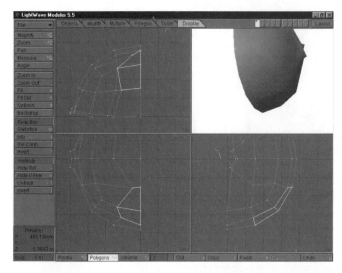

FIGURE **4.40** *Shaping the tail polygons.*

The next step is both simple and repetitive. You'll need to **Smooth Shift**, scale, and rotate the polygons until you have a tail like the one in Figure 4.41.

We need to add a muscular bulge at the base of the tail. To do this, select the lower polygons of the tail and **Smooth Shift** them. **Smooth Scale** them with an **Offset of 200 mm** to

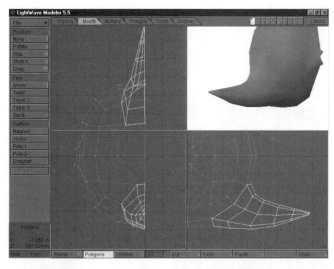

FIGURE **4.41** *The finished tail.*

size them down slightly. Tweak the points around the newly formed polygons so they smoothly blend into the body.

This is an action you will be doing repeatedly in the creation of creature details. When you move the Smooth Shifted polygons straight out from the body they create a bump edge around the entire group of polygons. This is desirable for some features, but it's not something you'll want for muscles and tendons that need to gain altitude gradually, forming a smooth slope. To do this, you need to drag the points of the polygons away from their origin and inward toward the body, building a gradual slope. Figure 4.42 show how your polygons should appear when finished.

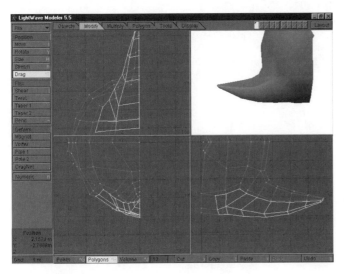

FIGURE **4.42** *Adding the muscle to the tail.*

Now we need to work on the spine a bit. Since we're dealing with a hybrid between an amphibian, a fish, and PAC-MAN, we need to incorporate details of all these creatures. Typically, amphibians have an apparent spine bulge down their back, so we need to add one to Munch. Select the row of polygons that run down the back to the tail and **Smooth Shift** them. Then stretch them upward to create height, and inward to create a sloping effect. Tweak the points on either end as you did with the tail muscle so they blend smoothly with the body, as shown in Figure 4.43.

Now that we have a spine, we need to tweak the polygons at the base of the tail so they don't appear too narrow. Hide all of the polygons except for the back of the body. Then select the polygons at the lower part of the spine and drag the points outward so they taper smoothly into the tail as shown in Figure 4.44.

Leave the spine as it is for now. We might add details later but we'll have to wait until we Metaform the object; the typical creature model will go through two instances of Metaform before it's complete. The first is to add enough polygons to create the fine details;

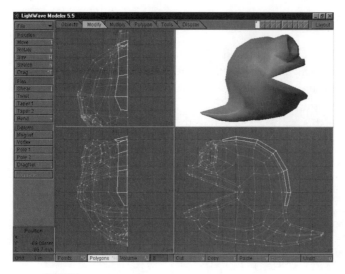

FIGURE **4.43** *Creating the spine.*

the second is to create the final smoothed mesh. If you were creating a simple creature you might need only one pass, but you'll find that detailed creatures require two passes.

Let's move on to the poison sacs behind the eyes. Basically, we need to create a kidney-shaped bulge behind the eyes. Start by selecting the three polygons immediately behind the eye on the side of the head and **Smooth Shifting** them as shown in Figure 4.45.

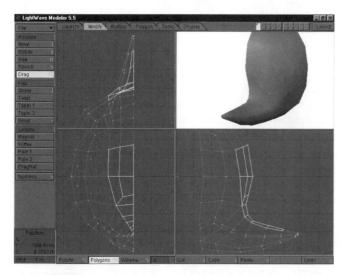

FIGURE **4.44** *Tweaking the base of the spine.*

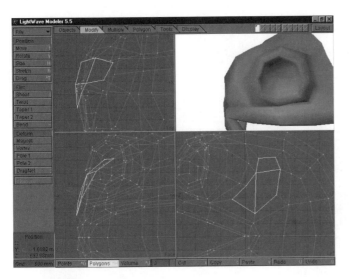

FIGURE **4.45** *Creating the poison sac.*

There is one problem; take a look at the **Shaded Viewport** and you'll see that the side of the sac is rather flat. This is because the polygon in the middle runs through two sets of polygons that surround the bulge. To correct the problem, we need to delete the lower two polygons of the sac as shown in Figure 4.46.

We need to add new polygons, which parallel the ones on either side of the sac, as shown in Figure 4.47.

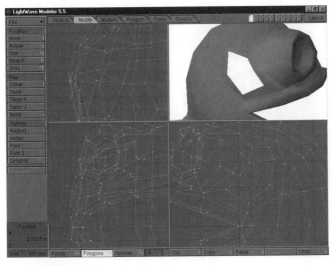

FIGURE **4.46** *Deleting the lower poison sac polygons.*

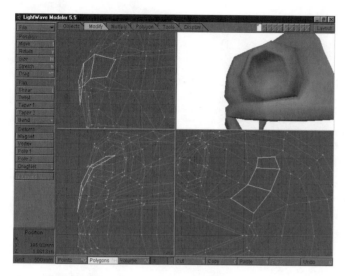

FIGURE **4.47** *Adding the new poison sac polygons.*

Now we have a rounded bulge. Let's keep moving ahead, though; we've got quite a few details to add to Munch. We need to add a tendon bulge around the back of the jaw, which is common in fish. This requires a bit of tweaking, but it's fairly simple.

Select the five polygons that follow the back of the jaw and **Smooth Shift** them. Then move them out a bit and drag the back of the points forward as shown in Figure 4.48, to form the body of the tendon.

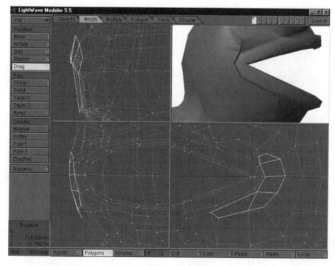

FIGURE **4.48** *Creating the jaw tendon.*

Select the four polygons at the base of the jaw and pull the rear points backward until they meet the front points of the tendon as shown in Figure 4.49. This creates a tight crease between the jaw ridge and tendon.

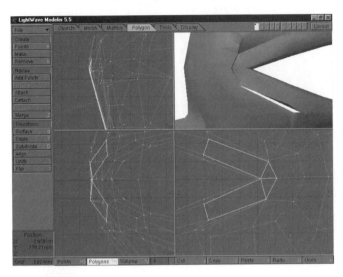

FIGURE **4.49** *Tightening the jaw crease.*

Now we have a rather large ledge where the poison sac meets the jaw. We have a little cleanup work to do here so that the blend between the tendon and the poison sac flows smoothly. Weld the points that are creating a V-shaped indent in the jaw line. The points you need to weld are shown in Figure 4.50.

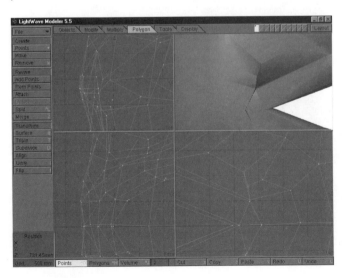

FIGURE **4.50** *Welding a few outlaw points.*

Now that we have the points welded, delete the floating point that's in the middle of the polygon, above the points we just welded. Delete the point so your model looks like the one in Figure 4.51.

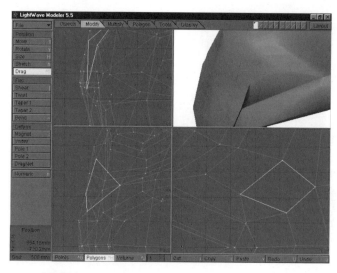

FIGURE **4.51** *Deleting excess points.*

It is time for some tricky tweaking to perfect the seam between the poison sac and the jaw ridge. First, move the lower points of the poison sac down so they meet the upper points of the jaw ridge as shown in Figure 4.52.

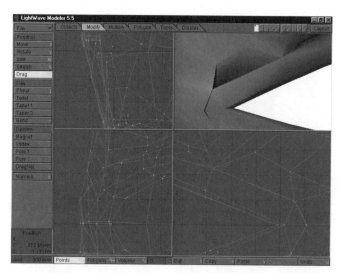

FIGURE **4.52** *Tightening the gap between the jaw and poison sac.*

Now we have just one more problem area to fix so the seam between the poison sac and jaw will be perfect. Take a look at Figure 4.53. We have a polygon that's causing a dent in the face. Move the points so the polygon is flush against the body by selecting the polygon and dragging the farthest point to the right over so that it lies behind the points on the left as shown in Figure 4.54. As you can see by looking at the **Shaded Viewport**, the line between the jaw and poison sac is very clean.

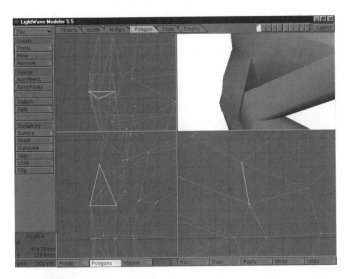

FIGURE **4.53** *A problem polygon.*

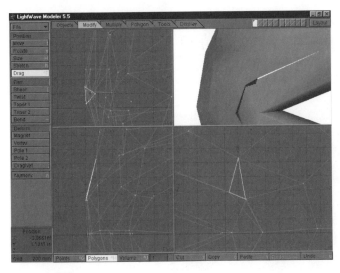

FIGURE **4.54** *Correcting the problem polygon.*

Now let's start adding the details that make our little creature a little more aquatic. Here's where we have a great deal of freedom to be creative. We could assume that Munch breathes through lungs like a typical amphibian, but where would be the fun in that? He would be much cooler if we added some gills so he could breathe in the water.

But what happens when he's airborne? Well, he just holds his breath until he can get to the nearest body of water. This, of course, gives him a very short range, which makes sense when you think about it. These guys have been hiding, undiscovered in the swamplands, for years. We haven't seen them because they have a very short range — they can't travel far from the water.

We need to add gills. This is another tricky procedure, so take your time and use the figures to help you determine the point placement. Select the four polygons on the backside of the mouth tendon and **Smooth Shift** them to create the gill. Move the polygons away from the body and drag the points on the leading edge over to the right to create a nice gradual taper on the front of the gill as shown in Figure 4.55.

To create the depression of the gill where it cuts into the body, hide the front to the body and then select the polygons at the back of the gill. Next, **Smooth Shift** the polygons and drag the points so we create a small edge on the gill as shown in Figure 4.56. Then give the new polygons a surface called **Gills** and change the color to pink so we can distinguish them from the body.

To inset the interior of the gill, select the gill polygons, **Smooth Shift** them, and drag the point so they are slightly smaller that the parent polygons. Move them back very slightly to reinforce the edge of the gill so it doesn't Metaform into a sharp edge. Next, **Smooth Shift** the polygons a couple of times, moving them back into the head each time. When we're done Smooth Shifting the polygons we should have something similar to the model in Figure 4.57.

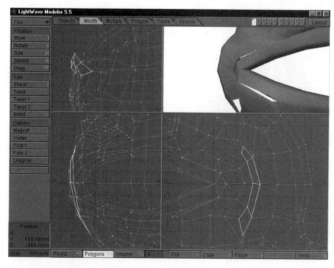

FIGURE **4.55** *Creating the gills.*

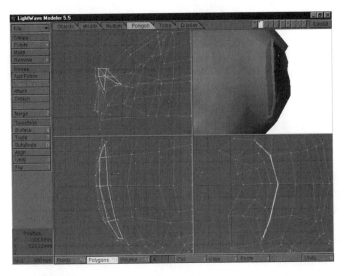

FIGURE **4.56** *Forming the thickness of the gills.*

We need to give the polygons on the back of the interior a new surface named Gill Back. Why? So we can give them a darker surface color to add more depth to the gills. To be completely accurate, we can also give it a lighter color when Munch's mouth is open, since light will be illuminating it from the other side. As you can see, it's very important to think about the surfacing of the creature while you're modeling so you can define the surfaces properly.

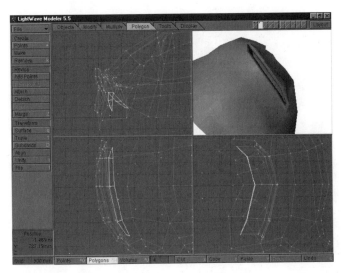

FIGURE **4.57** *Creating the interior of the gill.*

Now we're getting somewhere. You can see how this little guy is really starting to gain some personality. OK, what's missing? A number of things, but one in particular is a method of moving himself through the water. The tail could do it, but that's basically a rudder. To really get around this guy needs some sort of flipper. Actually, flippers will make him look even more aquatic and a lot more detailed. Besides, they'll be cool when he's animated.

Where do we put the flippers? Probably the best place is just in front of the gills, which will make it easier for him to use the flippers to change direction. Let's add the flipper to Munch.

Make sure that we hide all the polygons except the body. Then start the flipper by building the tendon base along the side of the body by selecting the two polygons just under the jaw bulge and **Smooth Shifting** them. Drag the points to create a wide line of polygons in the center. Then drag the shape of the flipper tendon so it's a bit more rounded, as shown in Figure 4.58.

Next, create the fold of skin around the base of the flipper. This is easily done by **Smooth Shifting** the polygons into the body a bit. Of course, we have to reinforce the rim as always; create the fold of skin as shown in Figure 4.59.

The next step is to build the base of the flipper by **Smooth Shifting** polygons out from the depression in the body as shown in Figure 4.60.

To create the flipper, simply make a series of **Smooth Shifts** and tweak the points to give it an organic shape. Create the flipper as shown in Figure 4.61.

Now we just need to position the flipper in a natural position by rotating it down and back a bit as shown in Figure 4.62.

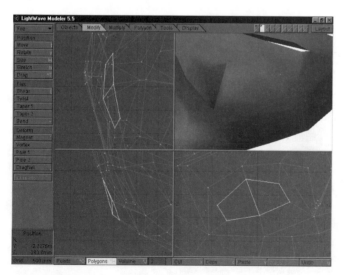

FIGURE **4.58** *Creating the flipper tendon.*

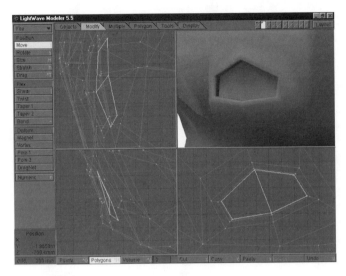

FIGURE **4.59** *Creating the skin fold around the flipper.*

Although this flipper position will be a bit more complicated to bone for animation, it's the accurate neutral position because it's in the middle of the flipper's range of motion. You always want to consider the range of motion when creating the moveable parts on your creatures.

The flippers are done, but we have a problem to correct. Take a look at the front of the flipper tendon and you'll see that we have two polygons that are large and stretch

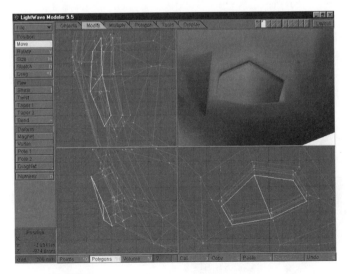

FIGURE **4.60** *Building the base of the flipper.*

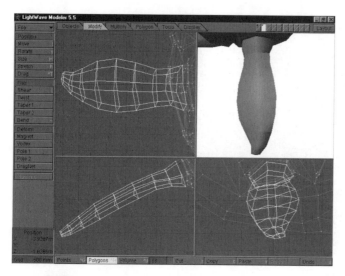

FIGURE **4.61** *Creating the flipper.*

across a long range. Even though it looks fine here, when you **Metaform** the object it will flatten the front of the flipper tendon. To resolve the problem, simply select both polygons and add a point in the middle; then select all three points across the middle and Split them. This will loosen the tension on this region, making it round when we apply Metaform. Figure 4.63 shows the finished result.

Whew! This is a lot of work, isn't it? Well, creating detailed creatures requires a lot of patience and perseverance. Don't worry, we're just about done.

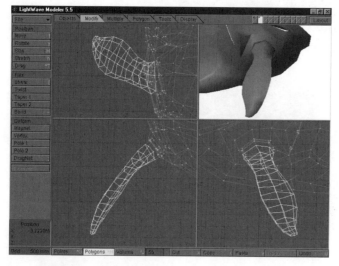

FIGURE **4.62** *Positioning the flipper.*

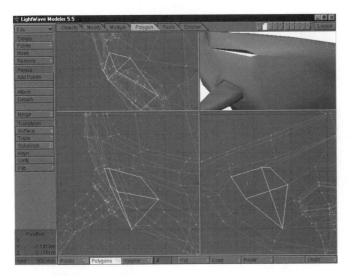

FIGURE **4.63** *Correcting problems.*

Now, add a whale-type flipper to the tail, which will make it easier for him to move through both water and air. It's fairly easy to add the flipper to the tail; select a few polygons in the middle of the tail near the tip and drag a few points to make them wider, as shown in Figure 4.64.

Now create the tail fin the same way we created the flipper earlier. Simply **Smooth Shift** the polygons away from the tail and drag the points to shape it as shown in Figure 4.65.

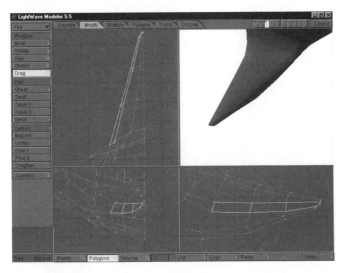

FIGURE **4.64** *Prepping the tail for the fin.*

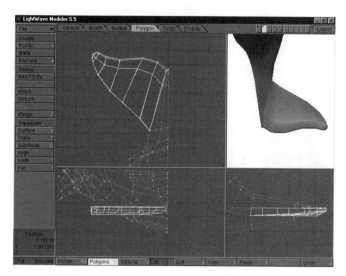

FIGURE **4.65** *Building the tail flipper.*

Now that's a tail fin! Let's take a look at what we have so far. Use the mirror command to complete the model. Press **SHIFT+V** to activate the **Mirror tool**, then press **N** to bring up the numeric requester. **Select** the **X axis** and then set the **position to 0**. Press **OK** to accept the changes and then press **Enter** to mirror the mesh. To merge the points on the seam press the **M key**.

Now we have a complete model. The next step to see the results is to Metaform the object. Press **SHIFT+D** to bring up the **Subdivide Panel** and then select **Metaform** and set the **Max Smoothing Angle to 179**. Press **OK** and the model will take on a more organic appearance like the model in Figure 4.66.

Pretty cool, isn't it? It's not quite finished yet, but you get the idea. You can see how useful Metaform can be for creating detailed models. Our fish had only 1,200 polygons before we Metaformed it. This lets us work with a limited number of polygons and still create incredible details.

Now we're finally going to take a shot at those teeth and gums.

MODELING MUNCH'S TEETH AND GUMS

You've probably seen many creatures with teeth that have merely been plugged into the gums without any concern for creating the gum details. You know — they simply put the teeth in the gums without creating the holes for the teeth. Well, we won't be doing that here. One of the main elements of detailed creatures is to add the subtle details that distinguish it from all the other models.

Munch, is a hybrid of amphibian and fish so we'll be adding a little chaotic bony ridge of teeth. The teeth are unlike ours. Instead of being individual teeth, it's actually a

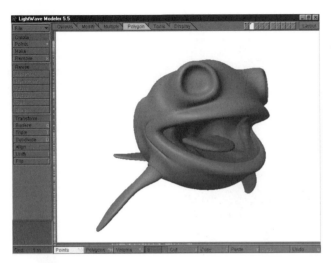

FIGURE **4.66** *A Metaform test on the model.*

single bone with a spiked edge on top. The first step in creating the teeth is to make the hole in the gums. Since we have a single object for the teeth, we'll be making one long, thin depression in the gums, the same way we did for the eyes and the fold of skin around the flippers.

First, hide all of the polygons except the front part of the lower gums. Then select the three polygons on the top of the gums and **Smooth Shift** them. Now move them up slightly and drag the points in a bit. Next, add some thickness to the top of the gums by **Smooth Shifting** the polygons and dragging them in a bit until we have something like Figure 4.67.

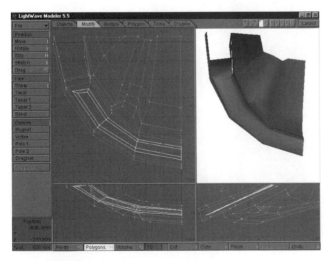

FIGURE **4.67** *Creating the gums for the teeth.*

To make the depression for the teeth, simply **Smooth Shift** the polygons a couple of times inward as shown in Figure 4.68.

Repeat the same steps to add the tooth depression in the upper gums and then we'll move on to the teeth. First, create a template for the teeth. Copy the polygons that form the tooth depression in the gums to another layer. Then **Metaform** the teeth to create the final shape as shown in Figure 4.69.

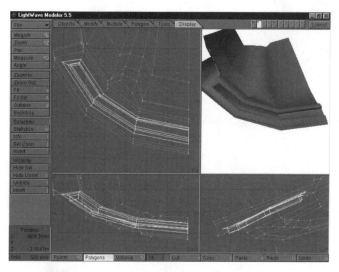

FIGURE **4.68** *Creating the depression for the teeth.*

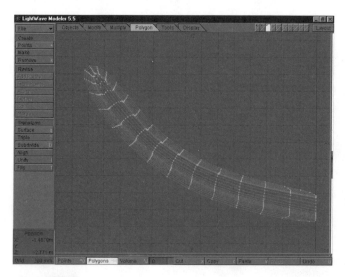

FIGURE **4.69** *The tooth template.*

With the template in the background layer, start laying down points over the template, following the segments in the template. Once the points are laid, select them in groups of four and create polygons. You should end up with something similar to the mesh in Figure 4.70.

Next, extrude the mesh to add the foundation for the teeth and start forming the individual spikes in the teeth. To do this, select the top polygon on the first segment and **Smooth Shift** it. Then scale the polygon and move it as shown in Figure 4.71.

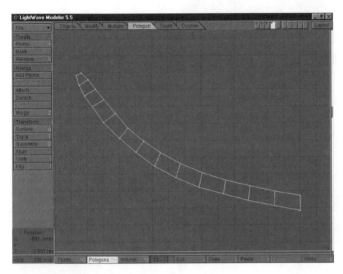

FIGURE 4.70 *The beginning of the teeth.*

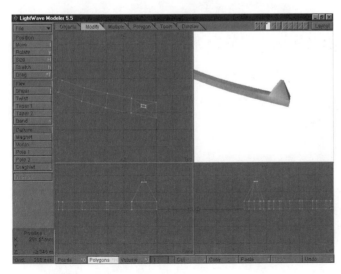

FIGURE 4.71 *Creating a tooth spike.*

Repeat the process for the remaining segments. Be sure to randomize the placement of the top polygon so the teeth are staggered a bit. Nothing looks more artificial than perfectly aligned teeth. Believe me, most creatures don't have a good dental plan. When you're finished, you should have something similar to Figure 4.72.

Now move the teeth into place. Select the tooth template as the background layer and rotate the teeth until they line up with the template as shown in Figure 4.73.

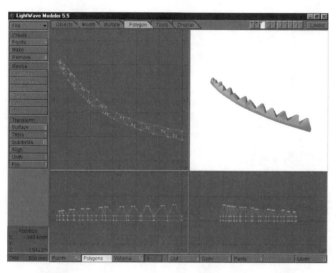

FIGURE **4.72** *The completed teeth.*

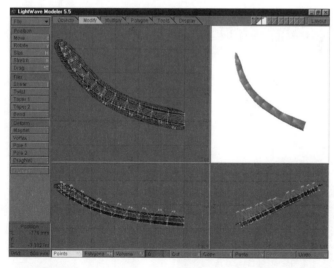

FIGURE **4.73** *The teeth aligned with the gums.*

Now we're getting somewhere. Repeat the same process to create the teeth for the upper gums. Be sure to keep the teeth on a separate layer since we will be Metaforming them separately from the body.

Select both the body and tooth layers to see what our creation looks like. You should have something like Figure 4.74.

Of course, the gums wouldn't be perfectly rounded so we need to add a little chaos. This requires a few more polygons so we'll need to Metaform the object to increase the mesh density. Before we Metaform the object, however, let's add one more detail that is really cool in deep-sea creatures — those really slick feelers that hang over the fish's head to attract prey. One of those little bobbers would really add some character to Munch, so let's add one.

First, select a polygon on the forehead as shown in Figure 4.75.

Smooth Shift this polygon several times to create the feeler. You can see the completed feeler in Figure 4.76. Create your feeler so it looks like the one in the Figure 4.76.

That's certainly a great addition to the model. I think we're finally done with the details we can add to the low-resolution model. Now we're ready to Metaform it so we can add more details. Before you Metaform the mesh, save the model as *Munch.lwo* so we have a backup of the pre-Metaformed model. You never know when you may want to go back and modify the model on the low-resolution level.

In fact, I typically save many version of the model as I'm working on it. I typically end up with at least 30 to 40 versions of the model by the time I've finished it. This allows me to go back to any point in the development and modify the model. In fact, you'll find that you can borrow parts from models to use in another creature you are developing. For

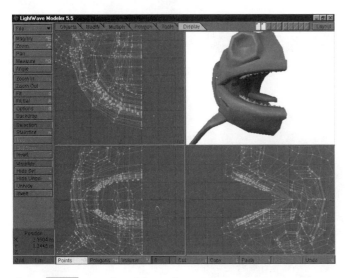

FIGURE **4.74** *Munch with his teeth.*

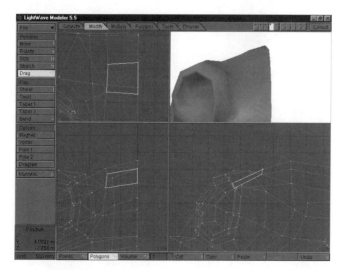

FIGURE **4.75** *Starting the feeler.*

example, a human head always has eyes, ears, nose, and mouth so one low-resolution head can be used to model literally any human head, man or woman.

Once you're done with the lower gums, repeat the same process for the upper gums.

We're almost done now. Actually we could have stopped anytime before now but where would be the fun in that? Part of being a modeler of high-detail creatures is the willingness to stick with it until you've added just about every conceivable detail your model can hold without looking cluttered. Fortunately, real creatures are very detailed

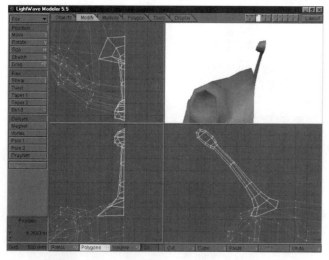

FIGURE **4.76** *The completed feeler.*

so it's nearly impossible to add too much detail. The more we add the more realistic our creation becomes.

Now that we've saved the model, let's **Metaform** it once to increase the mesh density. Next, hide all of the polygons except for the lower gums where the tooth hole is located. Then select the lower tooth layer and the gum layer simultaneously. Now we can tweak the gums and teeth a bit so they don't look too perfect. The best method is to select the points at the back of the gums and move them back a bit. Do this in several areas until you have something similar to Figure 4.77.

That's much better; now the gums look more natural and realistic. Speaking of realistic, there's a common feature seen on amphibians and fish that we're missing on our Munch model — ribs. In fact, most creatures have very prominent ribs so let's add some to Munch now that we have enough polygons to do it.

Start by selecting several polygons on the lower body, in front, and **Smooth Shift** them. Then scale the polygons and move them away from the body slightly as shown in Figure 4.78.

Repeat the same procedure to add a few more rib bones as shown in Figure 4.79.

You'll be glad to hear that we have just one more detail to add and we're done with Munch! All we need to do now is add an eyeball. This, of course, is the easiest part to add; simply create a sphere and size it to fit in the eye socket as shown in Figure 4.80.

Let's wrap this thing up by mirroring the mesh and merging the points. Start with the eyes. Go ahead and mirror the eyes along the X-axis so we have one on either side. Do the same with our teeth. Mirror the teeth along the X-axis and then merge the points. Smooth the teeth by **Metaforming** them once.

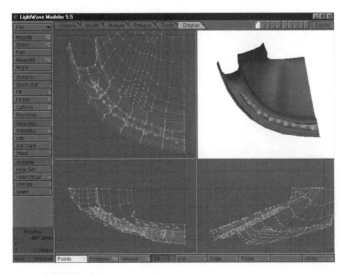

FIGURE **4.77** *Adding chaos to the gums.*

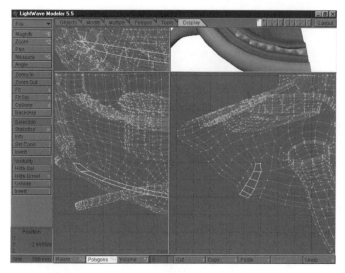

FIGURE **4.78** *Adding a rib bone to Munch.*

Finally, mirror the body along the X-axis and merge the points. Now we can perform the final **Metaform** on the body. Once the Metaform process is complete, select all three layers (body, teeth, and eyes) and save the object as *Munch Final.lwo*. After selecting all three layers you should have something that looks like Figure 4.81.

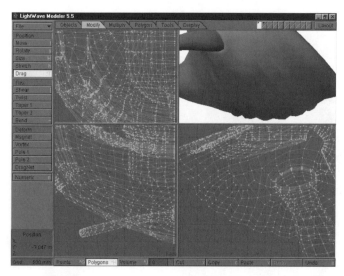

FIGURE **4.79** *Adding the rest of the ribs.*

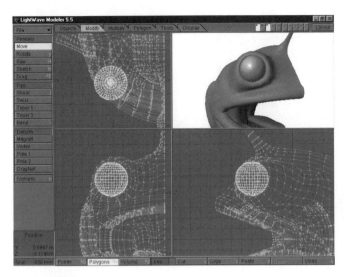

FIGURE **4.80** *Adding the eyeball.*

To get a better idea of the finished model, take a look at the rendered version in Figure 4.82

That's definitely not your typical PAC-MAN, now is it? You can see how we've used Metaform to bring a simple cartoon character to life. We need just one more detail to make Munch perfect.

FIGURE **4.81** *All of Munch's parts combined.*

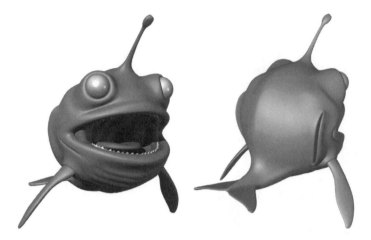

FIGURE **4.82** *A final render of the Munch model.*

Since Munch is so small and vulnerable, he needs some form of deterrent other than poison sacs. He needs something that will make him less appealing to predators. How about if we borrow the protection a blowfish uses? You know, those obnoxious little spikes that cover its body. That will certainly provide Munch with some serious protection since eating him would be like taking a bite out of a porcupine.

How do we create the spikes? First, **Undo** the **Metaform** we just performed and revert back to a half-mesh version of Munch. Then hide all the polygons except the body and simply start **Smooth Shifting** the individual polygons on his back, and scaling the top polygon to create a spike as shown in Figure 4.83.

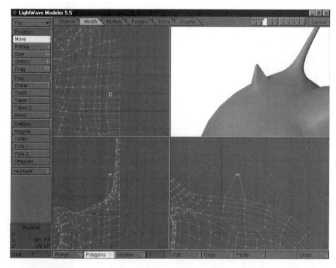

FIGURE **4.83** *Creating a spike.*

Repeat this process until you have added spikes to his entire backside. Be sure to make the spikes smaller as you approach the perimeter of the spikes and the tail. This will make the spikes appear more natural. When you are done, you should have something similar to Figure 4.84.

Now **mirror the mesh**, **merge the points**, and **Metaform**. Your completed model should look something like Figure 4.85.

Well, he certainly looks a lot better now. He's fairly well protected against predators. It's just amazing how simple details can be added using the Metaform modeling technique. **Save** the new version of Munch as "Munch Spikes.lwo."

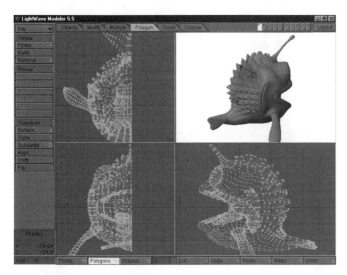

FIGURE **4.84** *Adding more spikes.*

FIGURE **4.85** *Munch with his completed spikes.*

The only step left in the process is to surface out the model with image maps to make him realistic. Fortunately, LightWave makes the surfacing process very simple. We already defined the surfaces as we modeled the creature so simply load it into Layout and apply the image maps. Of course, we have to paint the image maps but that's a subject for Chapter 9. Let's take a look at surfacing Munch.

SURFACING MUNCH

Since the focus of this chapter is on Modeling and not surfacing, we'll take just a brief look at how Munch was surfaced. For the purpose of this discussion, you'll need to load the *Munch2.lwo* object from the *Chapter4/Munch* folder companion CD. It has already been surfaced for you to expedite our discussion. Let's take a look at how we surfaced Munch.

Munch presents a unique surfacing challenge since the majority of his body is round. You could use a spherical image map but that would pinch at the top and bottom. A cylindrical map won't work either since it will pinch as well. The two remaining options are to surface the model with Planar or Cubic image maps. Since Munch is round, we'll use the Cubic mapping method.

Of course, if we want to add details to specific areas on his body we'll have to get a bit tricky. Although you typically want to use Planar image maps to surface parts of creature bodies with specific details, we'll explore the secrets of Alpha maps to create Munch's detail. Before we get into how Alpha maps are used, let's take a look at how the body surfaces were modified so we can properly map Munch. Take a look at Figure 4.86.

FIGURE **4.86** *The surface selections for Planar mapping Munch.*

The different surfaces of Munch's body are indicated with unique colors. As you can see, there were only a few surfaces selected to allow us to add detail to specific areas of his body. We created a unique surface for the nose since we'll be adding some small bumps and color changes to this region. We also gave the fins their own separate surface because we want them out of the way, so to speak. This will make more sense when we explore the power of Alpha maps. Let's take a look at how Alpha maps can be used to make your seamless creature surfacing a lot easier.

USING ALPHA MAPS TO SURFACE MUNCH SEAMLESSLY

Alpha maps are a highly misunderstood tool in LightWave. They are also the most powerful surfacing tool in your creature surfacing arsenal. Most people use Alpha maps to trim areas of an image map so they can put details like signs on walls, or labels on equipment. Although these are great uses for Alpha maps, they also barely scratch the surface of their true usefulness. You see, an Alpha map filters the image map, so it basically acts as a transparency map for a specific image map. The Alpha map uses shades of gray to filter the image map. Areas that are black are completely transparent and areas that are white will show up on the surface. Of course, gray areas will be semitransparent depending on the shade of gray.

We know how an Alpha map works, but how is it used to seamlessly surface creatures? The goal in surfacing your creature is to add occasional chaos and detail to its body. No creature has a consistent color across its entire body. In fact, fish and amphibians usually have a darker back and lighter belly, so you'll need to add these color changes if you want Munch to appear realistic. This can easily be accomplished with Alpha maps.

To surface Munch using Alpha maps we'll first have to give him a base coat of surfacing. For this we'll be using Cubic image maps since they will surface his organic body seamlessly. Figure 4.87 shows Munch with the Cubic image maps applied.

As you can see, the surfacing is fairly nice looking, but way too consistent. We need to add some subtle color changes on the back and belly to make Munch more realistic. To do this, we'll need to create several unique image maps with their corresponding Alpha maps. Let's take a look at one of the Alpha image maps that was used to create a light brown coloration on Munch's belly, which is shown in Figure 4.88.

Here we have two rather simple images. The one on the left is the color map and the one on the right is the Alpha map. You can see by the white spot on the Alpha map that we are filtering out all the color image map that is black. This allows us to place a brown spot on the belly of Munch without adding the black color. Take a look at what Munch looks like once all his color is applied with Alpha maps, in Figure 4.89.

That's quite an impressive looking creature, wouldn't you say? Notice the subtle, and not so subtle, color changes on his body. He certainly looks a great deal more realistic than the simple Cubic mapped version, doesn't he? As you can see, the belly now has a nice

FIGURE **4.87** *Munch with his basic Cubic map surfacing.*

light brown tint to it, while maintaining the original chaotic details of the Cubic mapped surface. How was this achieved? It's actually quite simple. When adding the color/Alpha image maps to the color layer we set the texture opacity to a value less than 100 percent, which makes the previous texture layer show through. This is a very useful technique for creating seamless, and stretch-mark free, details on your creatures.

Take this opportunity to explore the surfacing of Munch thoroughly. You'll be surprised to find that nearly all of his surfacing detail was added with very simple color/Alpha maps.

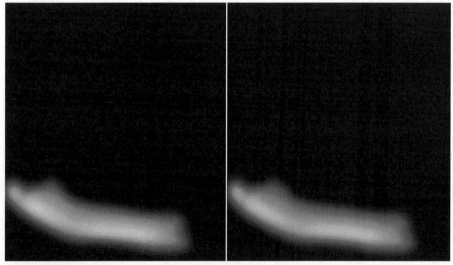

FIGURE **4.88** *Munch's belly color and Alpha image maps.*

FIGURE **4.89**   *Munch with all of his surfaces applied.*

When you're done with Munch, you should spend some time experimenting with Cubic image map bases, covered in layers of color/Alpha image map details on your own creatures. You'll be surprised at the amazing amount of detail you can add with this technique, all the while avoiding those awful seams and texture stretching.

We've gone from a simple creature concept to a photorealistic 3D creature in under 30 pages! As you can see, Living Toons are rather unique creatures that really catch your eye. It's rather cool to see a cartoon character literally come to life before your eyes.

This, of course, is a rather brief examination of creature surfacing. To get an in-depth look you'll need to read Chapter 9, which covers photorealistic creature surfacing.

IT DOESN'T END HERE

That's it for our LightWave modeling chapters, but it doesn't end here. It's up to you to explore the power and flexibility of Metaform. You should go back to the version of Munch before we Metaformed him the first time and see what kind of details you can add. Maybe some horns, scales, bumpy spots, or even another flipper. Basically, see what details you can add using the techniques you learned in this and the previous chapters.

Once you've added every detail possible to Munch, you should see what kinds of creatures you can create from scratch. Remember, you're limited only by your imagination. If you can think of it, you can model it with Metaform. There is absolutely no detail that you can't create with Metaform. I've used it to add individual hair follicles to creatures before — a bit neurotic but it certainly looked cool.

One last thing. Before you dive into your own creature creation be sure to explore Chapter 9 very thoroughly. It will greatly improve your creature surfacing, which is the defining element of a creature model. You can spend countless hours modeling a creature but if you skimp on the surfacing you'll end up undermining all of your modeling efforts.

PART

III

3D Studio Max Creature Modeling

by Shane Olson

This part covers character modeling with Kinetix 3D Studio MAX. You may complete the first tutorial with any release of MAX without the need for any additional plug-ins. The second tutorial, Modeling with Surfacetools, requires that you have MAX R2 along with Digimation's Surfacetools plug-in.

In the first tutorial, we cover the basics of patches, and how they work. You will be modeling a fairly simple goldfish character to get the hands-on experience you will need to create characters successfully on your own. Then, with the basic knowledge of patches under your belt, we will take a step forward in patch modeling and discover a whole new modeling method using a great plug-in for MAX R2 called Surfacetools.

Surfacetools is a spline-based modeling tool that, when implemented correctly, results in a simpler and more productive way of modeling with patches. You will test this new-found knowledge while we model an advanced 1920s gangster thug-type character in the second tutorial.

Sound like fun? Let's get started!

VISIT THE COMPANION CD-ROM FOR COLOR IMAGES.

All of the figures shown in this book are mirrored, in color, on the CD-ROM. I recommend you open the CD and view the images while you read the book, or download the images for faster reference. There will be details in the figures that you can't see in the printed image.

CHAPTER

5

Getting to Know Patches in MAX

© 1997, 1998 Komodo Studios

Bezier patches are a new and often untapped method of character creation. Modeling with Bezier patches is often compared to sculpting in real life with a medium such as clay or papier-mâché. The comparison is made because of the way patches are manipulated. Bezier handles that protrude from each of its four corner points, called *vertices*, control a Bezier patch. When manipulated, these handles distort the mesh smoothly like pushing or pulling clay. The result is a final character that is very smooth and organic.

Another similarity to clay is the underlying structure. When creating a character with clay, you usually start by creating a wire armature to support the structure of the model. In similar fashion, you create a patch model by starting with a type of armature that is made from splines. This armature also serves as a preview of what your final model will look like.

THE ADVANTAGES AND DISADVANTAGES OF PATCHES

Patch modeling has a lot of advantages over traditional modeling methods. In 3DS Release 4, there were no such thing as patches. Building an organic character was almost impossible. If you were crazy enough to attempt it, you usually had to use a third-party plug-in such as Metaballs. Even in MAX modelers have attempted to create organic creatures using other methods such as Lofting, Boolean, and Free Form Deform. When asked "How long did that take you?" they would usually rattle off some inconceivable number of hours. Even then they would usually add "I still couldn't get it to look like I wanted." If you find yourself making these statements, then patch modeling may be your key to avoiding that aneurysm you've been contemplating. Of course, a nice model can be created using other methods, but this way may save you a lot of heartache and frustration.

Do not be fooled into thinking that Bezier patch modeling is the end-all character modeling tool. It isn't! Patches do have their advantages, but they also have some downfalls as well. Let's take a look at the pros and cons of using patches.

THE ADVANTAGES OF PATCH MODELING

- **Patches are fun!** The number one advantage of patches is that, once you get used to them, they are very fun to work with. They are kind of like playing with taffy, except you don't get sticky and you can't eat them when you're done. Of course, they are also very challenging. You must have good strategy and proper planning before conquering patches.
- **Patches automatically "smooth" from one patch to another.** The organic smooth quality is what makes patches a great choice for modeling organic creatures. With

traditional modeling methods it was hard to get something to look organic but with patches, it's almost too easy.

- **Bezier patches are controlled by Bezier handles.** If you are used to using Bezier handles in a 2D-drawing program such as Macromedia Freehand, patch manipulation will be that much easier for you. The transition is the same, only this time you have six handles on every point instead of two (two for each axis). If you haven't had experience with Bezier curves, don't worry. They are very easy to get used to.

- **The Topology or "density" of patches can be changed on the fly.** Turning down the topology on your model helps increase the redraw speed, and also lets you work with a less complicated mesh. At any point in time you can turn up the face count and see what your final model will look like.

- **Mirroring the mesh to save modeling time.** You need to model only half of the character because you can mirror the other half as you go, saving you a ton of repetitive work. Say you were going to model a man. With patches you would have to model only half of his face, body, arm, and leg, then while you are modeling you can Mirror your mesh as an instance, and anything you do to one side will interactively repeat to the other side.

- **Seamless meshes.** The final output of your model can be a completely seamless character, which is preferred by most animators because it makes bones animation that much easier. Seamless means that there are no joints in your model, like at the knees, elbows, and knuckles. This makes for a much more believable and better-looking character.

Of course, to every silver lining there is a cloud. Beware; patch modeling is not the end-all character modeling tool. Let's take a look at the downside to using patches.

THE DISADVANTAGES OF PATCH MODELING

- **Patches automatically "smooth" from one patch to another.** Yes, this can be a disadvantage as well. If you are trying to get a hard edge, such as the tip of a fingernail, MAX automatically smoothes the faces together. You can get some very bizarre results trying to make something look like it has a crisp edge. In other words, try to avoid them.

- **Tight details.** Since you are working with an entire patch of faces, it is relatively hard to get into tight places. It's like trying to hammer a straight pin with a sledgehammer. The patches are just too large to get really small detail. We will be addressing this problem in the next chapter when we solve it using a new third-party plug-in called Surfacetools.

- **Material ID.** Material ID cannot be assigned to individual patches for mapping. You must first add an Edit Mesh Modifier, then add Material ID to groups of faces. This is bad because when you do this your model is no longer a patch model. It becomes a polygonal model that cannot have its topology changed the regular *Edit Patch* way. We will learn how to work around this problem with a charity-ware plug-in by Peter Watje in the next chapter.

- **Patches models can get very dense, and it is sometimes hard to manipulate individual vertices.** For example, say you were modeling a human and you were looking at it from the top. Now let's say you wanted to move a point that was on the foot. You would have to look through the entire mesh that made up the rest of the body, then try to decide which points belong to the foot since MAX doesn't allow you to hide patches like you can hide faces. You must either detach the patches and hide them, or build the appendages separate from the body and weld them on afterward. If you model them separately, you don't have to look through the entire model to see a point on the foot. Actually, it's not really a disadvantage but rather a pain-in-the-patch, so to speak.

That about does it for the pros and cons of patches. In the next few chapters we will be exploring the Patch Character Modeling Method fully, and you'll discover lots of tips and tricks along the way. This tutorial is intended to supplement the MAX manuals, not to replace them. I'm sure you've seen enough rewrites of user manuals. Let's get started!

CREATING A CHARACTER WITH PATCHES

This first tutorial is aimed at giving you a good foundation to create organic patch characters using the tools that come preinstalled in all versions of MAX. No additional plug-ins are required for this tutorial.

Here is an overview of what we will be doing in the following tutorial. Modeling with patches is a six-step process:

1. Finding Source Material for Your Character Design
2. Creating Axis Templates from Your Source Material
3. Importing Your Axis Templates into MAX
4. Tracing Your Axis Templates with Splines
5. Laying Patches One by One
6. Applying Image Maps to Your Creature

Let's start right in and begin taking the steps to creating a character model with patches. To explain how to create creatures in 3D Studio MAX, I had to design a character that was simple enough to cover all of the bases, but hard enough to make it challenging. Meet Edward, the solution to the challenge, shown in Figure 5.1. Edward is a little

FIGURE **5.1** *The finished Edward in all his shining glory.*

goldfish created specifically for this tutorial. He was built almost entirely with patches (except the eyes); he is a totally seamless and organic creature, making him a prime candidate for great character animation.

So who is Edward? That is a question you must ask yourself before you sit down and start modeling. Who is this character? Why does he exist? We ask these questions to help us understand more about our character, and in turn, create a fuller, more richly designed creature that people will understand and relate to. Sometimes the art director or script will have the biography already set up for the character. Let's take a look at the vision of Edward, through the eyes of an art director.

EDWARD'S BIOGRAPHY

Edward is a goldfish, but if we left it at that, Edward would be just a plain, boring goldfish, leading to a rather boring model. You see, Edward is a goldfish that has spent all of his life behind glass, in a fishbowl, with no one to talk to but himself. This means that Edward is rather bored, making him very curious. To keep himself from going insane, he spends his day staring at our world through the distorted glass of a fishbowl, which makes objects appear much larger and rather wacky, like those marvelous carnival mirrors do. Now I bet you're wondering how I know the view is distorted. Well, being the committed creature modeler that I am, I stuck my head in a fishbowl — yes, I emptied the water first. I have to tell you, it was tough getting that thing off my head.

So, what does Edward see as he gazes through the glass of the fishbowl? Many things actually, but he really find the television interesting. The only problem is trying to change the channels with the remote. I'll bet you're wondering what his favorite show is? Well, he really likes cartoons, particularly *The Simpsons* and *The Flintstones*. As you can see, this little guy has great taste in television shows. OK, so what else does he see? Well, he often sees the family cat, Sniffles, which is usually staring back at him with hunger in his eyes. Of course, Edward spends his days in utter paranoia hoping that Sniffles doesn't get lucky one day and have Edward au gratin for lunch.

Edward spends much of his day watching the world around him. His eyes have to be large and bubbly to see through the thick fishbowl glass. Edward exhibits two facial expressions, curiosity and fear. The large eyes make these easy emotions to create, and as far as his other details, well, he's a goldfish so we can rely on typical fish details for the rest of his body.

Now that we know a little about Edward, we can build him patch by patch, from head to tail, and fin to fin.

Edward is a simple character that took about three hours to model, not including maps. This tutorial is intended to decrease your learning curve, and get you past many frustrations so you don't need to invest as much time experimenting. Of course, the best way to learn patches is to experiment with them.

Ready to get your feet wet?

FINDING SOURCE MATERIAL FOR YOUR CHARACTER DESIGN

It is a good idea to find some source material before you begin. Source material is anything that can get you onto the path of creating your character. Most of the time, you will be receiving concept sketches and photographs from an art director that are considered source material. The source material for Edward was a handbook on caring for goldfish. It was chock full of color images that are great for reference. Another good source was a goldfish hunt on the Internet. Figure 5.2 is an example of the search.

FIGURE **5.2** *Edward's source material.*

You should always try to track down as much source material as possible. It's the foundation of your character. The source material for Edward was relatively simple due to the character, but you will find characters that require a great deal more source material such as Knuckles, the gangster we'll be modeling in the next chapter.

Now that we have our source material for Edward, we are ready to start creating our axis templates.

CREATING AXIS TEMPLATES FROM YOUR SOURCE MATERIAL

There are three axis template files that are included in the CD-ROM inside the *Chapter 5* folder, which have already been made for you. We will need these files to create the Virtual Studio in this exercise. It's a good time to check and make sure you have all of the following files.

- *fishside.tga*
- *fishtop.tga*
- *fishfront.tga*

Now that we have some resource material we must create three axis drawings to use as templates for our model. Axis templates are a very useful tool to help you understand the 3D volume of your character by laying the foundation for you.

You will trace these templates with splines to create a wire frame of your model. You could just start whipping out patches, but usually you end up with a mess of patches all over the place, which isn't good. Believe me, I've done it. As you get better with patches, you may want to skip this step, but for now we will make an axis template for each axis view of our character, which is a view from one of the object's three axes, like the front, side, or top view of Edward as shown in Figure 5.3.

We'll be mapping these three axis views onto boxes within MAX, with their maps showing in the shaded viewport. This will give you a template for creating your wire armature.

⇨ TIP

All of your axis views should be proportionate. Notice that in Figure 5.3 the front view is the same height as the side view, and the top view is the same length as the side view, and so on. This is very important for creating your axis view images. It will make things line up much easier when you implement them as templates.

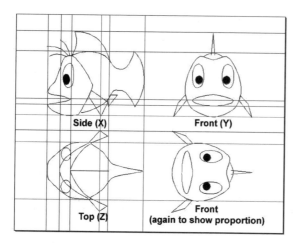

Side (X)   Front (Y)

Top (Z)   Front
              (again to show proportion)

FIGURE **5.3** *Axis views of Edward.*

There are three ways of creating axis views. You can draw them by hand, build them on the computer, or use existing photographs or photos that you took of the creature yourself.

USING DRAWINGS FOR AXIS TEMPLATES

If you are confident enough to draw your axis views by hand, it's a good idea to use grid paper and/or a ruler to help you get the proportions right. If you're going to create them with a computer program such as Macromedia Freehand, or Fractal Design Painter, use a guideline or a grid to help you.

Make sure, in your final draft, to use a dark enough medium (such as a black pen) and a light enough paper to give your drawings enough contrast. Then, when you scan in these drawings later, they will need little or no adjustments. You will need to get your images into the computer somehow, and scanning is the best option. If you don't have a scanner, most copy shops or service bureaus have scanning services that can help you out. (WARNING: Be prepared before you go to a self-serve copy shop — most of them charge you by the second!)

USING PHOTOGRAPHS AS AXIS TEMPLATES

If you decide that you would rather use photographs instead of drawings, that's fine. When looking for your photographs, try to get images as perpendicular as possible. If you find a side view of a fish, for example, make sure it is as orthographic as possible. Or, if you take a photo of a live creature or a sculpture yourself, follow the same guidelines. After you get that far, you should treat the images just like drawings. You need to scan them (unless they are already digital, like images from the Internet). After scanning, you need to follow the rules of proportion, and scale your images accordingly. Make sure that the top view is the same height as the side view, etc.

SUGGESTED AXIS TEMPLATE PREPARATION

Any type of template, whether it be a drawing or a photo, should be saved as a targa file type. Other file types will work, but probably not as well. The images should be no larger than 640 pixels per inch by 480 pixels per inch. 72dpi is recommended. The images should also have a very high contrast so you can see them well enough to trace in the shaded viewports of MAX. You can do this by adjusting the light-dark balance in a photo manipulation program such as Adobe Photoshop.

Now we're ready to import the axis templates into MAX.

IMPORTING YOUR AXIS TEMPLATES INTO MAX

We will build a *Virtual Studio*—basically a 3D room with two walls and a floor made from primitive boxes. Each axis template is then mapped onto its appropriate box (wall). Take a look at Figure 5.4 to see an example of a Virtual Studio.

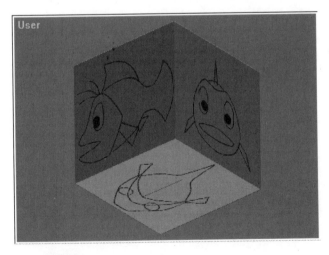

FIGURE **5.4** *The Virtual Studio.*

STEP 1. CREATING PRIMITIVE BOX WALLS

1. Click in the top viewport, and then create a Primitive Box that has the length and width of 200, and a height of 1. This will be used as the top view of the fish (the floor of the Studio). Name this box Top View.
2. Choose **Select** and **Rotate**, and then toggle **Angle Snap**. Now, in the front viewport, hold down **Shift** and rotate the box 90 degrees. Select **Copy** as the object type, and enter **Side View** in the Name Dialog box. This will be used as the side view template.
3. With the Side View box still selected, in the left viewport, hold **Shift** again and rotate the box 90 degrees. Then select **Copy** as before and name this box "Front View."
4. Your boxes should all be crossing in the center; move each box separately out to the edge of each wall until your configuration looks like Figure 5.5.

STEP 2. PREPPING THE MATERIALS

1. Next, we map the walls with the Axis Templates that we spent so much time creating. Open the Materials Editor. In the first Material Box, change the preview type to Cube so we can preview our maps better.
2. Now hold down **Shift** and copy your new material into its neighboring two squares for the other two maps. Your Material Editor should now look like Figure 5.6.

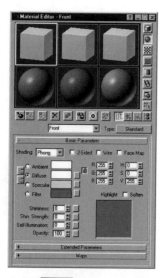

FIGURE **5.5** *The bare walls.*

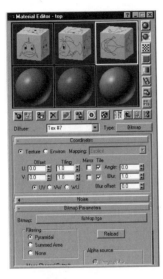

FIGURE **5.6** *Materials prepped and ready for images.*

3. For this part of the exercise, download the *fishfront.tga*, *fishside.tga*, and *fishtop.tga* maps from the CD-ROM that came with this book, and put them into your 3dsmax Maps directory.

4. Give each Material Slot a name that coincides to the wall it will be mapped to. Then name the first slot Front, the second slot Side, and the third slot Top.

5. Click on the **Maps** drop-down menu. Then click on the **Diffusion Map** slot and select **Bitmap** from the Map types list.

6. Click on the **Blank** bar to choose a bitmap. Browse for your **Maps** directory where you put the fish maps from the CD-ROM and select *fishfront.tga*, then click **OK**. The cube in the first material slot should now have the front view of Edward.

7. Click the second material slot, and repeat the same map selection process, but this time use *fishside.tga* as your bitmap selection. Follow the map selection process one more time, with the third slot, using *fishtop.tga*. Your Material Editor should now look like Figure 5.7.

STEP 3. ASSIGN MATERIALS TO BOXES

To view the maps in the shaded viewport, first you need to toggle the **Show Maps** in **Viewport** under the Diffusion map's submenu of each material. You shouldn't see the maps in the viewport just yet, because we need to apply mapping coordinates to the boxes first.

FIGURE **5.7** *Bitmaps loaded and ready.*

STEP 4. ASSIGN MAPPING COORDINATES TO EACH BOX

1. Click on the box that is facing you in the front viewport and add a UVW map to the modifier stack. Hey, there's Edward! But wait — he's upside down! For some unknown reason, MAX likes to default to upside-down mapping coordinates. This problem is easily flipped.

2. Click on **Sub-Object** under selection level. The mapping gizmo turns yellow, which allows you to apply basic transforms to the mapping gizmo. Notice the line extruding from the bottom of the gizmo. This line represents the top of the map. So, what we need to do is a **Select** and **Rotate**, and rotate the gizmo 180 degrees in the front viewport until it looks like Figure 5.8.

3. Repeat Step 4 for the other two boxes. If the map does not show up, try rotating the box in the left viewport 180 degrees until it is right side up.

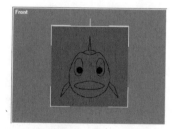

FIGURE **5.8** *Rotate the mapping gizmo.*

Great! Now you have built a Virtual Studio! Next, we will be tracing the axis templates with splines to create a wireframe for our model. You could do without the splines, and use the axis templates only, but viewing maps in your viewports is a memory hog, and splines take up a lot less memory. Besides, this step will prepare you for the next chapter, "Modeling with Surfacetools."

➪ TIP

If you are having trouble viewing all three walls with your system, try toggling the **View Map** in the **Viewport** button for the maps that you are not using. This will dramatically increase redraw speeds.

TRACING YOUR AXIS TEMPLATES WITH SPLINES

Now we are going to create a wireframe of our creature out of Bezier splines. When you create a wireframe of your model, you start to see your creature take shape. We'll start by learning a little bit about splines, and then we'll start tracing our character.

Before you begin throwing splines all over the place, however, you need to plan your project. You have to ask yourself "Where would be the best places to put the splines?" This is a tough question if you have never modeled with patches before. The basic silhouette is a good place to start. Place lines wherever you think you will need a reference point. Again, the best way to learn how to do it is to practice. You will develop these skills over time. Some people choose to use tons of splines, and some people use just one or two. In the following section, you will see where to place the splines. You may decide to follow along and place the splines as shown, or you are welcome to read through this section on splines and place them wherever you like.

BEZIER SPLINE BASICS, AND HOW THEY APPLY TO PATCH MODELING

If you have played around with MAX, you've probably dealt with splines before. If you haven't, take the time to do so now. The more you use them, the more you will understand them.

Bezier splines are lines created in MAX that usually are used for modeling methods such as Lathing or Lofting. They are also used as paths for cameras and such. We will be using them strictly as a reference for our patch modeling, a rather uncommon method.

Figure 5.9 shows the four different types of curve properties of spline vertices. Here are some definitions of splines.

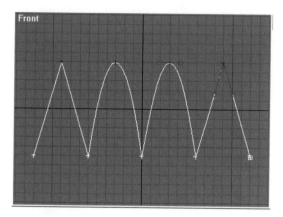

FIGURE **5.9** *Bezier spline curve types.*

- The entire line, including all handles and points, is called a *spline* or *Bezier spline*
- The line between two points is called a *segment*
- The points along the line are called *vertices*
- The lines with little boxes on the end, protruding from the vertices, are called *Bezier handles*

The vertices along the spline define the shape of the curve. You may assign one of four different properties to a single vertex. The Properties dialog box appears when you right-click on any particular vertex, or selected vertices. Examples are displayed in Figure 5.9, and go from left to right as follows.

- **Corner.** The Corner property type is used to make Hard Corners in your splines. They do not have Bezier handles.
- **Smooth.** The Smooth property type is used to create Smooth splines. They also do not have Bezier handles, and are calculated by the neighboring vertices before and after the vertex. It's a good idea to start with this property type as the default, and assign others as needed.
- **Bezier.** The Bezier property type is more commonly used to create smooth curves. Unlike the *smooth* property type, Bezier has handles that let you control the curve manually while maintaining the curve's smoothness.
- **Bezier Corner.** The Bezier Corner property type is the most commonly used vertex property. Bezier Corner is much like Bezier, except the handles move independently from each other, allowing you to manipulate both the incoming and outgoing segments separately.

To create a basic spline, go to **Create/Shapes/Line**. Then create the spline by clicking, or click-dragging your way around. When you click to place a vertex without dragging,

MAX assigns the Corner property type to the vertex. If you click-drag, MAX assigns a Bezier property type to the vertex, allowing you to control the curve as you drag. Use click on corners and click-drag where you want smooth curves. You will learn which ones to use over time. You can assign the other two vertex properties later by adding an Edit Spline modifier to your newly created spline. We will talk more about Edit Spline later.

MODELING EDWARD—OUTLINING THE FACE WITH SPLINES

Let's start by outlining Edward's face so we will have a reference to his gill and profile when it comes time to lay the patches. In the left or right viewport, outline the face until your spline looks something like the spline in Figure 5.10.

Don't worry if your outline doesn't look exactly like the one in Figure 5.10 — that's what **Edit Spline** is for! With your newly created spline selected, click **Modify**, then **Edit Spline**. The Max default takes you right into **Sub-Object Mode**, which is the Vertex level. Drag the vertices around to their proper locations, and assign new properties to any offending vertices and drag the handles around to make the spline match Figure 5.10.

Notice that in Figure 5.10, all of the vertices are selected so you can see their handles and placement. After you are finished tweaking your spline to match Figure 5.10, turn off **Sub-Object** mode. Now, using the same procedure that you used to outline the face, outline the rest of the fish as shown in Figure 5.11.

Notice that all of the "parts" are outlined separately. We trace the parts separately so we can manipulate them individually later, not affecting the other splines. The splines can be either open or closed, it doesn't matter. (Open means the ends are not connected; closed means the ends are connected.) When you get to the point where you are going to outline the eye, instead of using **Create/Shapes/Line**, use **Create/Shapes/Circle**, and click-drag a circle in the appropriate location. Then add an edit spline modifier and tweak the spline to match the outline of the eye.

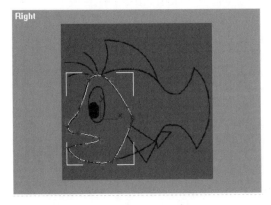

FIGURE **5.10** *Traced face using splines.*

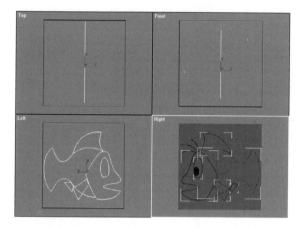

FIGURE **5.11** *A tracing of the side profile.*

⇨ **TIP**

> If you are having trouble viewing the outline, save what you have done and open *splines.max* on the CD-ROM included with this book. Then you can select any spline, go into **Modify/Sub-Object** mode, and see how the splines were created.

After you have finished outlining the entire side profile with all of the appendages (eyes, fins, etc.), take the time to do an Arc/Rotate Selection in the Perspective viewport to see what you have accomplished. As you can see, you have a flat two-dimensional fish. Let's add some volume to this poor guy.

Before we add volume, you must decide which side of Edward you would like to model. Remember that one of the benefits of patch modeling is that you have to model only one half of the character. Choose which half to model, left or right. You should decide based on what you feel most comfortable with. We're modeling Edward's left side; therefore, we will be tracing the rest of Edward, on his left side.

Let's add some volume. Since we've already drawn one fin, we don't need to draw it again in every viewport. Let's just use the same one we have already created, by moving the Pectoral Fin outward on the X-axis to its new location in the front viewport (his left side). You need to restrict the movement to the X-axis so the fin won't move from its original Y location in the side viewport. Take a look at Figure 5.12 to see the fin moved.

Select the Pectoral Fin in the side viewport. Change your top viewport to shaded mode so you can see the top view Axis Drawing. Now click **Select and Move**, and Restrict the X-axis. Then, in the top viewport, drag the fin out to the approximate location of the fin on the drawing.

Now we need to adjust the fin to match the axis templates. With the fin selected, click on **Modify/Sub-Object** to return to the **Edit Vertex mode**, then move the vertices

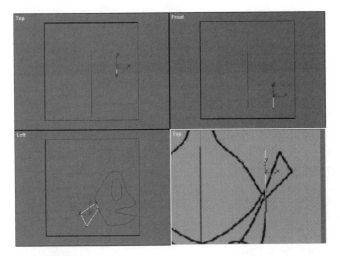

FIGURE **5.12** *Moving the pectoral fin to its new location.*

around until they match up as closely to the Axis drawings as possible in all viewports. Remember, the templates are for reference only, and do not have to be exact. See Figure 5.13 for final placement.

Now we need to give the body some volume. There are at least two ways of doing this. One way is to trace the silhouette of the fish from the front, creating a separate spline. This method works just fine. Keep the reference armature as simple as possible so you don't get lost in a sea of splines. Since we already have a spline drawn for the gill, let's use that one instead.

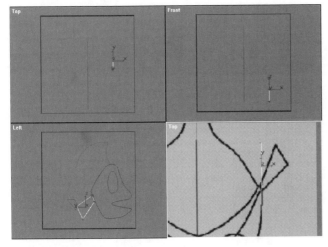

FIGURE **5.13** *Editing the fin in all viewports.*

Select the vertex or vertices that define Edward's gill. Then, in the top viewport with X-axis still restricted, pull the gill outward toward the pectoral fin. When you are finished, move the Bezier handles to make the spline fit the shape of the fish using the front shaded viewport axis template as reference until your final spline looks like Figure 5.14.

After you have reached that point, return to **Sub-Object** mode, and adjust the handles until your outline looks like Figure 5.14. You must use a little artistic judgment when creating your templates. We didn't follow the outline of the eyebrows with this spline because it's not representing the eyebrows. This spline is representing the gill line.

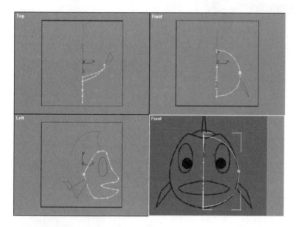

FIGURE **5.14** *Pulling out the gill.*

Now move the eye spline out to its new location and rotate it to match the other viewport templates. Do this using general transforms on the spline, not by moving the individual vertices. Look at Figure 5.15 to see the results.

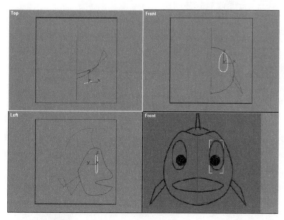

FIGURE **5.15** *Relocating the eye spline.*

Finally, the last spline! This spline will help you visualize the outer profile of Eddie. In the top viewport, outline the outer profile so your final spline looks like Figure 5.16.

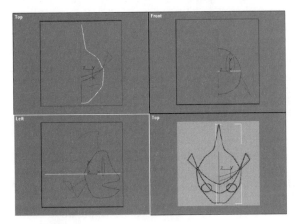

FIGURE **5.16** *Tracing the top profile.*

Now comes the exciting part — viewing the Finished wireframe! If you haven't done so already, save your scene now as *ed.max*.

Hide all of the Virtual Studio walls by selecting the walls, then go to **Display/Hide Selected** and select one of the splines (any one). Now hold down **Arc Rotate**, and select **Arc Rotate Selected**, to rotate around the selected spline in the perspective viewport, then click and drag in the perspective viewport to rotate your new wireframe armature. Cool, isn't it? You should have something that resembles Figure 5.17.

If you want to get an even better idea of what Edward will look like, select all of the splines, then mirror them in the top viewport as an instance with the X-axis constrained. If the new half is not located in the right spot, all you have to do is move it over.

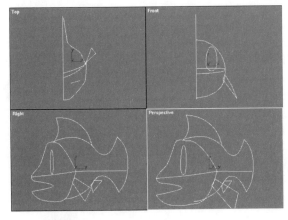

FIGURE **5.17** *The finished wireframe.*

Arc Rotate your selection again in the Perspective viewport, and you will see a good representation of how Edward will look. Make sure you delete the extra splines (right half) when you are finished looking at him. They will just get in your way otherwise.

NOTE

If you think you will need to add more splines to help you, like a mouth spline for example, do it now. Add or subtract as many splines as you think you will need to for reference. Don't worry; you can always add more splines at any time during the modeling process.

LAYING PATCHES ONE BY ONE

The time has finally come to create a patch! First, let's learn the basics of patches and how they work.

Bezier patches are much like Bezier splines. They have vertices and handles to manipulate them. The only difference is that the vertex now has three pairs of handles instead of just one. This is where things start to get interesting. First, save your wireframe, then open a fresh scene in MAX.

To create a patch, go to **Create/Standard Primitives/Patch Grids** then click on **Quad-patch**. In the front viewport, click and drag a patch out to form a square.

There are four parts to a patch:

- **The Inner Mesh.** The inner mesh is the actual grid of polygons that you will be manipulating.
- **Edges.** A Quad-patch has four edges. These edges are basically splines surrounding the Inner Mesh.
- **Vertices.** A Quad-patch has a vertex on each corner. Each vertex has Bezier handles protruding outward that control the edges, which in turn control the Inner Mesh.
- **Lattice.** The lattice is a type of framework that surrounds the patch. The lattice is what really makes the patch do what it does. All of the calculations are based on the position of the lattice. We don't need to be concerned with the lattice because it usually just gets in the way. We'll talk about the lattice and its uses later in the chapter.

That's the anatomy of a Quad-patch; now let's take a look at Tri-patches. Tri-patches have the same properties as Quad-patches, except they are triangular (they have three sides). Tri-patches are great for tight spots and rounded objects, but beware! Use Tri-patches only when absolutely necessary. Tri-patches can be very confusing and they easily cause wrinkles and ripples, which are usually undesirable.

The best way to figure out how patches work is to experiment with them. Click **Modify/Edit Patch**; then select any of the four vertices and start pulling, tweaking, and pushing them around. See the extra lines that don't really make sense? That's the lattice. Unselect the **Display Lattice** checkbox and you'll see that the annoying lines are gone.

Now you can really get a handle on things. Start pulling the handles around. Don't be afraid to change viewports. The main thing you're trying to accomplish is getting to know patches. When you're done experimenting, take a look at some general rules listed next.

RULES FOR MODELING WITH PATCHES

Looking at the samples in Figure 5.18, see if you can point out the mistakes in the patch labeled Wrong.

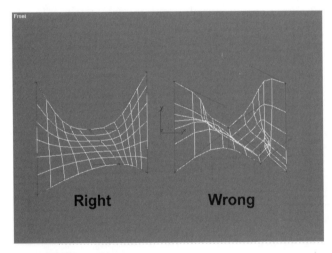

FIGURE **5.18** *Patch samples — right and wrong.*

Not terribly easy is it? Well, to make it easier take a look at the rules of modeling with patches.

1. **Make sure you check every single viewport!** Your model may look perfect in one viewport and be completely whacked in the other. Be careful, and go one patch at a time manipulating each vertex in each viewport before continuing. (You won't be able to see this mistake in the previous samples.)
2. **Always move vertices first, handles second!** If you move the handles first, you will be wasting your time. Move all of the vertices to where you want them in all viewports, then adjust the handles in all viewports. You will increase your modeling speed greatly if you get into this habit.

3. **Don't overlap handles from neighboring vertices unless necessary.** Overlapping handles often cause pinches and folds in your mesh.

4. **Spread the grid lines evenly between vertices.** This will ensure a nice smooth surface and also help with mapping coordinates later.

5. **Use Tri-patches only when absolutely necessary!** Tri-patches are wrinkle makers and are to be avoided as much as possible.

6. **Keep handles from adjoining patches perpendicular to each other in all viewports.** This is the best way to guarantee a smooth model!

7. **Always make sure the normals are facing the correct way.** Normals are the side of the face that the material gets mapped onto. If your materials are facing the wrong way, you'll be modeling your character inside out. For example, if Edward was built inside out, his scales would be on the inside of his body, and the outside of his body would be invisible. This mistake often happens with the very first patch laid. Make sure that the first patch is facing the way you want.

8. **Use only as many patches as you need to complete the model.** Strategically estimate how many patches it will take and where you will put them. This way you will have the lowest polygon count possible while still retaining the surface quality. Remember that you can always turn up the topology to get more polygons. We will cover Topology later in the chapter.

9. **Use your Shaded Perspective viewport as much as possible.** You will see problems you might otherwise miss. It also helps you visualize vertex placement.

10. **Make sure that all of the handles defining the center edge of the entire figure are protruding straight out from the edge.** If the handles protrude straight out from the center spline, you should not have pinches or creases running down the center of your model.

11. **Collapse the Modifier Stack!** Collapsing the stack means that any time your machine starts to bog down, most likely it is caused by the Edit Patch Modifier in the Modifier Stack. MAX likes to store every move you make into the Edit Patch Modifier; this has nothing to do with the undo levels, however, and shutting down and restarting MAX won't help. You *must* collapse the whole stack and reapply an Edit Patch Modifier. It's easy, so you should do it often. This will greatly reduce your file size as well. Also, when you collapse the stack, make sure to delete and remirror the other half of your model because after you collapse the stack, the other half is no longer an instance and will not update.

If you follow these rules when creating your character, you can't go wrong.

In addition to the rules, be aware that patch vertices have properties just like spline vertices, except that patch vertices have only two properties instead of four — Coplanar and Corner. You can get to the properties by right-clicking on a single vertex or set of selected vertices.

- **Coplanar** works just like a Bezier on a spline. If you move one handle, all of the handles move to retain smoothness. Use this property if you want large, smooth turns in your mesh.
- **Corner** works just like a Bezier Corner on a spline. Each handle works independently of the others. Use this property when you want to make sharp, tight turns in your mesh.

That's enough about the technical side of patches — the best way to learn is to do it! Let's start modeling Edward!

CREATING EDWARD'S BODY

Start by laying the first patch. Open the *ed.max* scene that you built earlier in the chapter. If you do not have it, load *edspline.max* from the Chapter 5 folder on the companion CD-ROM.

Remember, in this tutorial, we're modeling the left half of Edward. If you were to model the right half of Edward, you would choose the left viewport instead of the right. In the right viewport, go to the **Create/Standard Primitives** pull-down menu and select **Patch Grids**. Then select **Quad Patch** and drag out a patch in the front viewport. Your viewport should now look something like Figure 5.19.

To manipulate the Patch, click on **Modify/Edit Patch**. Following the rules of patch Basics, manipulate the vertices and the handles to match Figure 5.20.

Be sure to use the spline guidelines that you made. That was the easy part; here is where it gets tricky. Let's add some volume. A good rule of thumb is to make the gridlines of the patch follow the contour of the object that you are modeling.

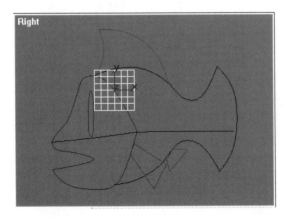

FIGURE **5.19** *Laying the first patch.*

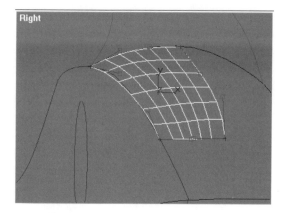

FIGURE **5.20** *Manipulating the patch to fit.*

Remember Rule #1 of patch basics? Here is where you get to apply it! Select the bottom two vertices of the patch; in the front viewport pull the vertices to your right until they are close to the spline that represents the outer body of Edward. Now adjust the handles to match Figure 5.21.

This is a perfect time to make sure that your patch is facing the right direction. Turn on **Shade** mode in the Perspective viewport, do an **Arc Rotate Selected**, and rotate the viewport around the object. Does it look right to you? Or are the Normals on the inside of the patch instead of the outside? If they are, you must pull the bottom two vertices in the opposite direction to correct the problem. Now that you've got your first patch home, let's give him a brother.

To add a patch to your existing patch, you must first select an edge. Click on **Vertex** under the **Sub-Object** menu to open the drop-down list, and select **Edge**. Now recheck the Lattice checkbox to make the lattice visible again. We need to make the lattice visible

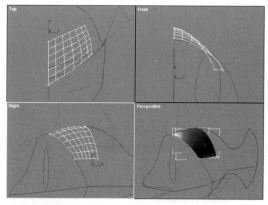

FIGURE **5.21** *Moving the vertices on the third dimension.*

so we can see which edge is selected. If the lattice is turned off, it's hard to tell. (This is the only use that I have found for the lattice).

Now select the rear most edge on the patch as shown in Figure 5.22. The edge of the lattice will turn red to indicate that you have selected it.

Click the **Add Quad** button and presto! A new patch is created, as shown in Figure 5.23.

Notice that the new patch protrudes from the contour of the leading edge. Take this into consideration when deciding when and where to add patches. You'll understand after you have added a few patches. To make the new patch conform to the shape of Edward's back, return to **vertex** mode under Sub-Object, and manipulate the vertices in all viewports to match Figure 5.24.

Try mirroring the model to check out the volume (shape) of Edward (no, you won't need a mirror for this exercise).

There are many benefits to mirroring your model early in the creation process.

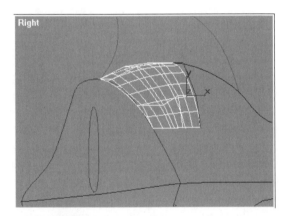

FIGURE **5.22** *Selecting an edge.*

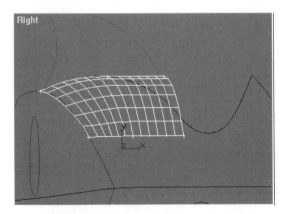

FIGURE **5.23** *Adding a patch.*

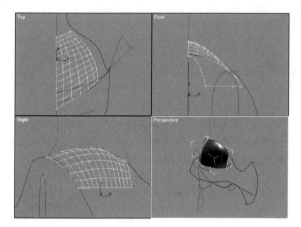

FIGURE **5.24** *Manipulate the new patch to fit.*

- **You get instant interactive feedback on what your final model will look like.** If you mirror your model as an instance, everything you do to one side (even adding patches) happens to the other side. Very intuitive indeed!
- **You get a good idea of the overall volume of the object as a whole.** If you waited until after you were all done modeling to mirror it, you might not like the outcome, because you wouldn't have been able to see what the whole model looked like while you were creating it. But if you mirror early, you will have a chance to correct mistakes as you go.
- **When modeling opposite sides of objects (like the opposite side of a leg), you can still see the outline of the patch, while the inner mesh is the color of the mirrored object.** If you didn't have the mirrored object, you would see only an outline because the normals would be facing the other way. It helps to see the normals of the mirrored object when you need to spread the grid evenly across the surface.

To mirror the model (as shown in figure 5.25), follow these steps:

1. Turn off **Sub-Object** mode.
2. Constrain the X-axis and make the top viewport active by right-clicking on it.
3. With the left half of the fish selected, click the **Mirror** icon.
4. Select the **Instance Radio** button.
5. If the new right half is not lined up correctly, do a Select and Move, and move it over to the centerline.
6. Now Re-Select the right half and return to **Modify/Sub-Object** mode.

Now that we've got volume, let's continue to add more patches.

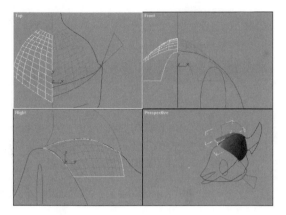

FIGURE **5.25** *Mirrored model.*

Following the same procedure that you used to add the second patch, add a third patch. Turn on the Lattice, select an edge, then add a Quad-patch. Get used to adding patches, because you will be doing it a lot!

Whoa! Look at Figure 5.26. The new patch went out of bounds. This happened because the newly created patch is based on the contour of the edge it was created from. This happens all of the time, so to fix it, return to **Vertex** mode and pull the vertices to their proper location, then adjust the handles to match as shown in Figure 5.27.

If you are having a hard time getting your model to look like the samples, have patience; skill will come with practice. Let's finish the row down to the tail as shown in Figure 5.28.

Good job! Just one more thing to fix. Take a look at the bottom edges of the patches in the right viewport. They aren't running parallel to the center spline line. They could stay

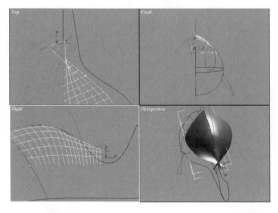

FIGURE **5.26** *Adding a third patch.*

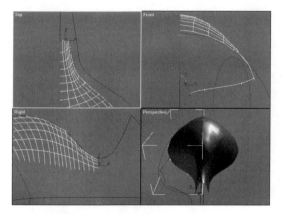

FIGURE **5.27** *Adjusting the offending patch.*

this way, but the model will be cleaner if they are parallel. As you can see, you can always go back and edit your model and make changes any time you want. Nothing is set in stone.

Take some time now to fix the bottom edge of the patches to prepare for the next row. Your edited model should resemble Figure 5.29.

Now that the first row is complete, move on to the second row. Select the bottom edge of the first patch and add a Quad-patch as shown in Figure 5.30.

Just like before, move the vertices up to the spline, then manipulate the handles so the spline fits. Do you see a pattern forming here? This is what modeling with patches is all about. Adding patches one by one, row by row, until you're done.

Now trim those sideburns! Move the bottom two vertices until they rest on the spline guideline as seen in Figure 5.31.

Again, just like before, add a new patch to continue the row. But now you need to weld up that seam!

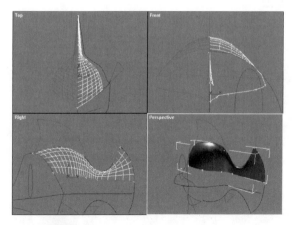

FIGURE **5.28** *The finished row of patches.*

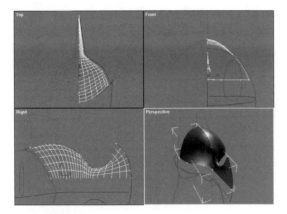

FIGURE 5.29 *Straightened up edges.*

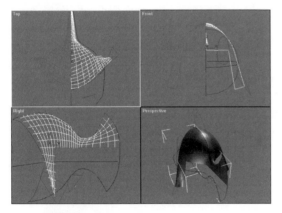

FIGURE 5.30 *Adding a second row of patches.*

This is the next step in the patch modeling process — welding vertices. The biggest mistake made when welding vertices together is not matching them up in every viewport. This is a must!

The easiest way to match vertices is to drag a selection box around two or more vertices to turn them red. Quickly scan each viewport to see which vertex needs to go where. Then adjust one vertex at a time in each viewport until all of the vertices occupy the same space.

⇨ TIP

Use 2D snap to help you snap onto vertices. You can set up the snap settings by choosing Views/Grids and Snap Settings. Make sure that Vertex is set to the highest priority. You can play around with the settings to see what works best for you.

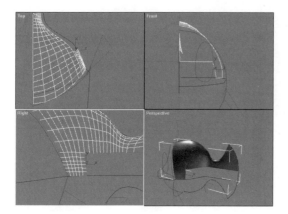

FIGURE **5.31** *Adjusting the vertices.*

Under Topology, turn the Weld Threshold to 3.1. This increases the "weld zone" around a vertex in case you didn't get the vertices close enough. If you turn it up higher than 3.1, you are liable to grab and weld unwanted vertices; but if you keep it at 1.1, it shouldn't do anything at all. . You'll find that 3.1 is a safe number to use when welding. When you are ready, click **Weld**. Use the shaded viewport to see if your weld took effect or not. An example is shown in Figure 5.32.

Now that you have welding down tight, finish up the second row. Keep adding, adjusting, and welding, adding, adjusting, and welding, until you finish up the second row. If you did it correctly, it should look like Figure 5.33.

Keep adding more patches and move to the next row. When you get to the third patch, take a look at Figure 5.34.

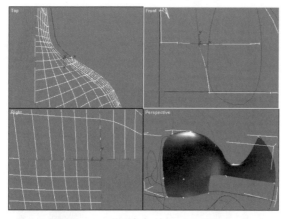

FIGURE **5.32** *Comparing welded and nonwelded vertices.*

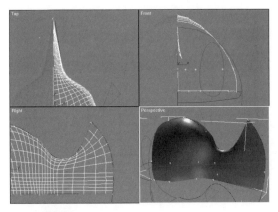

FIGURE **5.33** *The completed second row.*

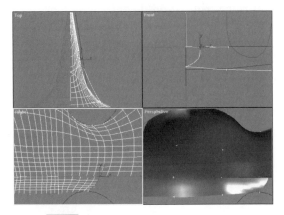

FIGURE **5.34** *Tail contour.*

This third patch starts to form the shape of the bottom of the tail. Examine the front viewport in Figure 5.34. Make sure your edge matches the edge in the image, then add a final patch and you're done with the tail!

Does your model look like the one in Figure 5.35? If not, take a break, come back and try it again. Keep adjusting the vertices and handles until you get it looking the way you want.

Now is a good time to show you the Topology Slider. The Topology Slider allows you to adjust the patch topology. This means that you can adjust the amount of faces or detail your object has. This is a great benefit over other methods of modeling because you can model with a low-resolution model to increase your redraw speed. Then, when you want to see the detail, crank it up!

As an experiment, turn off **Sub-Object** mode. Go to **File/Summary Info** and see how many faces your model has. It should be around 1760. Click **Close** to close the Summary window. Now, under the Modifier Stack, click the down arrow on the Topology spinner

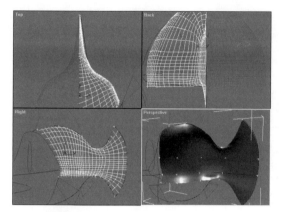

FIGURE 5.35 *The body halfway done.*

until it reads 3. You should see your polygons being reduced on the fly. Take a look at the Summary Info again. The face count is now around 800. This is one of the great benefits of patch modeling — you can turn the topology up or down any time you want.

Now you're ready to add another row of patches. Add a patch starting at the rear instead of the front of Edward as shown in Figure 5.36. This will prepare for the anal fin that is going to be attached to the next row — good strategic planning. You have to plan where you put your patches.

Another downfall of patches is that if you add detail to one side of the model, you must carry the same amount of patches all the way around the model. For example, if Edward didn't have fins (besides the fact that he couldn't swim), you could model the bottom half just like the top half. But since he does have fins, you'll have to add a few more rows of patches to compensate.

So go ahead and throw that patch on there, and finish off the row. Your new added row should look like Figure 5.37.

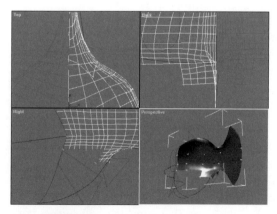

FIGURE 5.36 *Adding another row.*

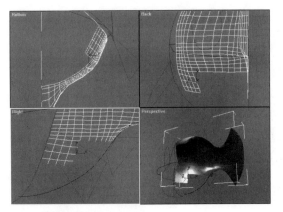

FIGURE **5.37** *The completed row.*

This next row gets tricky because now the patches are starting to roll around the back. They give you a false sense of depth, so add the next patch starting at the front this time, as in Figure 5.38.

Finish off this row just as before, except this time, there are a few things to note. Take a look at the gill line in Figure 5.39. The patches are placed slightly inside the gill line because you're going to create a ridge to define the gill later. Also notice that you still should be following the contour of the fish with the patches. For example, in Figure 5.39 top and bottom viewports are switched so you can get a better view. Notice how the leading edge has the same curve as Edward's rear end. You get much smoother results if you follow this technique.

For the last row, since there aren't any fins to get in the way, drag this patch all the way to the bottom. Check out Figure 5.39.

Now add a patch to the front as shown in Figure 5.40 to make a triangular hole.

This is a good time to learn about Subdivide. What is Subdivide? Subdivide divides an edge, creating two patches from one. Why do we need to subdivide? Take a closer look at

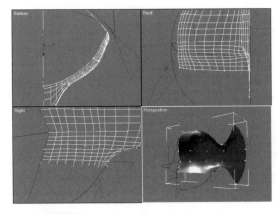

FIGURE **5.38** *The next patch.*

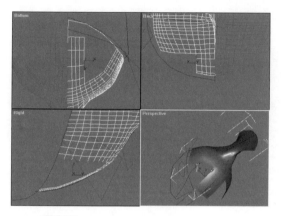

FIGURE **5.39** *Add a patch to the rear.*

Edward in Figure 5.40. You'll notice that there isn't anywhere to weld the front patch to the back patch, but if you subdivide the back patch, you'll create a set of vertices to weld to.

WARNING

If you have a series of patches in a row, Subdivide will divide all of their common edges! This can be an advantage or a disadvantage depending on how you use it.

Switch to Edge selection level and turn on the Lattice. Now select the edge of the long rear patch as shown in Figure 5.41.

With **Propagate** selected, click the **Subdivide** button. You should see the polygons double. Return to **Vertex** mode; there should be a new set of vertices anxiously waiting to

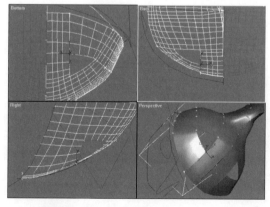

FIGURE **5.40** *Make a triangular hole.*

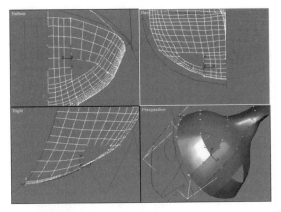

FIGURE **5.41** *Select edge to subdivide.*

be welded. Weld the vertices together so Edward looks like Figure 5.42. Now he looks like
he has exhaust ports.

Now fill in the hole. Select any edge and add a Tri-patch this time instead of a Quad-
patch. (This is one of those rare times when it's okay to use a Tri-patch.)

You're finally done with the main body! It's time to move on to the face.

MODELING EDWARD'S FACE

Start near Edward's brow and work your way in. The only problem is that there aren't
enough edges to build from, so you need more patches for the detail of Edward's face.

Remember Subdivide? Go ahead and select the edge that is shown in Figure 5.43.

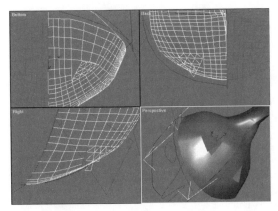

FIGURE **5.42** *Filling in the hole with a Tri-patch.*

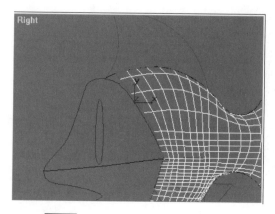

FIGURE **5.43** *Subdividing for more patches.*

Notice that the lattice is not shown when the edge was selected. Sometimes you can tell which edge you selected just by where the axis icon is located. With the edge and **Propagate** selected, click **Subdivide**. Propagate sends the divide all the way down the spine of the fish. If Propagate was turned off, it would divide only one patch and you would be left with a seam.

Let's model the brow. Here comes the tricky part. This is where you get to start using Bezier corners to make creases and valleys. Take a look at Figure 5.44; it shows the new patch formed into the top of the brow. If you combine artistic sense with a little skill you can do it. The vertices and handles are displayed so you can see how it was done.

With that first tough patch laid, you have two places to add a new patch, either from the body or the brow. Remember the retaining contour rule? If you add the new patch from the Brow patch, it will retain the same shape so you don't have to manipulate it as much. Go ahead and make the new patch look like the one in Figure 5.45.

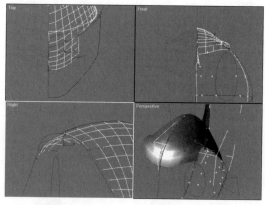

FIGURE **5.44** *Modeling the brow.*

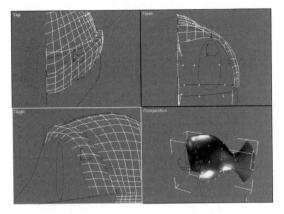

FIGURE **5.45** *Continuing the brow down the face.*

Moving down the bridge of the nose, add a patch and move the outer corner inward to start forming the eye socket as shown in Figure 5.46.

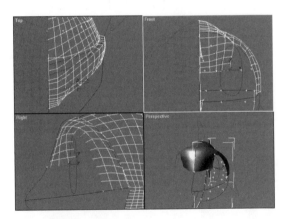

FIGURE **5.46** *Creating the bridge of the nose.*

Yes, we need to use another Tri-patch! Add a Tri-patch from the brow; then weld the free vertex. Start to form the eye socket more, as in Figure 5.47.

Add two more patches to form the nose and the top lip as shown in Figure 5.48.

Getting the hang of it? Now add three patches to form Edward's top lip as shown in Figure 5.49.

Notice that where the last patch meets the gill line, there is an extra set of vertices to deal with. Remember how to resolve this problem? Subdivide! Select the edge that you want to subdivide, and press the **Subdivide** button. Continue adding and manipulating patches to form the lower jaw as shown in Figure 5.50.

Keep working your way up toward the chin and lower lip. Use Figure 5.51 as a guide.

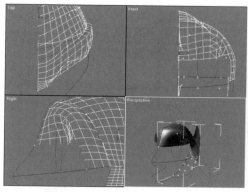

FIGURE **5.47** *Forming the eye socket.*

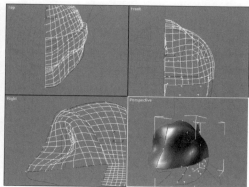

FIGURE **5.48** *Adding the nose.*

Finally, add the last patch to complete the body. To adjust the corners of the mouth, unhide your **Virtual Studio**, and turn on the **Show Maps** in viewport for the front wall. Use the template as a guide to adjust all of the vertices that make up the mouth. It should look like Figure 5.52.

To make the inside of the mouth, select the inside edge of the top lip, add a patch, then move the two free vertices to the back of the throat and adjust their handles as shown in Figure 5.53.

Do the same thing with the lower part of the mouth, only this time you will need to add a Tri-patch to finish it off as shown in Figure 5.54.

Well done! The body is complete! Now it's time to add some fins to Edward so he can swim.

Start with the dorsal fin. To give the dorsal fin volume, in the top viewport, pull the center vertex outward as shown in Figure 5.55.

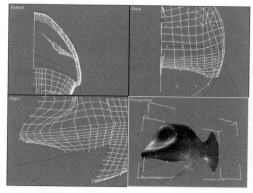

FIGURE **5.49** *Adding the lip.*

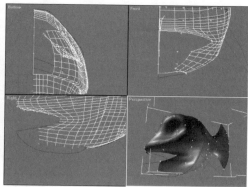

FIGURE **5.50** *Building the lower jaw.*

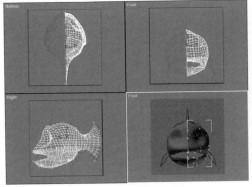

FIGURE **5.52** *Finishing the lower lip.*

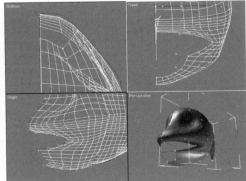

FIGURE **5.51** *Continuing working up to the lip.*

With the hole established, add a Quad-patch to the front and a Tri-patch to the back to create the fin. Look at Figure 5.56. Use the Corner vertex property to get the sharp transition from the body to the fin.

Now add the anal fin. Remember when we added the extra patches in the rear to prepare for the anal fin? Well, now is the time to tack that little fin onto the body. Using the same procedure as the dorsal fin, go ahead and add the anal fin so it looks like Figure 5.57.

Notice that the fin doesn't match the template exactly. Remember that the template is only here for reference; it doesn't have to match exactly.

Now get ready for the pectoral fins; they're tricky! Keep in mind that you could have left a hole for the fins while modeling Edward's body, but I wanted to show you this neat little trick to add appendages wherever you want.

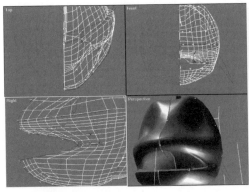

FIGURE **5.53** *Undercutting to form the inside of the mouth.*

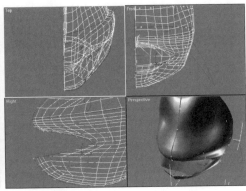

FIGURE **5.54** *Creating the lower half of the mouth.*

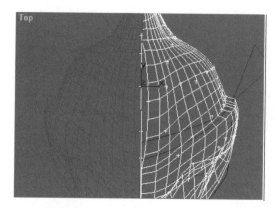

FIGURE **5.55** *Creating a hole to mount the dorsal fin.*

First, make a hole to attach the fin. Turn on Show Lattice and go to the patch level in the Modifier stack and select the *two* patches that are shown in Figure 5.57 (the two right below the centerline just behind the gill).

Click the **Detach** button and accept the default name for it. Then click on **Sub-Object** and select the **Attach** Button. Choose the detached set of patches and reattach them. Then return to **Sub-Object** mode and weld the eight vertices as shown in Figure 5.58.

Now pull the two vertices apart to create the cross-section of the fin. To create the actual fin, in the right viewport, create a new Quad-patch. Then add an Edit Patch Modifier to the newly created patch and move the vertices to match the fin profile so it looks like Figure 5.59.

Subdivide the edge of the fin that is closest to the body so you have a total of three vertices on each end, then mirror the fin to make the other side. Next, turn off **Sub-Object**

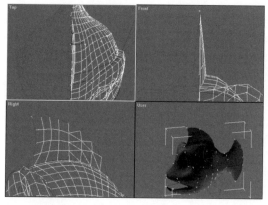

FIGURE **5.56** *Tacking on the anal fin.*

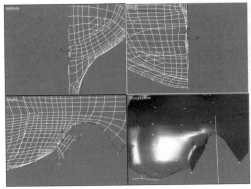

FIGURE **5.57** *Selecting a patch.*

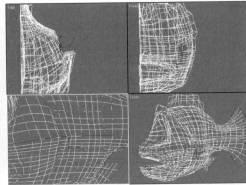

FIGURE **5.58** *Make a hole.*

mode and attach the mirrored half to the first half. Now weld all of the vertices together except for the two in the center of the edge closest to the body. You will need to pull these two vertices outward to match the cross-section of the body.

Now that the fin is completed, using basic transformations, **Select** and **Move** then **Select** and **Rotate** the fin to match the templates. Line up the fin to the hole as closely as possible, then go into **Sub-Object** mode and move the vertices so they match the hole more closely.

Select the left half of Edward and attach the fin. Go to **Sub-Object** mode and weld all of the vertices to their matching partner. If you are having a hard time seeing the vertices, use **Arc Rotate Selected** and **Zoom** in the **Perspective Viewport** to get a closer look.

Good job! Your final model should look something like Figure 5.60.

The only things left to model are the eyes and the tongue. Start with the tongue (even though goldfish don't have tongues). Since Edward likes to talk to himself, he needs one.

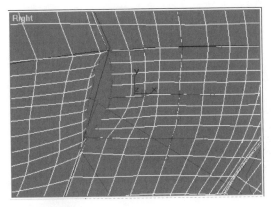

FIGURE **5.59** *Create the new fin separately.*

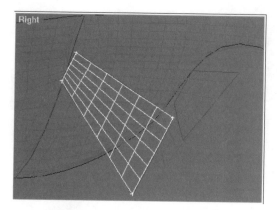

FIGURE **5.60** *The completed body.*

To start, make a primitive cylinder in the Front viewport as shown in Figure 5.61.

Now apply an **Edit Patch** to the cylinder, which will convert it into a patch model. Select the center vertex and pull it out as shown in Figure 5.62.

Now that you can see how the cylinder can be manipulated just like a patch grid, move and adjust the vertices and their respective handles until your final model looks like Figure 5.63. Now Edward can talk up a storm!

What about Edward's eyes? Eyes are easy because they are simple primitive spheres nonuniformly scaled along the Y-axis. The eyelids are just two copies of the eye chopped in half and rotated.

To get the eyelids to conform to the eyeball, **Select** and **Link** the eyelids to their parent eyeballs and that's it! Now there are just two things left to do before you put maps on Edward. First, we need to collapse the modifier stack. Second, weld the two halves of

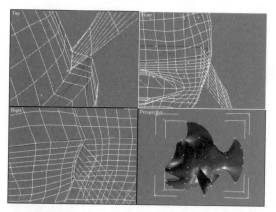

FIGURE **5.61** *Create a cylinder for the tongue.*

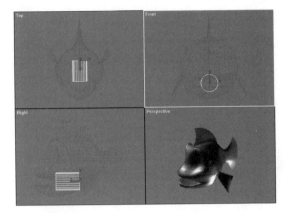

FIGURE **5.62** *Pulling out a vertex for the tongue tip.*

Edward together. Start by selecting one of the halves and attaching it to the other half. Then go into **Sub-Object** mode and start welding vertices together. Just make sure you get them all. You wouldn't want Edward to leak.

Congratulations! You've completed you first patch model! Your finished model should look like Figure 5.64.

Now that Edward is modeled, he needs to come to life with a little surfacing. Here's how we surface Edward.

APPLYING IMAGE MAPS TO YOUR CREATURE

Before you do this section of the tutorial, make sure you do a **Save As**, and save a new version of Edward as *edmap.max*. If you are just starting at this point, or would like a sample

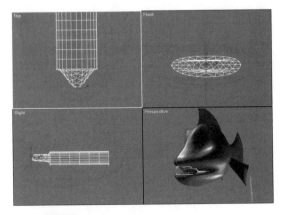

FIGURE **5.63** *Finishing the tongue.*

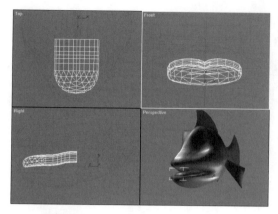

FIGURE **5.64** *Edward.*

model to work with, open the *edmap.max* scene included in the *Chapter5/Edward* folder on the companion CD-ROM.

Also, make sure you make any necessary revisions before proceeding any further because there is no going back. Before Edward is mapped, he needs a few changes, like more rounded fins. Figure 5.65 shows the changes you should make.

Turn up the topology to 5.5, which is enough for detail, but not too much. Add an Edit Mesh Modifier to your stack. Now your model is a polygonal mesh that can be edited only by polygon tools. You can go back to the patch level and change things, but it's dangerous. You could mess things up.

Grab a piece of paper and a pencil, because you are going to need to log your maps. Change Vertex to Face on the Sub-Object level, and select all of the faces that make up the

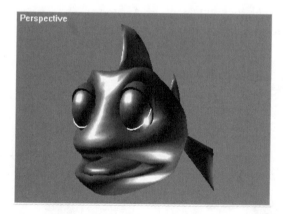

FIGURE **5.65** *Edward's facelift.*

dorsal fin. Make sure you get all of them, and not any extras. It may help to create a camera and orbit around your model to make sure you got them all.

Holding down the **Control** key adds to your selection, and holding down the Alt key subtracts from your selection. Scroll down the Edit Mesh menu until you find the Material ID dialog box. In the ID: text block type 2 and press **Return**. This assigns material ID#2 to the selected vertices. Now scroll back up to the top and click the **Hide** button to hide the faces so they are out of the way.

Remember that piece of paper? Write down the following:

1. Body
2. Dorsal fin
3. Tail fin
4. Anal fin
5. Pectoral fins
6. Face
7. Mouth

This is a list for the material IDs for each of Edward's body parts. You make these selections based on how you want to set up the mapping coordinates. Try to use the coordinates that will logically fit each part the best. I chose to map each fin with planar mapping coordinates, the body with cylindrical mapping coordinates, and the face with planar mapping coordinates.

Before applying mapping coordinates, you need to finish assigning material IDs, just like you did with the dorsal fin. Go ahead and select each part separately, and assign it a Material ID. Name them according to the List. Remember to hide each piece as you go.

Remember to use the Camera view and Zoom/Orbit to get into the mouth to select the faces.

⇨ TIP

The default Material ID is 1, which is why I made the body a material ID of 1. That way, when everything is hidden, only the body will be left and it's already assigned an ID.

When you are all done, click **Unhide All** in the Face menu. Click the **Select by ID** button and select each set separately to see if you assigned everything correctly. That way you can see if the numbers are correct, and you can make sure you got everything. If you missed a face, just select it and give it an ID.

⇨ **CAUTION**

Try not to type a number in the ID dialog box accidentally when trying to select By Material ID because you will change the ID to the number you accidentally entered.

ASSIGN MAPPING COORDINATES TO YOUR SELECTION SETS

To apply mapping coordinates to all of our selection sets by Material ID, go back into **Sub-Object** mode if you are not already there. Do a Select by ID, and select **ID#1**. The body should turn red. With the **Sub-Object** button still depressed, add a UVW Mapping Modifier onto the stack. The default map is Planar. Change this to Cylindrical, then rotate the mapping gizmo until it is facing the correct direction.

The end with the line protruding from it is the top of the map. Turn the map so the line is on the same end as the face. When in **Sub-Object/Gizmo** mode, the green line represents where the map splits. Rotate the gizmo so that the line runs down Edward's tummy. You can turn on Rotate Snap to make it a little easier. Now click on **Map Fit** to make it snap to the selected faces.

When this is done, move down the list to #2, the dorsal fin. Add another Edit Mesh onto the stack, and select by ID #2. The dorsal fin should turn red. Apply Planar UVW Mapping to the selected faces, and then Rotate the Mapping gizmo until the line is facing upright.

Add another Edit Mesh Modifier and keep going down the list adding Mapping Coordinates to the rest of the parts. It's hard to visualize where the maps are located on the pages of this book, but to get a hand on view, open the *edmap.max* file in the *Chapter5/Edward* folder on the companion CD-ROM.

Then take a tour through the stack to see how I did it. It's OK if it gives you a warning. Click **OK** and move on. When you apply mapping coordinates, it doesn't do anything that would harm the mesh if you were to go up and down in the stack.

Now that you have tried this, you can get your reference maps from each piece. I use reference maps to help me paint my image maps. I get these by using a Plug-in by Peter Watje called *Unwrap*. Unwrap "unwraps" the object into a 2D file that you can then use as a reference for you map placement. Take a look at unwrapping a mesh.

UNWRAPPING YOUR OBJECTS

You can find the Unwrap plug-in inside the *Chapter5/Plugin* folder on the CD-ROM. Install it into your *plugins* directory. Once it's installed, go to the utility section of MAX and scroll down to Unwrap Object Texture. You can unwrap each piece based on Material ID.

Just select **Use Mat ID** and enter a number in the ID spinner. Keep the defaults, select **Pick Object**, pick Edward, and away you go! Save each map based on their Material ID. For example, name Material ID #2 *dorsalfin.tga*. Saving them as targa files works best.

MAKING YOUR SURFACE MAPS

Open up your favorite painting program, such as Fractal Design Painter or Photoshop. Then open up your first map, which in this case is *body.tga*. As you can see, Unwrap unwrapped the grid to give you a good reference to paint from. Figure 5.66 shows the unwrapped body grid and the map I painted based on it.

Go ahead and paint your maps. Now apply the maps to Edward to make him look good.

APPLYING YOUR SURFACE MAPS

First, open up the material editor and under the first map slot, click the **Standard** button. Change the Standard Material to Multi/Sub-Object. This allows you to assign more than one map to an object.

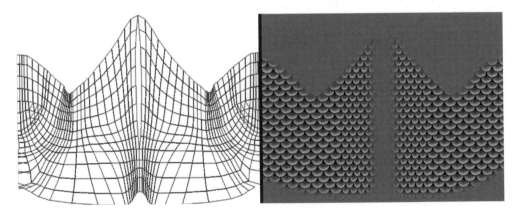

FIGURE 5.66 *An unwrapped mesh and its image map.*

A list of maps appears. Change the number of maps to Seven since this is how many parts you have. Now go through and name each map appropriately. Assign the whole map to Edward; all of his materials should appear when you render him. You should have something that looks like Figure 5.67.

FIGURE **5.67** *Edward with his scaly suit.*

Well, that wasn't too bad, was it? Of course, Edward was a rather simple character. Life gets a little more complicated when surfacing complex characters, which you'll discover in the next chapter when surfacing Knuckles, the gangster. After that, I strongly suggest you visit Chapter 9 to explore the issues regarding creature surfacing. It will open your eyes to a number of great techniques for creating awesome character and creature surfaces.

MOVING ON TO BIGGER AND MEANER THINGS

Well, that's it! Edward is complete! With the power of patch modeling in your toolbox you can model just about any organic creature that comes your way. During this tutorial, you probably experienced some frustrations, but thankfully, Peter Watje wrote his third-party plug-in to make the process of modeling with patches much easier! We will be covering this "new" tool in the next chapter. So take a well-deserved break, and come back when you are ready to conquer Knuckles using Surfacetools!

6 Breaking Knuckles— Creature Creation with Surfacetools

Now that you have mastered the art of traditional patch modeling, it's time to learn how to do it the easy way! You learned how to use patches first because patch modeling is the basis of Surfacetools. Surfacetools is a third-party plug-in developed by Peter Watje for Digimation. You can purchase Surfacetools for around $85 by visiting *www.digimation.com*.

Surfacetools has two vital features, CrossSection and Surface. CrossSection behaves much like Skinning in other 3D programs. It connects the points (vertices) in a series of splines to create a complete spline wireframe of your object. Surface allows you to convert any set of splines that make up a three- or four-sided frame of splines into either a Quad-patch or a Tri-patch. Both tools are covered extensively throughout this chapter.

The difference between Surfacetools and basic patch modeling is that with patches you are modeling with the patch itself, but with Surfacetools you are modeling with the outlining splines. Once you have laid the splines you add a surface modifier to turn the splines into a completed patch model. It may be hard to grasp at first, but when you get the hang of it, you'll be creating characters in no time!

To follow this tutorial the way it was intended, you'll need a copy of Surfacetools and 3D Studio MAX Release 2 (MAX R2). You may want to go through the chapter first to see if Surfacetools is for you. This tutorial also works with MAX R1 and the original version of Surfacetools. There are some minor differences in MAX R2 that I will point out as the tutorial progresses.

Get ready to create the more advanced character in Figure 6.1. Meet Knuckles!

Don't be overwhelmed by the complexity of this character. He looks mean on the outside, but he is really a gentle giant. From what you learned about patches in Chapter 5, you'll soon realize that Knuckles would take forever to do with patches. On the other

FIGURE 6.1 *Knuckles, ready to take care of business.*

hand, with the combination of the CrossSection and Surface tools this ornery little guy is rather simple to complete, and in a reasonable amount of time, too.

The first step in creating a character is to learn more about his personality and environment, so let's get to know Knuckles.

KNUCKLES' BIOGRAPHY

Knuckles is a thug who worked for an organized crime boss named Chillie during the early 1920s, in the time when there were tommy guns, mobsters, and detectives like Dick Tracy trying to catch you in the act. Knuckles is the guy that Chillie sends out to take care of someone who has crossed the line, or neglected to pay a loan. If you find yourself owing Chillie some money or he finds out that you've been smooching with one of his gals, you'll likely find yourself face-to-face with Knuckles, which will likely leave you looking at the stars, if you can even see after the pummeling.

So what does a guy like Knuckles look like? Well, it really depends on his personality. Knuckles isn't the sharpest tack on the board — actually, he probably wouldn't even be on the board. Yes, it's safe to say that knuckles won't be winning a Nobel Prize anytime soon. So you know that he's not bright, but what else do you need to know about him? Actually there is much to learn if you want Knuckles to look the part. For example, Knuckles is a lover of food, particularly Italian, and is often found shoveling in the stromboli at Luigi's on the corner of Fourth and Main Streets. For this reason you are likely to see a colorful collage of food stains on his clothing. You can bet Knuckles doesn't make regular trips to the dry cleaner's, well, unless he owes Chillie money.

Knuckles is a large guy, standing about 6'7" and weighing in at a solid 350 pounds. He sports huge arms and a rather portly midsection — it's safe to say that he has a huge stomach hanging out of his pants. In fact, it's so big that he can't tuck in the front of his shirt so it just hangs there. He's also quite a slob but I wouldn't tell him that to his face, particularly since you'll need a stepladder to look him in the eye

He's an invincible giant, or is he? Actually he has an Achilles' heel just like Superman. You see, Knuckles is somewhat like the guard dog that is subdued by a steak. To evade the bone-crunching grasp of Knuckles you merely need to present him with — you guessed it — a stromboli. Nothing warms his heart like food. Of course, you'd better bring enough — the last thing you want to do is tease a guy like this with an appetizer because you'll end up being the main course!

Let's wrap up this biography with the obvious features. You can assume that Knuckles would most likely be bald (to raise the intimidation factor). He would definitely have several teeth missing as a result of fighting while he was a youth. Since he's a mobster you can assume he'll be dressed in the stereotypical, double-breasted pinstriped tuxedo, with those marvelous wingtip shoes.

Since you know that Knuckles is a slob, you'll have to make him all messed up—shoes scuffed, stains on his clothes, and sleeves rolled up so they don't get in the way. Then, of course, fingerless gloves to top it all off. Oh yeah, and a cigar too.

Here is an overview of what you will be doing in the following tutorial. As it is with patches, modeling with Surfacetools is a six-step process.

1. Find source material to base your character from.
2. Create axis templates from your source material.
3. Import your axis templates into MAX.
4. Trace your axis templates with splines.
5. Add the surface modifier to your model.
6. Apply image maps to your creature.

Remember the preparation steps in the last chapter? The steps are basically the same for using Surfacetools. The first thing you need to do is find some good source material for Knuckles.

FINDING SOURCE MATERIAL FOR KNUCKLES

It can be a little tough to find source material for a character like Knuckles, considering that he exudes cartoon personality, but with more realistic details. When developing this character, I watched movies like *The Godfather* to get a good idea of how to dress him. To

FIGURE **6.2** *A hand-drawn character sketch of Knuckles.*

create his unique look I borrowed ideas from some cool game characters and a couple of cartoon characters. Basically, he's my Frankenstein's Monster.

Figure 6.2 is a character sketch of Knuckles that I drew to get a good reference to create my axis templates.

As you can see, this sketch embodies the concepts outlined in Knuckles biography. Notice how he has that brilliant look on his face, and that massive stromboli-stuffed belly that's hanging over his belt. Of course, he's missing several teeth and sporting those stylish fingerless gloves. This is a pretty good visual of our friend Knuckles.

You don't always need to use a photo as your source material; you can use anything you wish. In my case, I drew the source material myself since I wasn't going to find a single source for Knuckles.

Now that you have a character sketch, it's time to create templates.

CREATING AXIS TEMPLATES

Two axis template files are included in the CD inside the *Chapter6\Knuckles folder*. You will need these files to create the Virtual Studio in this exercise. It's a good time to make sure you have the files *thugside.tga* and *thugfront.tga*.

This tutorial uses two axis templates instead of three. The reason for this is that if you look at the character from the top, there isn't much more information than you can get by just using the front and side views, except for maybe the hand, so the hand was drawn palm forward. Typically, for animation purposes, the standard pose for a bipedal (two-legged) character is feet shoulder width apart, arms out to the sides, with palms facing downward, mouth and eyes open. The reason bipedal models are posed this way is when you use tools such as Bones to animate them, the mesh doesn't tear or wrinkle. So you will model the hand facing outward first, then rotate it so it faces downward later.

⇨ TIP

Like before, all of your axis views should be proportionate. Notice that in Figure 6.3, the front view is the same height as the side. This is still *very* important for creating your axis view images. It will make things line up much easier when you implement them as templates.

The axis templates for Knuckles were created with Macromedia Freehand using the source drawing as a guide. Refer back to Chapter 5 and review the Suggested Axis Template Preparation for more information on how to set up your templates.

Now that you have your axis templates, you're ready to import them into MAX R2.

FIGURE **6.3** *Axis templates for Knuckles.*

IMPORTING YOUR AXIS TEMPLATES INTO MAX 2.0

In the last chapter, you learned how to create a Virtual Studio to use as a template for building a patch model. Creating a creature with Surfacetools isn't any different. You'll need to create a Virtual Studio for Knuckles just like you did for Edward. The Virtual Studio building process won't be covered here as extensively as it was in the last chapter, but the steps will be covered. Refer back to Chapter 5 to refresh your memory on how to import your templates into MAX. The only difference is that you will be creating only the side and back walls.

The steps are as follows:

> **Step 1.** Create primitive box walls.
>
> **Step 2.** Prep the materials.
>
> **Step 3.** Assign materials to boxes.
>
> **Step 4.** Assign mapping coordinates to each box.

Once you have completed these four steps you will have a completed Virtual Studio for Knuckles that looks like Figure 6.4.

➪**TIP**

> Make sure that the boxes are the same size as the axis template images. Under UVW mapping, click Bitmap Fit to ensure that the images are at their original proportion.

FIGURE **6.4** *Knuckles' Virtual Studio.*

Now that you have your Virtual Studio constructed, you can begin the actual modeling process by tracing your axis templates with splines.

TRACING YOUR AXIS TEMPLATES WITH SPLINES

In the last chapter, you used a spline wireframe as a template for building patches. This time, the actual splines themselves will be used as the final model. It's basically the same process, only this time the spline building is the production phase and the patch building will be done for you. To use the splines as the final model, you will need to make them more dense, creating more splines to define the object.

Take time out now and get to know how Surfacetools works. Save the scene you have done so far as *knuckles.max*, and open a new scene. Do a File/Refresh to get a fresh layout; then follow the short Surfacetools tutorial provided next.

SURFACETOOLS PRIMER

Surfacetools comes with two modules. The first module is called CrossSection, which connects splines together at common vertices to build a wire frame of your model. **To understand how CrossSection works, follow this simple CrossSection tutorial.**

Before starting this tutorial, make sure you have both the *Crosssec.dlm* and *Surface.dlm* installed into your MAX2 plug-in folder.

CrossSection Tutorial

1. Open a new file in MAX2.
2. In the front viewport, create a circle, any size.
3. Click **Modify/Edit Spline**.
4. Under Sub-Object, change Vertex to Spline, then select the spline (circle). It should turn red.
5. In the Left viewport, constrain the **X-axis**, then hold down Shift and drag the spline to the right. You should have two splines that look like Figure 6.5.
6. Repeat this process five times until you have a total of seven splines. It doesn't matter how far apart they are at this point.
7. Click **Sub-Object** to turn it off.
8. Under Modify, click on **More**, then choose **CrossSection** from the list.

MAX automatically connects the splines at their common vertices. In other 3D programs such as Softimage or Alias, this process is known as *skinning*. This process dramatically speeds up modeling time. All you need to do is create the cross sections and MAX fills in the rest. Now let's play with the splines a little.

Click on **CrossSection** in the Modifier stack, then pull down to Edit Spline again. The cross section lines disappear. Click on **Sub-Object** and alter the original splines any way you want to by rotating, scaling, or moving vertices, segments, or splines. Then go back up to CrossSection in the stack to see the result.

Go ahead and experiment with them now.

⇨ **TIP**

You may also add another Edit Spline modifier on top of the CrossSection modifier to manipulate the newly created cross-splines.

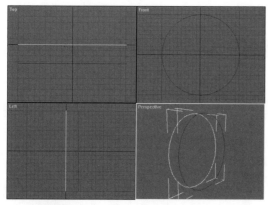

FIGURE **6.5** *The duplicated spline.*

Now that you have learned how the CrossSection modifier works, take a look at some guidelines to go by.

Follow these general rules for creating splines to use as cross sections:

CrossSection Rules

These general rules should be considered while you build any set of splines to be used with the CrossSection modifier.

Splines must be in ordered sequence. Each spline must either be copied one after another creating an ordered sequence, or they must be attached individually in an ordered sequence. If you add CrossSection to an out-of-sequence set of splines it will attach the splines in the order that they are arranged, creating a serious mess. Look at Figure 6.6 for an example.

Splines should have the same number of vertices. CrossSection will still work with an uneven amount of vertices, but you will save yourself a lot of headaches if you keep the vertex count the same for all splines in the sequence. The easiest way to ensure success is by duplicating the spline at the Sub-Object/Spline level.

Splines should not overlap. Overlapping splines cause collisions when you add the CrossSection modifier.

Use CrossSection whenever possible! CrossSection is the key to productive spline modeling. We will be examining when and where to use CrossSection when we create Knuckles. You could spend many hours connecting splines manually, or you could have CrossSection do it in one click.

Remember to use these rules as you create your model, and you will save yourself a lot of frustration.

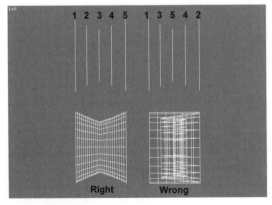

FIGURE **6.6** *Example of an ordered sequence and a nonordered sequence.*

The second tool that comes with Surfacetools is called Surface. Let's use Surface to surface our splines and turn them into patches.

SURFACE TUTORIAL

The Surface modifier works by surfacing any set of splines that make up either a square or a triangle, and replaces them with either a Quad- or a Tri-patch. The beautiful thing about Surface is that it is a modifier, which means that you are able to go to a lower level in the modifier stack, make changes, and then return to the Surface level in the stack to see the changes made. This is probably the greatest benefit of Surfacetools.

Follow this tutorial to get a hands-on look at Surface.

With the spline object selected, go to **Modify/More/Surface**. The normals are flipped, so click on the **Flip Normals** checkbox to flip them. See the strange lines going down the sides of your cylinder? Those are caused by Surface surfacing the interior with patches. To fix this problem, click the **Remove Interior Patches button**.

Notice that there is also a Topology spinner, which works just as it does when you are working with patches. It increases and decreases the amount of polygons across the surface. Try it out.

The following rules will help you use Surface:

Surface Rules

These rules apply to the spline model *before* the Surface modifier is applied, instead of after you have applied the surface itself.

Each area of intersection must be either three- or four-sided. You must create three- or four-sided areas because the Surface modifier functions by placing either Tri- or Quad-patch objects in the areas outlined by the splines.

Pay close attention to where you place your vertices on your splines. If vertices are placed on a spline and don't serve to connect with another spline to create a three- or four-sided area, the Surface modifier won't function correctly. You will end up with pieces missing from your face where the unattended vertices lie.

Never weld coincident endpoints. This is probably the most annoying part of modeling with Surfacetools. Every time you manipulate two or more ending vertices that occupy the same space, MAX asks if you want to weld coincident endpoints. While modeling, keep your pinky finger on the **Tab button** and thumb on the space bar; then every time that dialog box pops up, press **Tab** to change my answer to NO, and press the space bar to select the highlighted button. You do not want to weld endpoints because it will confuse you when you want to adjust the splines and they are connected.

You'll be building Knuckles piece by piece, in the following order.

1. Coat
2. Stomach
3. Shirt
4. Shoes
5. Pants
6. Sleeves
7. Arms
8. Hands
9. Head

The first eight objects are relatively easy to create using CrossSection. Save his hands and head for last because they are the most difficult to model. Start slow and work your way up to the heavy stuff. CrossSection is hard to use when creating a detailed surface with hills and valleys so you will be creating the crossing splines manually, which takes more time.

⇨ TIP

It is very hard to see the detail in the following figures. The best way to study the model is to open *knuckles.max* scene that is supplied on the companion CD, and dissect the parts that you wish to study. Or for your convenience, the figures are also included in full color inside the *Figures folder* on the CD.

Start by modeling Knuckles' double-breasted suit coat.

CREATING THE DOUBLE-BREASTED COAT

Just like modeling with patches, you have to model only half of the character and mirror the other half, so you will be creating half of the coat. Start by creating contour lines that define the shape of the coat from the bottom up to the armpit. Then use CrossSection to connect these lines. Go only to the armpit because if you went all the way up to the shoulder, you would cover the hole that you need to connect the arm.

Start by creating a contour spline defining the CrossSection that makes up the bottom of the coat as shown in Figure 6.7. Make the spline with two lines and a cap to give the coat thickness. If you start at the bottom of the coat and work your way up, you automatically will create splines in the correct sequencing order needed to CrossSection correctly.

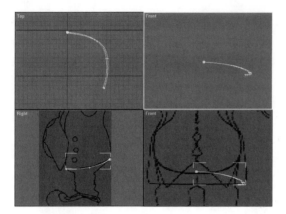

FIGURE **6.7** *CrossSection spline defining the starting point of the coat.*

Now, using the two axis views as templates, create the first spline as shown in Figure 6.5. Leave the spline open where it will be connected with the other half of the coat. If you close the spline, Surface will create unnecessary patches running up the seam.

If you are using MAX R1, you must add an Edit Spline to the modifier stack before completing this next step.

Once this spline has been created, go into **Sub-Object/Spline mode** and select the newly created spline. With the spline selected, constrain **Select** and **Move** to the **Y-axis**. While holding the **Shift key**, move the spline upward to about the location shown in Figure 6.8.

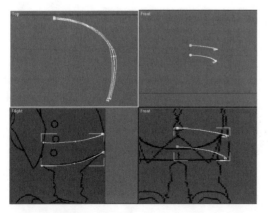

FIGURE **6.8** *Duplicating and manipulating a second spline.*

Now switch to the vertex mode and manipulate the vertices until they match Figure 6.8. Then, following the same procedure, duplicate three more splines and manipulate them until they look like Figure 6.9.

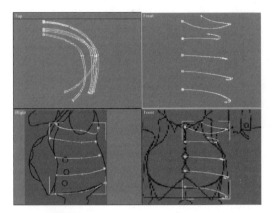

FIGURE **6.9** *Duplicating and manipulating the remaining splines.*

Now that you have the splines ready to go, exit out of **Sub-Object mode** and click on **More/CrossSection**. Under Spline Options, click **Smooth**, which creates smooth transitions between splines. Your spline cage should now compare to Figure 6.10.

If you have strange lines going all over the place, it's probably because your splines are not in a sequenced order. To ensure that your splines are in a sequenced order, trash the CrossSection modifier by clicking on the garbage can. Then detach all of the Splines separately and reattach them to the first spline, one by one, from bottom to top. Now reapply the CrossSection modifier and they are in the correct order!

To see what your model looks like so far, click **More/Surface**. Your model should look like Figure 6.11.

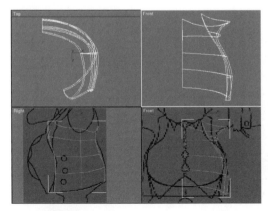

FIGURE **6.10** *Applying the CrossSection modifier to the splines.*

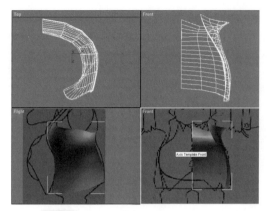

FIGURE **6.11** *Preview of the coat.*

If your model doesn't look like Figure 6.9, don't worry, you can always go back and edit your splines. To edit your splines, open your Modifier Stack and select **Editable Spline**. Then click on **Sub-Object mode** to adjust the vertices to their proper location. You can toggle back and forth to see your progress. Make sure that you make good use of **Arc Rotate Selected** to view your model as you work. This is an invaluable tool to help you see mistakes.

Use the same method to create the shoulder piece. Since the shoulder will be part of the lower half of the coat eventually, you need to create the first spline from one of the splines on the coat. The shoulder section of the coat does not need to have thickness, so you will be creating only the outer section.

First, select the coat and enter **Sub-Object/Segment mode**. Now select the outer segment on the back of the coat as shown in Figure 6.12.

With the segment selected, under the Edit Segment menu, check the box marked Copy. Then click **Detach** to separate a copy of the segment in the exact location as the

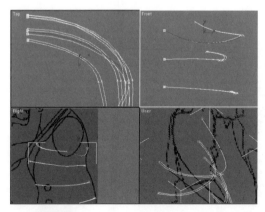

FIGURE **6.12** *Selecting the back segment.*

one selected. Accept the default name and choose **OK**. Then exit **Sub-Object mode** and select the new spline. You may have to select it by using Select by name.

Following the same procedure that you used to create the lower half of the coat, hold Shift and duplicate the spline several times, each time adjusting and moving them to form the shoulder section. Use Figure 6.13 as a placement guide.

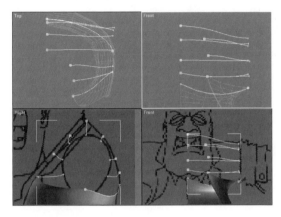

FIGURE **6.13** *Placement for shoulder splines.*

Notice that the last spline in the series, where it will connect to the front of the coat, has not been created yet. That's because you want another perfect match to the front spline of the coat. Use the same procedure that you did when extracting the first spline from the back of the coat to get the final spline.

To do this, select the lower half of the coat. Go into **Sub-Object/Segment mode** and select the outer front spline as shown in Figure 6.14.

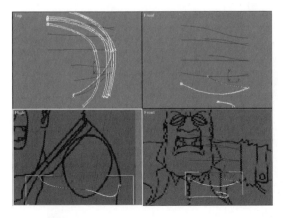

FIGURE **6.14** *Selecting the front segment to be detached.*

Now detach all of the newly duplicated splines from the first spline and reattach them in the order shown in Figure 6.15.

After you have attached the Splines, apply the CrossSection modifier. OOPS! Take another look at Figure 6.13. The splines are crossing at the last spline on the front of the coat. How did that happen? Let's examine the last spline in the series.

Go back down to **Editable Spline** in the stack and click on **Sub-Object/Vertex**. There's the problem! All of the splines have the first vertex (indicated by a box around the vertex) on the collar side of the spline, and the last spline's first vertex is in the armpit.

To fix this problem, click the vertex that you wish to make the first spline, and simply click on **Make First** in the Edit Vertex menu. Now turn off **Sub-Object** and return to CrossSection in the stack to see the result. Your splines should now look like Figure 6.16.

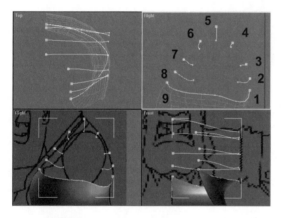

FIGURE **6.15** *Spline attachment sequence order.*

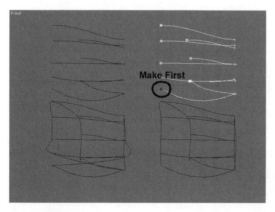

FIGURE **6.16** *The corrected splines.*

Add a surface modifier to preview the shoulder section. Now it gets a little trickier. You need to put a collar on the coat. First, extract a curve from the upper part of the coat to create the upper part of the collar.

This time you need to extract a curve from the splines that CrossSection generated. To do this, add an Edit Spline modifier to the stack above the CrossSection modifier, just like you did when creating the shoulder piece. Go into the **Sub-Object/Segment mode** and select the front segments that will make up the collar curve as shown in Figure 6.17.

Detach the segment with the Copy checkbox checked. Then exit **Sub-Object mode** and select the newly created spline. Duplicate and arrange three more splines to mimic Figure 6.18.

FIGURE **6.17** *Selecting the collar segments.*

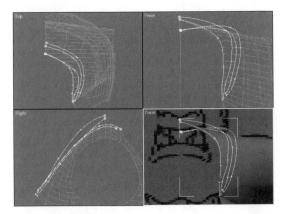

FIGURE **6.18** *The collar spline arrangement.*

Now apply a CrossSection modifier and a Surface modifier and toggle between the two to check your progress. It's kind of tough to get the collar to wrap around the shoulder. Have patience. If you are still having trouble, examine the *knuckles.max* scene inside the *Chapter6\Knuckles folder* on the CD.

The completed upper collar should look like Figure 6.19. Notice how it curves under to create thickness.

Now you can create the lower collar using the same method. First, extract the lower collar curve as shown in Figure 6.20.

Exit **Sub-Object mode** and click on the new spline to select it. Then duplicate the new spline three more times as before. Finally, arrange the splines to match Figure 6.21.

Now add CrossSection and Surface modifiers to the selected splines. See Figure 6.22 for the finished collar.

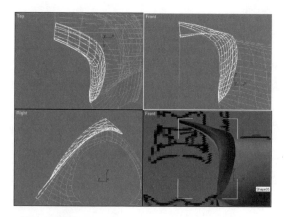

FIGURE **6.19** *The completed upper collar.*

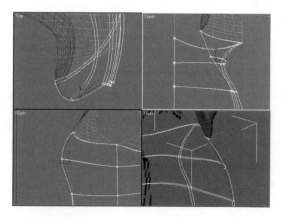

FIGURE **6.20** *the lower collar segments. The completed upper collar.*

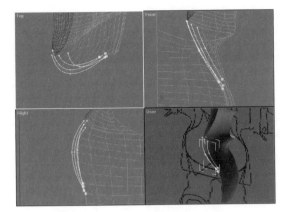

FIGURE **6.21** *The duplicated and adjusted curves to create the lower collar.*

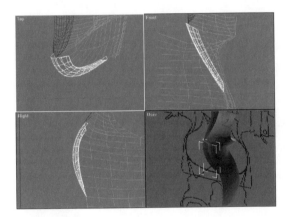

FIGURE **6.22** *Collar after modifiers have been applied.*

The coat is almost finished. Next you need to create the sleeves that are all bunched up at the top of the arm. Imagine what a nightmare creating this crumpled sleeve would be with traditional patch modeling methods. On the other hand, with Surfacetools it's surprisingly simple. To start, all you need to do is extract a curve from the shoulder as shown in Figure 6.23.

Then you duplicate that spline several times, and move the vertices around randomly to create the lumps and bumps as shown in Figure 6.24. Take the last spline, scale it down slightly, and bring it into the center of the sleeve to create the thickness of the coat sleeve.

Finally, add a Surface modifier and you're done with the sleeve. See Figure 6.25 to see the final result.

All that's left on the coat is the buttons. There are about four different ways of creating buttons, but since you are using Surfacetools to create everything else you may as well create the buttons using the same method.

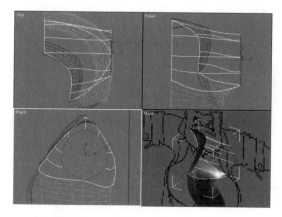

FIGURE **6.23** *Extracting a curve from the shoulder.*

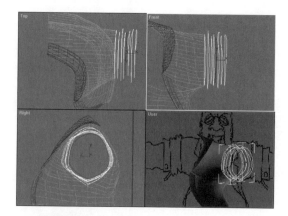

FIGURE **6.24** *Duplicating and moving the splines.*

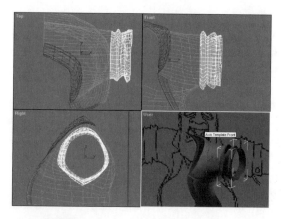

FIGURE **6.25** *Adding a surface modifier to the sleeve.*

To create a button, make a circle spline as shown in Figure 6.26.

Duplicate the spline once to create the thickness of the button, add CrossSection and Surface modifiers, and you're done.

After you are done creating the button, Select it, and make two instances of the button by holding Shift while you drag it upward. Now simply Select and Rotate each button into position. Your final set of buttons should resemble Figure 6.27.

Take a look at the whole coat. Select the entire left half of the coat and mirror it as an instance on the X-axis. Move the new half into position. It looks pretty good, but you need to correct some corners, as you can see in Figure 6.28.

To fix the problems, select the offending object, go into **Sub-Object mode**, then correct the problem. If the problem is being caused by the CrossSection and not the beginning splines, just add another Edit Spline on top of the CrossSection modifier and move the handles into place. Make sure that you do a Marquee selection while selecting vertices

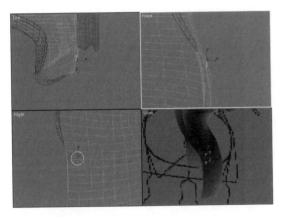

FIGURE **6.26** *The circle spline for creating a button.*

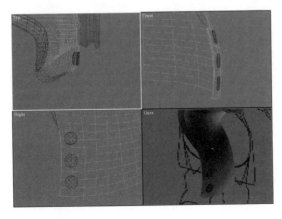

FIGURE **6.27** *The completed buttons.*

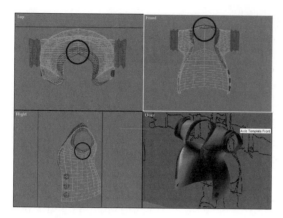

FIGURE **6.28** *Corner problems that need a little smoothing.*

in this mode, so you can be sure to select both of the vertices at each intersection. Figure 6.29 shows the tailored coat.

Now that the coat is completed, move right on to creating Knuckles' portly stomach. The stomach is a piece of cake! Well, it's actually many pieces of cake, stromboli, spaghetti, meatballs . . . well, you get the idea.

You simply need to build a series of splines that define the gut, just like you did with the bottom of the coat. First, make one spline, then duplicate the curve several times as shown in Figure 6.30. Use the coat side and front view templates as your guide.

Add CrossSection and Surface to your splines. Now there's a nice round belly ready to fill with stromboli! Look at Figure 6.31 for the final stomach model.

At this time, you may mirror the stomach if you wish to see the entire thing, but it isn't necessary.

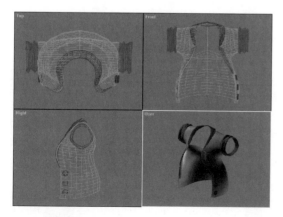

FIGURE **6.29** *The repaired mesh.*

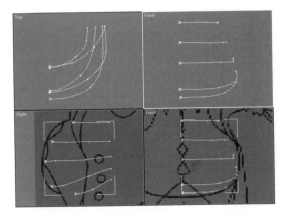

FIGURE **6.30** *The splines that make up the stomach.*

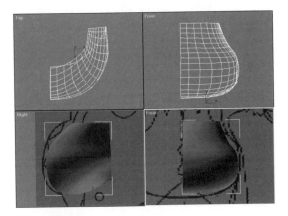

FIGURE **6.31** *Knuckles' stomach mesh.*

It's time to move on to the shirt, which isn't as easy. Basically, it's like the stomach, but this time you have to deal with more splines. Be prepared to move up and down the modifier stack several times to get it just right because you may have collision problems, such as the stomach poking through the shirt.

To start the shirt, create a single spline as shown in Figure 6.32. Use the stomach and coat as a guide.

Like you did for the stomach, duplicate the spline several times and manipulate them into place. Don't duplicate all of the splines at once—just one or two at a time so you have less to worry about at one time.

For the spline that creates the bottom of the shirt, duplicate the base spline and pull it down. Beware; this will make your splines out of sequence. To fix the sequence problem, detach all of the splines one by one and reattach them from bottom to top, in sequence.

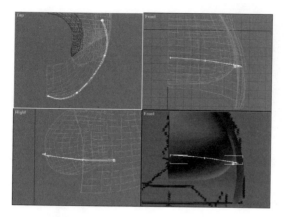

FIGURE **6.32** *The base spline for the shirt.*

The top two splines that create the collar were rotated to follow the contour of the neck. This is a very hard thing to do, and to do right. Take your time and be patient.

Your final spline cage for the shirt should look like Figure 6.33.

Now, to complete the shirt, we need to add some irregularity to the centerline of the shirt as shown in Figure 6.34.

You just need to add the old familiar CrossSection and Surface modifiers to complete the shirt as shown in Figure 6.35.

Next, create the shirt collar the same way you created the collar for the coat. First extract a curve to create the collar from. Select the spline that makes up the inner line of the shirt and extract it.

Then delete all but the top three segments. The leftover spline is what you will use to create the collar. Take this new spline and duplicate it three times. Adjust each spline and its vertices as shown in Figure 6.36.

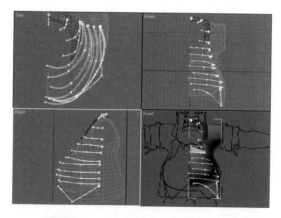

FIGURE **6.33** *The spline arrangement for the shirt.*

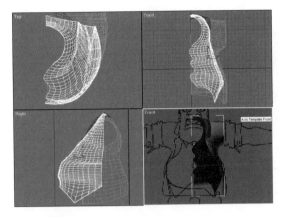

FIGURE **6.34** *Adding irregularity to the shirt centerline.*

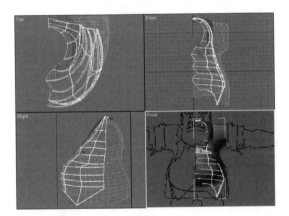

FIGURE **6.35** *The shirt mesh.*

To finish the collar, add a CrossSection and Surface modifier and you're done with the shirt.

Now mirror it to see the final result. If you need to, make any final adjustments now. Step back and look at your progress. Do a **Zoom Extents All** and take a look at your work. Does it look like Figure 6.37 Great job!

Now that the coat is complete, hide it by selecting the entire coat and going to **View/Hide Selected**. Next you will be creating the shoes, which are a little bit different because you won't be using CrossSection. You will be creating all of the splines manually. You'll be creating only half of the shoe and then mirroring it, just like you've done with everything else.

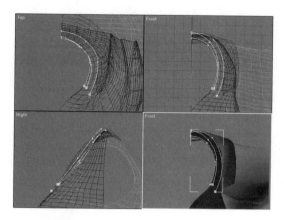

FIGURE **6.36** *The adjusted splines for the collar.*

The reason you can't use CrossSection is because of the rounded ends at the toe and heel are better created manually to avoid problems. Besides, you need to get primed for the hand and the head both also created in this manner.

Start by outlining the shoe silhouette in the side view. Then create a spline that describes the outer curve from the top view.

Pull out a vertex to create the curve where the opening of the shoe will be, as shown in Figure 6.38. Pay close attention to where you place the vertices. It needs to have the same amount on both the top and the bottom because this is where you will be placing the intersecting splines.

With that done, duplicate and move the lower/outer spline to create a center profile to define the middle of the shoe as shown in Figure 6.39.

The next step is to create the intersecting spline. The easiest way to do this is to create one spline (the one on the toe first), adjust it until you're satisfied, and then duplicate it

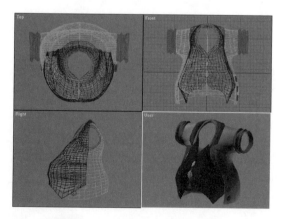

FIGURE **6.37** *The completed double-breasted suit coat.*

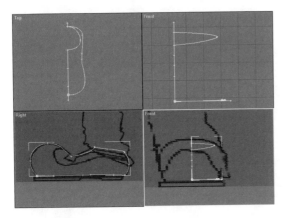

FIGURE **6.38** *Outlining the shoe profile.*

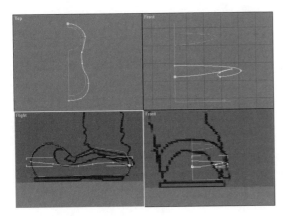

FIGURE **6.39** *Creating a spline to define the middle of the shoe.*

down the length of the shoe three more times. Now adjust the new splines to fit. They should look like the ones in Figure 6.40.

Make sure that everywhere two splines intersect, the vertices occupy the same space. This is very important for Surface to work properly. To aid you in the effort, click on **3d Snap**, which will show you a little blue cross indicating when you are on a vertex.

Use Snap only when connecting vertices and not during general manipulation. Snap will automatically snap either to a vertex or the center grid line, whichever is closer, so if you are not near a vertex when you make a move, it will snap to the centerline, creating wild splines.

If you properly snapped all of your vertices and splines to create a three- or four-sided area, Surface should work just fine. Add the Surface modifier; the half-shoe should look like Figure 6.41.

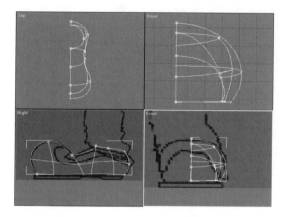

FIGURE **6.40** *Creating intersecting splines.*

Now let's give Knuckles some soul! To create the sole for the shoe, use CrossSection this time. Start by extracting the curve that makes up the bottom silhouette of the shoe. Then Hide the shoe as shown in Figure 6.42.

Next, duplicate the spline three times: once for the outer-rim of the sole, once to give the sole its thickness, and once in the center to make the bottom of the sole. Bring some vertices up to create the notch in the bottom of the sole as shown in Figure 6.43.

Now add the CrossSection modifier and choose **Linear** to make the edges of the sole square. The CrossSectioned version looks like Figure 6.44.

Finally, add a Surface modifier and you're done. Now you need to add some shoelaces. The shoelaces are not made using Surface tools, but are created by lofting a circular spline along a path. If you are not familiar with lofting along a path, consult your MAX R2 manual for more detailed information.

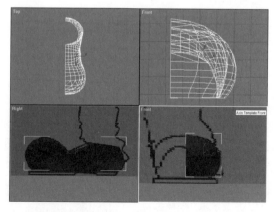

FIGURE **6.41** *Half of the shoe surfaced.*

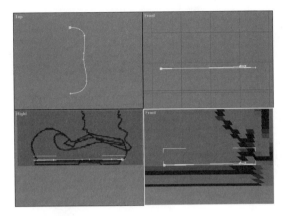

FIGURE **6.42** *The starting spline for the shoe sole.*

First, create a circle approximately the circumference of the shoelace, then create a spline path where you want the lace to be located. With the path selected, click on **Create/Loft Objects** and then **Select Shape**. Select the shape and there you go, a shoelace! Now simply duplicate the shoelace two more times and adjust them so they match Figure 6.45.

To create the eyeholes for the shoelaces, create a primitive Taurus and adjust it to fit. Then copy the Taurus two more times; then adjust and mirror them. The finished laces are shown in Figure 6.46.

The pants are just as easy to create as the rolled-up sleeves were. They follow the same concept. Start by creating a spline encircling the outer perimeter of the shoe opening as shown in Figure 6.47.

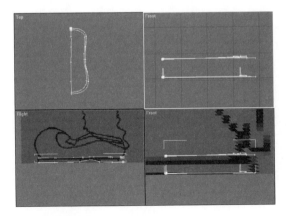

FIGURE **6.43** *The sole splines.*

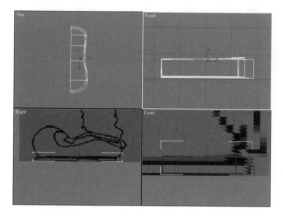

FIGURE **6.44** *The CrossSectioned sole.*

As you did with the coat sleeve, duplicate the spline enough times to get the detail, then randomly adjust the vertices creating all of the dips, folds, and wrinkles that occur when a man of this stature wears slacks like these.

Make the top two splines touch in the middle to create the crotch. Have the top curve in the stack wrap around the contour of the belly. The row of splines should look something like Figure 6.48.

Add a Surface modifier. Remember, if it didn't turn out the way you wanted, you can always go back and edit the curves. Now he's looking more assembled. You can mirror the pants if you would like to get an idea of what they will look like when completed. The final pair of pants can be seen in Figure 6.49.

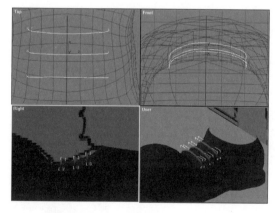

FIGURE **6.45** *Lofted shoelaces.*

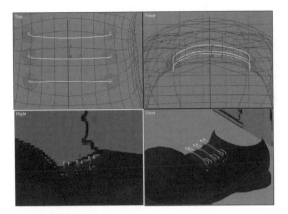

FIGURE **6.46** *The finished shoelaces with eyelets.*

Next you need to create a shirt sleeve poking out of the coat. To create this sleeve, extract the curve from the inside contour of the folded sleeve of the coat. Then duplicate this curve just enough times to create the sleeve. Scale and move the last curve inward to create the thickness of the sleeve. The array of splines should mimic that of Figure 6.50.

Add a Surface modifier; see Figure 6.51 for the finished sleeve.

How about those massive arms Knuckles uses to pummel his victims? Let's see how they are modeled.

Start just as you have been, by extracting the inner curve from the sleeve object. Duplicate the spline several times down the length of the arm as shown in Figure 6.52.

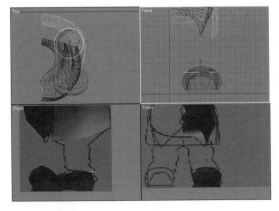

FIGURE **6.47** *The beginning spline for the pants.*

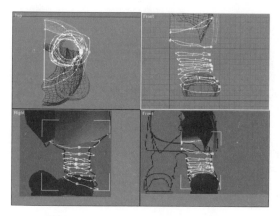

FIGURE **6.48**   *The splines randomly adjusted to create the folds in the pants.*

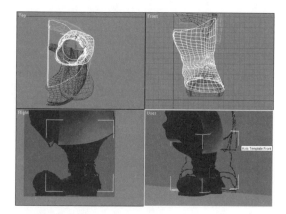

FIGURE **6.49**   *The surfaced pants.*

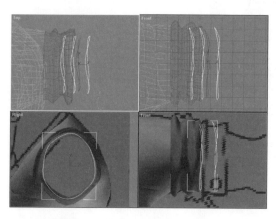

FIGURE **6.50**   *The shirt sleeve contour splines.*

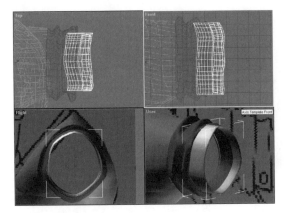

FIGURE **6.51** *The surfaced shirt sleeve.*

Using the templates as your artistic eye, manipulate the vertices to create the shape of the muscles and elbow. You will notice the band around the end of the arm near the wrist. This is the wristband for the fingerless gloves on his hand. It's easier to create the band now rather than manually later.

Figure 6.53 shows how I chose to model the arm. It's not very realistic, but I was going for cartoon-y. Create your arm however you wish.

Now that we have the greater portion of the body completed, it's time to move on to the hands.

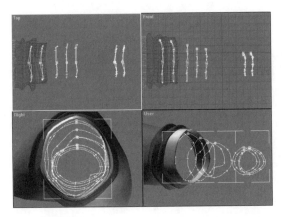

FIGURE **6.52** *The splines that make up the arm.*

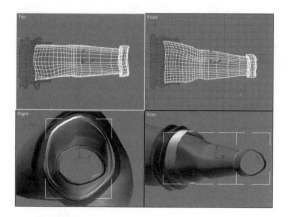

FIGURE **6.53** *The final rendition of the arm.*

CREATING KNUCKLES' HANDS

Creating the hands and head require a different technique than the regular CrossSection method. The CrossSection modifier will be used very little. Instead, you will be creating the intersecting lines manually. You must create them using this method because these shapes are very complex. CrossSection could be used, but it would take a lot more time. Instead, you will start by tracing the outer silhouette of each shape, then combining them into a whole object.

Since the objects are so complex, it would be best to create separate Virtual Studios for each, so save what you have so far, open a new scene, and get to work on the hands.

To complete this section of the tutorial, make sure you have both files *handtop.tga* and *handside.tga*.

Remember how to create a Virtual Studio? If not, return to the beginning of this chapter and follow the section on creating a Virtual Studio.

The Virtual Studio for the hands has two axis templates, one for the top view and one for the side view. Create two boxes and map them with their appropriate axis templates. Your Virtual Studio for the hand should look like Figure 6.54.

Start by creating half of a finger; mirror it, and then duplicate it twice to end up with three fingers. Why only three fingers? Most cartoons have only three fingers and a thumb so that's how we'll build Knuckles' hand.

To make a finger, start by outlining the silhouette in the right or left viewport as shown in Figure 6.55.

Pay close attention to where you place the vertices. You must have the same amount on both the top and the bottom. Stop where the knuckle joins the main portion of the hand.

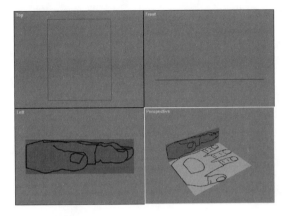

FIGURE **6.54** *Virtual Studio for the hand.*

With that done, create a circle that represents the fingernail as shown in Figure 6.56. If you wish, you can also create a spline just underneath the tip of the finger to add depth to the fingernail.

Now, outline the finger in the top viewport, making sure to keep the same number of vertices. Your final outline should look like Figure 6.57.

Now comes the fun part. Create all of the intersecting splines manually to create a completed finger. Make sure you use 3D Snap to help you snap the vertices to one another. It's easiest to create the line first with the appropriate amount of vertices, then snap each vertex to its mate. That way you shouldn't need to switch viewports (but keep

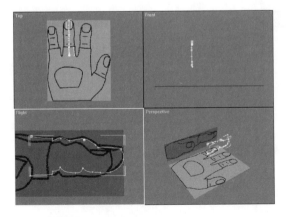

FIGURE **6.55** *Outlining the side of the finger.*

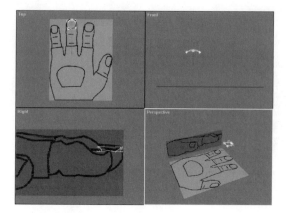

FIGURE **6.56** *Creating the fingernail.*

on the lookout for wild splines in the other viewports). Figure 6.58 shows the spline finger with its intersecting splines.

Mirror the finger and attach the two halves. When you mirrored the finger, it created two center splines. One is unnecessary so go ahead and delete it now. If you would like to see how the finger is looking so far, and want to make sure all of your vertices are connected, go ahead and add a Surface modifier. It should look something like Figure 6.59.

Duplicate and rotate the finger to create two more fingers. To make them smaller, do not scale them outside of **Sub-Object mode**! This will disturb the orientation and mapping coordinates. Instead, go to **Sub-Object mode** and scale each finger on the spline level. I

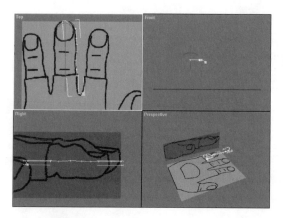

FIGURE **6.57** *Outlining the top of the finger.*

FIGURE **6.58** *Finger splines ready for mirroring.*

have changed the finger to a skin color to give me a better idea of how the final model will look. Figure 6.60 shows all three fingers rotated into position.

Now that the fingers are in place, create the thumb by simply duplicating one of the fingers, and rotating it into position. Then make the appropriate adjustments in **Sub-Object mode**. The placement of the thumb should match Figure 6.61.

Quickly, create the hole in the glove by creating a spline the shape of the hole as a separate object. Duplicate the spline to create thickness, then add a CrossSection modifier to connect the splines. Refer back to Figure 6.61 for the placement of the splines. Finally, attach the new object to the rest of the fingers.

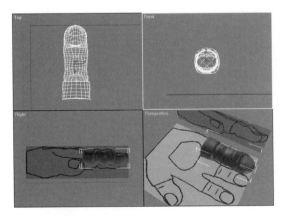

FIGURE **6.59** *The surfaced preview of the finger.*

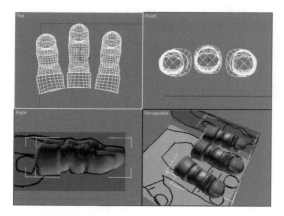

FIGURE **6.60** *All three fingers in place.*

To create the end of the glove where it will connect to the arm, first create a separate spline with eight vertices and shape it according to Figure 6.62. Then duplicate the spline and scale it down slightly to create thickness. Now add a CrossSection Modifier to connect the lines. Next, attach the wrist object to the rest of the hand.

If you can get past this part, you can create anything with Surfacetools! You need to connect all of the vertices with splines on the hand to make sort of a web defining the hand.

This is very hard to illustrate in the book, so your best bet is to open the hand.max file that is included in the *Chapter6/Knuckles folder* on the CD. Save what you have done so far, open up the *hand.max scene*, and select the hand mesh. Hide the two Virtual Studio

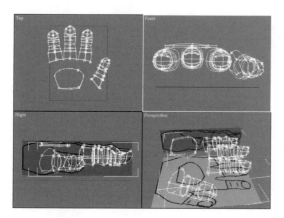

FIGURE **6.61** *Thumb and glove hole placement.*

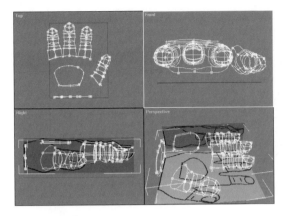

FIGURE **6.62** *The wrist spline attached and ready to go.*

walls so you can get a clear view of the hand. With the hand selected, go to the spline level of the modifier stack. Then use Arc Rotate Selected and rotate the hand in the perspective viewport to see exactly how the splines were created.

Using your newfound knowledge, reopen your own hand scene and have a crack at it! It takes time, but once you get the hang of it, it's a snap! The finished spline hand should look like Figure 6.63.

To complete the hand, start by creating a line connecting the wrist to the glove hole, then creating another one from the glove hole to the middle finger. Next, create a line defining the bottom of the hand, and create splines to define the right and left edges of the hand. When you finish framing in the hand, fill in all of the rest of the splines. The trickiest part is the area between the thumb and forefinger. Take your time and have patience. Figure 6.64 shows the hand completed and ready to be welded onto the arm.

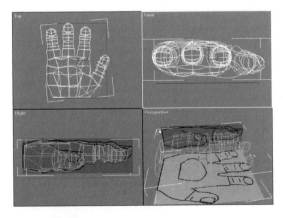

FIGURE **6.63** *The completed spline hand.*

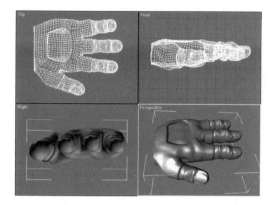

FIGURE **6.64** *The surfaced hand.*

If you can create that hand with Surfacetools, you're ready to conquer anything! Now, put those skills to a test! The final mountain you must overcome is the head.

CREATING KNUCKLES' HEAD

As with the hand, you should view and dissect the finished head in MAX before starting. It is much easier to decipher how it was done with your own eyes, rather than having it explained to you. But don't worry, that doesn't mean I'm not going to explain how it was done, it just means that it will help you understand what I'm talking about if you actually have the model right there in front of you. So to start, save what you have done, and open the scene *head.max* located in the *Chapter6/Knuckles folder* on the CD.

To create the head, once again you need to create a Virtual Studio. By now, you should know how to create a Virtual Studio in your sleep. If you need some help, refer back to the beginning of this chapter.

To complete this section of the tutorial, make sure you have both of the files *head-front.tga* and *headside.tga*.

The Virtual Studio for the head has two axis templates, one for the front view and one for the side view. Create two boxes and map them with their appropriate axis templates. Your Virtual Studio for the head should look like Figure 6.65.

The process for building the head is the same as it was for creating the hands. Start by laying in the major splines, defining the main areas, such as the silhouette from the front, side, and top. Then place the horizontal splines defining the contour of the face. After that, create the vertical intersecting splines. Finally, add a Surface modifier to see the results.

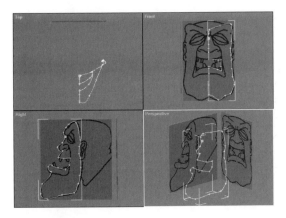

FIGURE **6.65** *Virtual Studio for the head.*

Just as with the hands, you should open the *head.max scene* in the *Chapter6/Knuckles folder* on the CD then dissect the head mesh by going down to the Line level in the modifier stack, so you can see how the splines were assembled.

Create a spline that defines the profile of the face and the jaw line as shown in Figure 6.65. This will serve as a starting point.

Create only as many vertices as you need to define the shape. You will be adding and deleting vertices as you go, so it's not important where you place them right now.

At this point, you'll want to start placing lines to define the smaller details such as the lip, eye, and ear. The reason we need to do this now is because it is easier to create the rest of the head around these smaller details, rather than building the head first, then adding the details later.

Start with the lower lip. First, create two splines running down the length of the lip, joining at the corner of the mouth as shown in Figure 6.66. Pull the center spline outward to create depth.

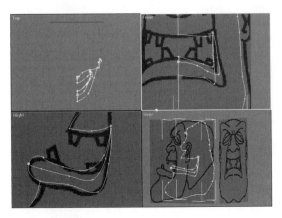

FIGURE **6.66** *Creating the lip splines.*

Now make intersecting splines running across the lip as in Figure 6.67.

Now move on to the eyes. Create two splines creating the outer parameter of the eye and then create two more splines defining the eyelids as shown in Figure 6.68.

To create a line to define the back part of the eye socket, create a spline arcing toward the inside of the head from one corner of the eye to the other. Next, make a spline defining the lower portion of the brow. Figure 6.69 shows the new eye socket and the eyebrow splines.

Now comes the tricky part. You need to create two intersecting splines to finish the eye. Make sure you make good use of the different Bezier vertex properties to get the shape exactly how you want it. Feel free to refer to the *head.max scene* again if you are having

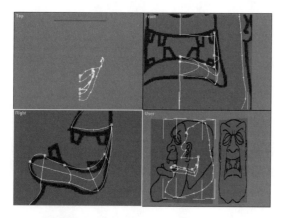

FIGURE **6.67** *Finishing the lip.*

FIGURE **6.68** *Creating the eyelids.*

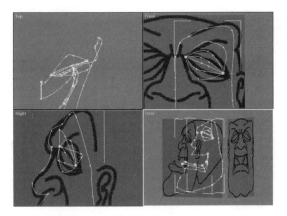

FIGURE **6.69** *Eye socket and eyebrow splines.*

trouble understanding how the splines were created. The finished eye section should look like Figure 6.70.

With the eye and lip done, connect them to create the smile crease. Make a line starting from the bottom center of the eye. It should curve around to form the curve in the nose, then continue it down toward the corner of the mouth as in Figure 6.71.

Create two lines to define where the nostril will be as shown in Figure 6.72. Then create a third line to create the depth of the nostril.

Create a curve that runs down the length of Knuckles' nose, up his nostril, and coming to its final resting place in the tip of the upper lip as shown in Figure 6.73.

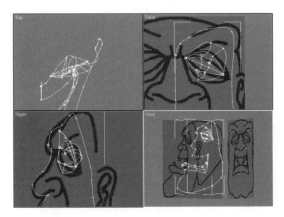

FIGURE **6.70** *The completed eye socket.*

FIGURE **6.71** *The spline connecting the eye to the lip.*

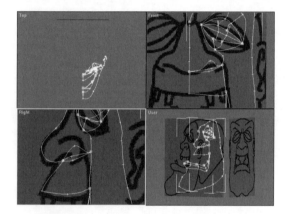

FIGURE **6.72** *The nostril.*

FIGURE **6.73** *Nose spline.*

Perfect! Now all you need to do is create two lines going across the bridge of the nose to fill in the detail. Figure 6.74 shows the final nose splines.

Now move onto the most difficult part of the head, the ear! This is one of the few parts of Knuckles' face where you can use CrossSection to make the job easier. Start by tracing the ear as a separate object from the face as shown in Figure 6.75.

Duplicate the spline several times as shown in Figure 6.76. These lines will define the complex curves and fold of the ear.

Scale and move each line until you are satisfied with the look. Add both the CrossSection and Surface modifiers to check your progress. The ear up to this point should look something like Figure 6.77.

FIGURE **6.74** *Creating the bridge of the nose.*

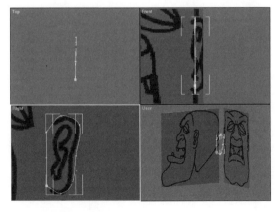

FIGURE **6.75** *Tracing the ear.*

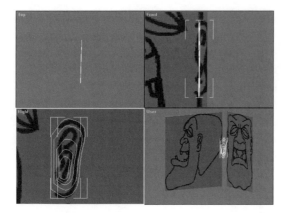

FIGURE **6.76** *Duplicating the ear splines.*

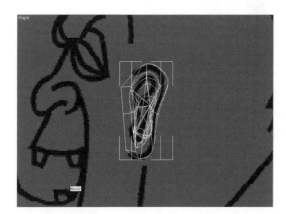

FIGURE **6.77** *Adding the CrossSection modifier.*

Return to **Sub-Object mode** and manipulate the vertices to create more detail like the nib where the ear connects to the head, and give the top of the ear a little bend to make it more realistic. The final ear should look like Figure 6.78. Refer to the *head.max scene* on the CD for additional reference.

All the main pieces are now in place. Now you need to create all of the lines to define the rest of the head. Start by creating a spline that runs down the length of the jaw, the top connecting to the corner of the eye and the bottom connecting to the lower jaw. The new line is shown in Figure 6.79.

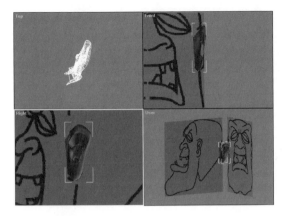

FIGURE **6.78** *The final ear.*

Create two more lines to define the lower jaw, one going from the back part of the lip down to the jaw, the other going from the front of the lip down to the jaw line as shown in Figure 6.80.

Next, create intersecting lines all the way up the side of the jaw and across the brow. Start at the bottom and work your way up. Figure 6.81 shows the intersecting splines attached to the side of the face.

Add a Surface modifier to see your progress. If some of the patches are missing, return to **Sub-Object mode** and use 3D Snap to fix the offending vertices. Return to the Surface to see if the problem was remedied. At this point, Knuckles' face should look like Figure 6.82.

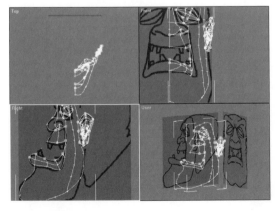

FIGURE **6.79** *Defining the jaw line.*

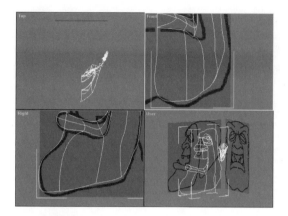

FIGURE **6.80** *Finishing the jaw.*

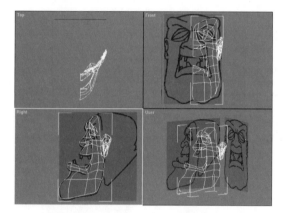

FIGURE **6.81** *Creating the intersecting splines.*

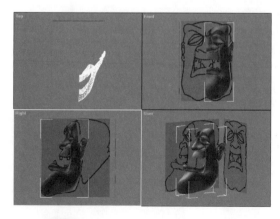

FIGURE **6.82** *Adding the Surface modifier.*

Next you need to move onto that big, bald, head of his! Start by creating a spline that defines the silhouette of the top of the head and the two fat rolls at the neck as shown in Figure 6.83.

Next, create a spline that leads off of the corner of the jaw line that defines where the neck will end, as shown in Figure 6.84. This will be the anchor line, where all the splines will end.

Create three splines leading from the three splines creating the brow, and shape them to the head as shown in Figure 6.85.

Next, create two lines running in the opposite direction across the top of the head and down the side as shown in Figure 6.86.

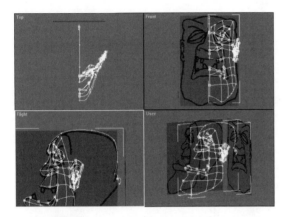

FIGURE **6.83**   *Creating the silhouette spline.*

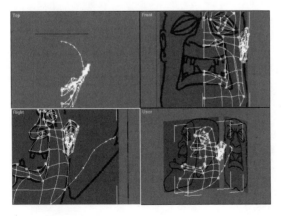

FIGURE **6.84**   *The anchor line.*

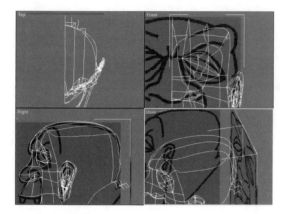

FIGURE 6.85 *Shaping the head.*

The rest of the splines will be intersecting lines filling in the detail down the side of the face. Create the first line, adjust it, duplicate it, and repeat. Take a look at Figure 6.87 for final placement.

You're almost done with the main part of the head! To create the fat rolls and the double chin, create a line defining the chin line, then create another two lines creating the curve in the neck as shown in Figure 6.88.

Now create the intersecting lines as shown in Figure 6.89.

Here's a little trick to get the folds in the fat rolls of the neck. Change the vertices that will be creating the valleys to Bezier corner. Grab the handles and pull them upward to change the orientation on the incoming and outgoing splines as shown in Figure 6.90.

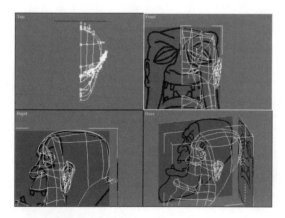

FIGURE 6.86 *Creating the intersecting lines.*

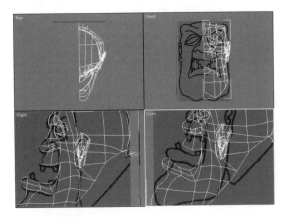

FIGURE **6.87** *Filling out the detail.*

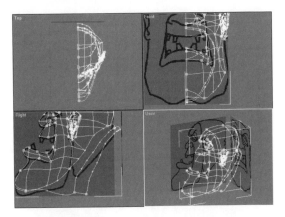

FIGURE **6.88** *Creating the neck and chin.*

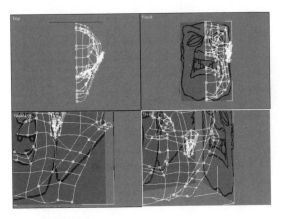

FIGURE **6.89** *More intersecting lines.*

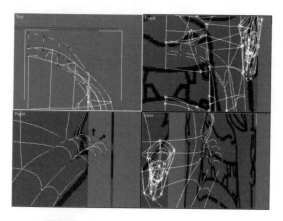

FIGURE **6.90** *Pulling up the Beziers.*

Now the outer head is complete. Move on to creating the inside of the mouth, including the gums, tongue, and teeth.

Start by extracting the spline that defines the mouth as a copy for reference. De-select and hide the face mesh. Now select the new, extracted spline. Do this to get all of the other confusing splines out of the way. You will be building the mouth from this new spline. Then you can unhide and reattach the rest of the head. As long as you don't touch the spline you just created, it will be a perfect match.

Start creating the mouth by placing a line that defines the inner silhouette of the mouth as shown in Figure 6.91.

Duplicate that new spline and move it toward the cheek. Adjust the newly created spline to line up with the vertices on the top and bottom lips.

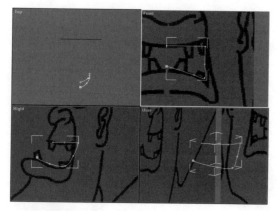

FIGURE **6.91** *Creating the mouth.*

To create splines that will define the gums, place three splines along the bottom of the mouth that continue back then up along the top of the mouth as shown in Figure 6.92.

Now for the hard part, connecting all of the splines together as shown in Figure 6.93; refer to the *head.max file* on the CD to get a better idea of how it was done.

Now push and pull the vertices on the center gum spline to create tooth sockets at random places along the gum line. Figure 6.94 shows the final mouth and gum line.

Move on to the tongue. This is the other part where you can use the CrossSection modifier. Create a C-shaped spline to form half of the tongue as shown in Figure 6.95.

Duplicate this spline several times and Apply a CrossSection modifier to create the intersecting splines. To create the tip of the tongue, add an Edit Spline modifier and enter

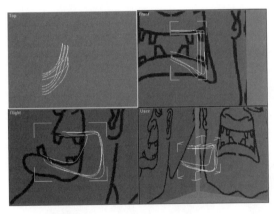

FIGURE **6.92** *Building the inside of the mouth.*

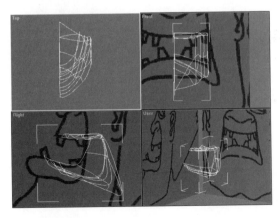

FIGURE **6.93** *Building the intersecting lines for the mouth.*

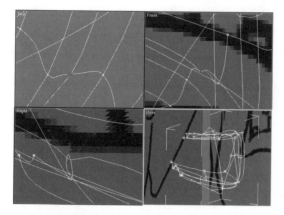

FIGURE 6.94 *Making the teeth sockets.*

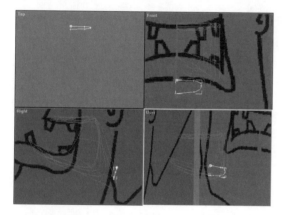

FIGURE 6.95 *The spline that will form the tongue.*

Sub-Object mode/Spline. Delete the last C-spline leaving the other splines out in the open and disconnected. Using 3D Snap, snap all of the remaining points into one point at the tip of the tongue as shown in Figure 6.96.

All you have to do is add a Surface modifier and you're done! But first you have to seam Knuckles together and map him.

SEAMING KNUCKLES

Before you apply any surfacing to Knuckles you have to seam him together. Open your scene that contains Knuckles' body. Select the entire left half of Knuckles and delete it.

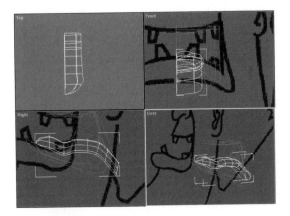

FIGURE **6.96** *Building the tip of the tongue.*

Now mirror the entire model again to ensure a fresh mirroring. Start by seaming the coat first.

Select the coat, go to **Modify**, and trash the Surface modifier of each section except for the collar pieces. Now select **Attach**, and attach the opposite half of the coat including the upper half, and the rolled up sleeves. Select **Sub-Object/spline**. When you mirrored the coat, it created two centerlines in the same location. You need only one spline; select one of the center splines and delete it.

Zoom in on each set of intersecting vertices that run down the center of the coat and make sure they are occupying the same space. Use 3D Snap to help.

After you are done, add a Surface modifier to the entire coat and you get a completely seamless object! Repeat this process with the stomach, shoes, pants, and shirt.

To complete Knuckles, you have to merge the hand and head scenes with this scene.

MERGING SCENES TOGETHER

To merge the scenes together, do a Save-As and save the new scene as *merged.max*. Click on **File/Merge** and select the head scene. When the list appears asking what you would like to import, choose the face mesh only and click **OK**.

The head of Knuckles should appear. It may not be in the correct location, and may possibly be too large or too small. First, trash the Surface modifier from the modifier stack of the head. To correct the proportion, with the head selected add an X Form modifier from the More modifier menu. A yellow box should appear around the head. Now scale and move the head into position. It should match Figure 6.97.

FIGURE **6.97** *The X Form modifier.*

When you are sure of your positioning, click on the **Edit Stack** icon and Collapse the modifier stack. This should leave you with a clean editable spline. You add an X Form modifier because if you were to scale and move the head without it, MAX might ruin your mesh. X Form insures that the transforms are a permanent addition to your model.

To continue, mirror the head and seam it together. You may now choose to modify the neck to fit inside the collar a little better by choosing **Sub-Object**, and manipulating the vertices to fit.

Merge the hand scene exactly the same way. Go to **File/Merge** and select the hand scene. When the menu pops up asking what you want to merge, select the hand object only. With the hand imported, add an X Form modifier and **Move/Scale** it into position. Remember to face the palm down, not forward, because that is the character neutral position, making it easy to add bones and animate him later.

Finally, mirror the hand. After seaming and merging, the final character should look like Figure 6.98. You just need to do a little tweaking and you're done with the modeling part.

To make the eyes, simply create two primitive spheres and fit them in the eye sockets. Unlike Edward, Knuckles' eyelids are built in so you don't have to worry about making them. Next are the teeth, which are created by using a Free Form Deformation modifier. To do this, create a sphere, add the FFD 3x3 modifier, then move the points around until you get a tooth shape that you are pleased with. When you are done with the teeth, place them in the sockets that you created earlier.

The last thing you need to do is tweak the shirt and add some buttons. Select the shirt and go into **Sub-Object mode**. Select the vertices on one half of the shirt where it overlaps and pull it forward. Now select opposite vertices on the other half of the shirt and pull them backward. Now you have an overlapping shirt that needs some buttons. Create

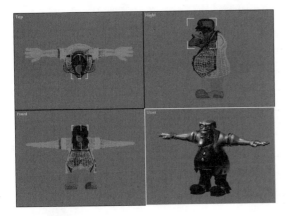

FIGURE **6.98** *Seamed and merged.*

some primitive cylinders and throw them on the shirt. Knuckles should look like Figure 6.99 before we surface him.

Let's add the final touch to Knuckles — surfacing.

FIGURE **6.99** *Ready to be surfaced.*

SURFACING KNUCKLES

Unlike Edward, Knuckles is composed of several different parts. Material IDs were assigned to Edward because he was all one object, but with Knuckles that isn't the case. Knuckles is made up of many different objects and each object already has its own material ID. The only objects to which you must assign separate Material IDs are the gloves, the inside of the mouth, and the white sections on the shoes.

To select separate material IDs, add an Edit Mesh modifier to the object (in this case, the hand) and select the faces that you would like to have a different Material ID. For the hand, make the glove Material ID 2. Figure 6.100 shows all of the faces for the glove selected. Follow the same procedure to assign material IDs to the inside of the mouth and the white parts of the shoes.

Use procedural maps for Knuckles' coat, so no image maps are required. Therefore, no mapping coordinates are required either. Follow the settings in Figure 6.101 and apply the material to the coat.

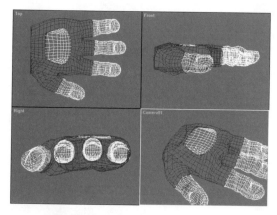

FIGURE 6.100 *Selecting faces for Material ID.*

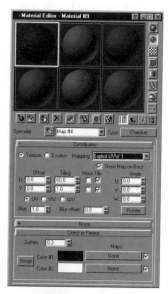

FIGURE 6.101 *The material settings.*

Procedural maps were also applied to everything but the face. You may choose to add maps if you wish by simply adding mapping coordinates to each object and mapping them accordingly.

To give Knuckles a little more personality, create an image map for his face, which means you will need to add mapping coordinates. To do this, select the head, add a UVW Mapping modifier, and choose cylindrical mapping. Then select **Sub-Object** to activate the gizmo, and rotate the gizmo so it is facing upward. Now click on Fit to make the Mapping gizmo snap to the object. Finally, rotate the gizmo in the top viewport so the green line is at the back of the head. This green line signifies where the map will split when you use the Unwrap Utility.

Speaking of Unwrap, take a look at what it does.

UNWRAPPING THE HEAD

As with Edward, you will want to use the Unwrap utility to unwrap the head object for reference when you create the maps. You can find the Unwrap plug-in inside the MAX2/Plug-in folder on the CD that came with this book. Install it into your plug-ins directory.

With it installed, go to the utility section of MAX and scroll down to **Unwrap Object Texture**. Now you can unwrap the head. Keep the defaults, select **Pick Object**, pick the head, and that's it! Now you have a painting template for your head image map.

Next, create the image map. As you did with Edward, open your favorite painting program such as Fractal Design's Painter. Then open up your head map, which in this case is head.tga. As you can see, Unwrap unwrapped the grid to provide a good reference template for painting. Figure 6.102 shows the unwrapped head grid and the map I painted based on it.

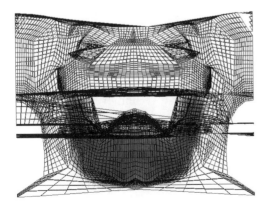

FIGURE **6.102** *Knuckles unwrapped head.*

Paint your maps however you wish, or use the ones that are supplied in the *Chapter6/Knuckles/Maps folder* of CD. Copy these map files to your maps directory in MAX for easier access. You should read Chapter 9, "Photorealistic Creature Surfacing," to learn more about creating character image maps.

Let's apply the map to Knuckles' face.

APPLYING IMAGE MAPS

To apply Knuckles' face map, open up the Material editor under the first map slot. Then click on **Diffusion Map** and add the newly created Color Map. Following the same procedure, add the **Specular Map**, **Shininess Map**, and the **Bump Map**, all of which were created using the unwrapped head as a guide. Now assign the new map to Knuckles' head. You should now have a fully surfaced Knuckles that resembles the character shown in Figure 6.103.

FIGURE **6.103** *Knuckles in all his glory.*

Of course, you can always apply image maps to all of Knuckles' surfaces to make him even more interesting. You can find a full image-map surfaced version of Knuckles in the color insert of this book.

IT DOESN'T END HERE!

Now that you have a handle on creating characters using patches and splines, it's finally over — or is it? It is for me, but now it's your turn to turn up the heat and create your own creature creations with 3D Studio MAX. Don't limit yourself to the details covered in this part; do some experimenting and see which details you can create with patches and splines. The possibilities are limitless.

Dive into Chapter 9, "Photorealistic Creature Surfacing," and after memorizing it, come back and see if you can add photorealistic surfacing to Edward and Knuckles. They'll be waiting for you.

PART IV

Animation Master Creature Modeling

By Robert Ward

This part covers modeling characters with Hash software (MH3D and Animation Master; since both packages contain all the functionality discussed in this chapter, I'll refer to both as AM). What sets AM apart from most other software on the market today is total reliance on splines and spline patch modeling. In fact, the official Hash mantra is "Say no to Polygons." Hash splines are very simple, but very powerful. A model generally starts by laying down one point, which becomes a spline, and building from there by adding more and more splines and connecting them together into patches.

Although we will cover the ins and outs of Hash-spline modeling, you should already be familiar with the software, what defines a legal patch, and how to perform all the basic functions such as attaching and detaching control points (CPs), lathing objects, rotating objects, etc. If you are not, crack open that software manual now and read through all the explanations and tutorials.

We're going to go through a quick overview of Hash-spline modeling, and then model two characters. The first will be a somewhat simple (deceptively simple, that is) ghost character, and the second a more complex, lean, muscular action hero. We'll proceed as though we've been given a small stack of design sketches from our art director that give the feel of the characters. Not every detail has been included so we'll have to make some decisions and assumptions about them.

CHAPTER

7

Getting to Know Spline Patches

There is a lot of material to cover, some of it a bit complex if you haven't modeled a character with AM before, but perseverance will get you over any hurdle. It's more important for you to get the general principles than the specifics of the given character. With the principles at hand you can build virtually anything you desire.

Again, we won't be discussing software basics such as how to lay down CPs or connect points, so refer to the software manual if you aren't comfortable with its basic functions. We will discuss the pros and cons of the various forms a patch can take, how to think about spline detail, and how to model rounded forms with patches.

THE FORMS A PATCH CAN TAKE

Patches can take a few forms. Some are problematic, but others are very useful. Read on to learn how and when to use them, and how to minimize the potential negative effects they can have on a surface.

4-POINT PATCHES

The most basic patch is the 4-point patch, formed by the intersection of four splines — two vertical and two horizontal. Figure 7.1 shows an example of this type of patch.

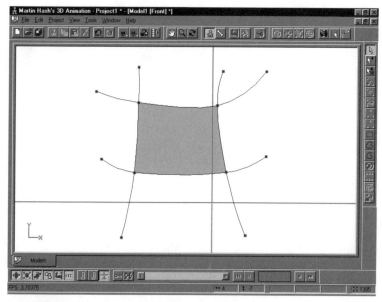

FIGURE **7.1**   *An example of a basic 4-point patch.*

The overwhelming majority of patches in a model will be of this type. Generally, these never cause creasing; however, it's almost never possible to cover the topology of a form completely with 4-point patches alone, so you must occasionally resort to 3-point patches.

3-POINT PATCHES

Three-point patches are problematic because they generally cause a crease on the surface of the model, which is a rather ugly artifact. They may not show up in all viewing angles, but if your model is to move, they definitely will appear. You must plan ahead, and if you must use them, place them in an area where creases normally occur, such as at the corners of the mouth, or in an area where they will not be conspicuous such as in the armpit. Figure 7.2 shows a wireframe of a 3-point patch, in addition to a rendered example of the type of creasing you can expect to see.

As you can see, the creasing can be a serious problem when attempting to create a smooth surface. You should try to minimize the number of 3-point patches in your model.

4-POINT PATCH WITH A DANGLING SPLINE

A less common patch is the 4-point patch with a dangling spline. This is a 4-point patch with a fifth spline attached to one of the CPs. These generally occur in areas like the eyes

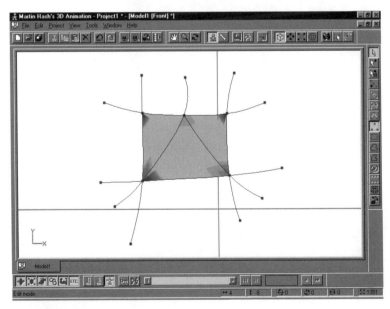

FIGURE **7.2** *An example of a 3-point patch with creasing.*

or the mouth where a circular spline is placed amidst a gridlike layout of 4-point patches. You can minimize the creasing effect these cause by continuing the fifth spline through the CP belonging to the 4-point patch, which gives you a dangling spline that will not be attached to anything. Then use this dangling spline to adjust the curvature of the surface so it flows smoothly into the continuous splines around it. This takes some practice and experimentation to get right, but generally, place the CP of the dangling spline at the location it would be if it were continuous with one of the other splines. Figure 7.3 shows a wireframe example of this type of situation on the left, the same wireframe with the dangling CP adjusted to minimize creasing in the middle, and a rendered example of the type of creasing you might see on the right.

Like many details in modeling with a given package, the handling of creasing is a matter of experience.

Let's take a look at two features of Hash patches that really make them stand out from the crowd.

HOLES

Since patches are defined by three or four points, any patch with five or more points will not render. These patches are referred to as *holes*. A hole can also be constructed with three

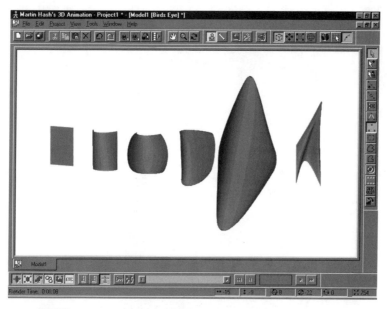

FIGURE **7.3** *Examples of a 4-point patch with dangling spline.*

or four points; since a renderable patch must contain two or more splines, any patch constructed with one spline (with its ends attached) will not render, and again, you get a hole. Figure 7.4 shows an example of a 10-point hole and a 4-point hole.

Holes are such an important part of modeling characters that we strongly recommend that you straighten them out in your mind now.

HOOKS

Hooks are a special case. They are Hash's answer to reducing spline count or complexity in a model. They allow you to attach a terminating spline to the middle of another spline without creating a 5-point patch, which allows you, for example, to attach a hand with a wrist that contains 12 splines to an arm that contains 8 splines. Without hooks, you would have to continue those 12 splines into the arm, and through the torso. Figure 7.5 shows an example of a cylinder with 8 splines attached to a cylinder with 12 splines through the use of hooks.

There are a couple issues surrounding the use of hooks. One, you can't manipulate a hook directly. It will move with the spline it's connected to, but you cannot grab it and move it. The second issue is that export to DXF format is problematic. The software will attempt to export patches containing hooks, but these will contain polygons with more than four sides, which won't export properly. Models with no hooks export perfect DXF

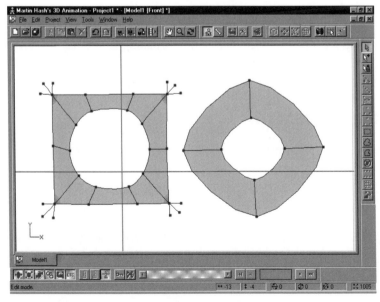

FIGURE **7.4** *A 10-point hole and a 4-point hole.*

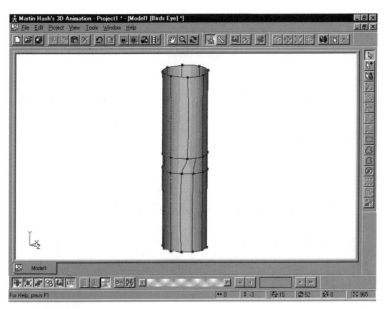

FIGURE **7.5** *An 8-point cylinder attached to a 12-point cylinder through the use of hooks.*

files containing all Quads, so if you plan on exporting your models, it's probably best to abstain from using hooks completely. For this reason the ghost character will be built without hooks.

There you have it. With these patch types as your arsenal, you can build nearly anything you imagine. Of course, building and animating are two different things. Animation must be planned into the model design, so let's take a look at planning.

PLANNING FOR ANIMATION

When looking at a design sketch you have to ask yourself or the art director, "How will the character be animated?" Will it basically be used just for walk cycles and render out at 50×50 pixels, or will it be capable of speech and a wide range of acting? If it's going to be used as a tiny sprite in a game you can probably get by with very little spline detail and focus on arm, leg, and hip motion. This means more splines in the joints of those areas. If it will be capable of speech or expressing emotion — most likely the face will contain a great number of splines outlining the shapes that will be animated — you can't animate points that aren't there.

It's important that you take the time to consider how the model is used before you begin the actual modeling. If not, you could find yourself spending unwanted hours trying to add detail to your model, which is typically next to impossible.

Since we're on the subject of spline volume, let's take a look at the economy of splines.

ECONOMY OF SPLINES

Economy of splines is always an important consideration if you plan to animate your character. The idea is to keep the number of splines to the minimum that will allow you to get the desired detail, and will allow you to animate the character. It's a thin line to walk, but once you get down to animating you'll be glad you did. You can keep the spline-count manageable by:

- Preplanning (lay out your splines on paper schematically before modeling)
- Using hooks
- Adjusting the bias and magnitude to alter a surface instead of adding more splines

All the forms in Figure 7.6 were created from the same 4-point patch with adjusted bias and magnitude. The best way to get a grip on what these controls do is to turn on the bias adjustment handle and play with it.

Note that the preceding examples could all have been built using additional splines instead of bias adjustment. Why use one technique over the other? Using bias reduces the necessary number of splines, but sometimes you don't *want* to reduce it. Extra splines

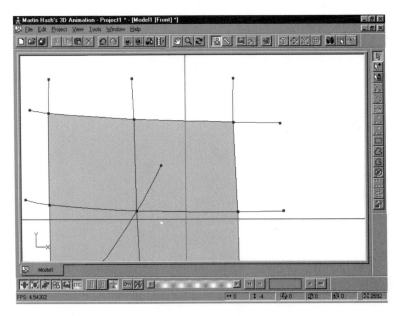

FIGURE **7.6** *4-point patches with adjusted bias and magnitude.*

generally give more control in muscle animation than bias adjusted splines. Do some tests for this point and discover it for yourself.

AREAS OF GREATEST DETAIL

Most often the areas with the greatest detail will contain the greatest number of splines. Usually these are the face and hands. Sculptors have the luxury of starting with a general form and progressively adding levels of detail as they work. Patch modelers have no such luxury. Generally you're forced to work from the detailed areas outward. This is not a forced rule, however. As you gain experience, you might wish to develop a technique where you build a simple form first, then progressively add splines in those areas that need them. In the long run, this technique can be more time consuming, however, and it's more likely that you would work yourself into a corner.

If you find that your understanding of some aspect of the preceding discussion is a bit foggy, open a model window and experiment. If bias adjustment is your sticky point, create a sphere and adjust to your heart's content. Once you feel comfortable with splines and patches, we'll move along and build something.

Modeling Rounded Forms: Building a Nose

Let's build a section of a nose to get a feeling for modeling "in the round." Figure 7.7 shows a few views of the section we will model.

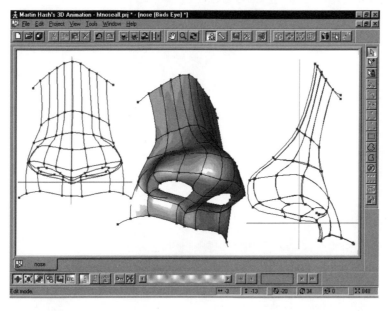

FIGURE **7.7** *Three views of a section of nose.*

As you can see, the middle of the nose is rounded, so you want a spline running down the center to define the roundness and one spline on either side to define its outer shape. If the nose were flat in the front, you might want two splines for the center, and two for the outer contour.

Start the nose by building the center shape in the Right view. Figure 7.8 shows this spline.

Next, construct a pair of splines in the front view to define the outer shape of the edge of the nose. Figure 7.9 shows these splines. Note that they contain the same number of CPs as the center spline.

To build splines in three dimensions, construct the shape in one view, then adjust the CPs at a view 90 degrees from the first. For instance, if the spline were built in the front or back view, adjust it in the right or left view.

For every point you lay down in the front view (X- and Y-axes), you have to estimate its position in the right or left view (Z-axis). When working with templates, landmarks such as creases in a face or a cheekbone help you place points in three dimensions, but without a template you're left to intuition and your knowledge of the object you're modeling. You might know that in the front view of a model the base of the jaw is in line with the center of the lips, and in the right view it's at the midpoint of the skull. This doesn't provide precise coordinates but allows you to proceed point by point without blind guesswork. It takes quite a lot of practice but once you get the hang of it, any form you want to model will be within your grasp.

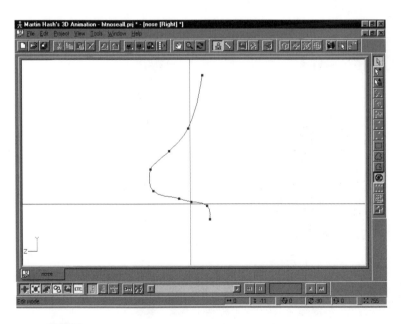

FIGURE 7.8 Spline outlining the center of the nose, right view.

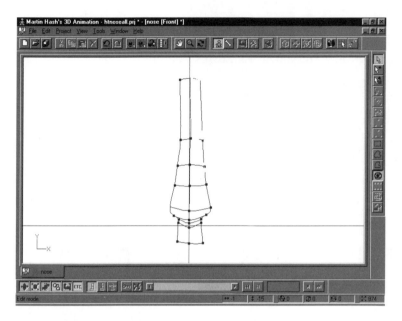

FIGURE **7.9** *Splines defining the outer shape of the nose's edge.*

Let's continue with our nose. Go to the right view and adjust the two new splines as you see in Figure 7.10.

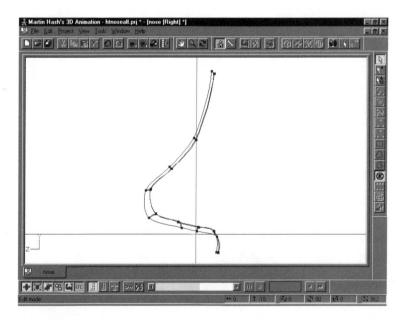

FIGURE **7.10** *Splines adjusted in the right viewport.*

⇨ TIP

Keep your mesh very neat as you work — this means, in the case of Figure 7.9, lining up your CPs in the right view. This will make it much easier to adjust and add splines as you work, and to animate your mesh when you are finished. Even a simple mesh that does not have its CPs lined up is far more difficult to animate than a complex mesh that does.

Switch to the front view. (Your fingers should always be ready to jump to the numeric keypad to switch views so you don't need to have two views open at once.) To construct the nostrils lay down two splines as shown in Figure 7.11. Note the number of CPs — you'll need these to attach additional splines for the body of the nose.

Adjust these in the right view, creating the shape of the nostril as seen from the right. Remember to line up your CPs — it should appear as though there is only one spline outlining the nostril. Figure 7.12 shows how this looks.

Now you need to extend a second pair of contour splines from the nostril splines as shown in Figure 7.13.

Here is a tip for patching the horizontal splines. When connecting one CP to another, the CP you grab will jump to the location in 3D space of the CP you are connecting to. A quick way to work is to lay down a horizontal spline, connected to nothing, with as many CPs across as there are vertical splines, then simply grab each CP on the floating spline and connect them to the vertical spline, from right to left. (A reminder,

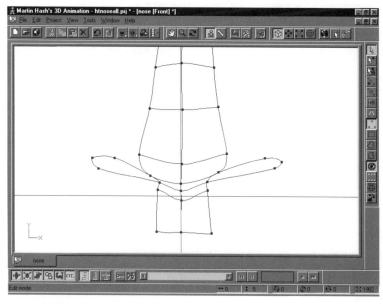

FIGURE **7.11** *Two splines for the nostrils.*

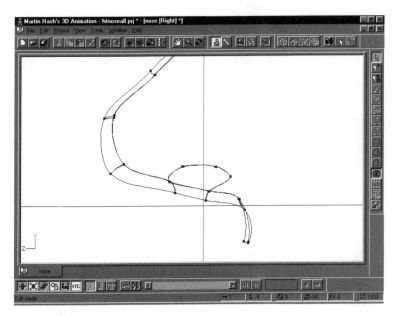

FIGURE **7.12** *The nostril splines as seen from the right.*

you grab a CP with the left button, and attach by right-clicking in Windows, and with the tilde key on the Mac.) As you work, you may find this or some other method more comfortable for you.

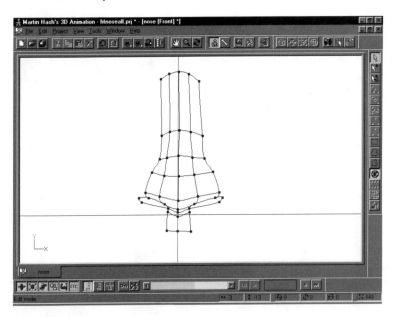

FIGURE **7.13** *Second pair of contour splines.*

Again, adjust these in the right view. It can be difficult to grab the CP you want in the right view since a spline laid down in the front is flat. Don't be afraid to move other CPs out of the way as you search for the one you want. It will eventually become second nature to nudge CPs around and quickly find the one you want. Figure 7.14 shows these splines adjusted.

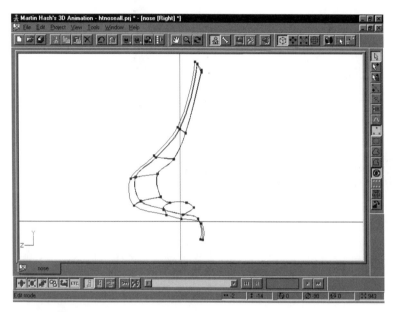

FIGURE **7.14** *Adjusted in the right view.*

Next you need to build a second rim around the nostrils as seen in Figure 7.15.

Note that this is one continuous spline. To check this, select one portion of the spline and press the comma key. This should select the whole spline. If it doesn't, it means that what appears as single spline-loop is actually two splines attached to each other. If so, you need to break the splines where they attach and then reattach them.

Continue the process of running splines off the nostril loops and adjusting them in the right view until you arrive at what you see in Figures 7.16 and 7.17.

Figure 7.18 shows the completed nose. There are three versions of this nose on the CD-ROM in the *Chapter07/Primer directory*. Each looks virtually identical, but there are subtle differences in the way the splines are arranged. Load each of these and see if you can tell the difference.

One final step in constructing the nose is to build the inner funnels of the nostrils. Simply grab all five CPs of each nostril, extrude them, scale down a bit, and pull them up into the nose. Be sure to check their placement in a side view.

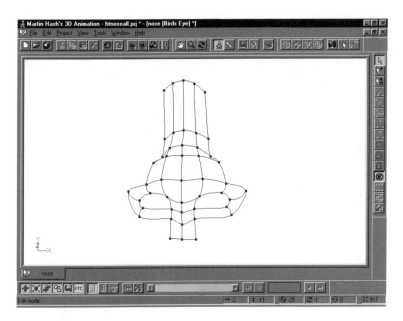

FIGURE **7.15** *Second rim around the nostrils.*

You can then turn on shaded-wireframe mode and adjust it to your liking, rotating it around a bit as you go. Figure 7.18 shows the completed mesh in front and right views with shaded-wireframe mode on and off.

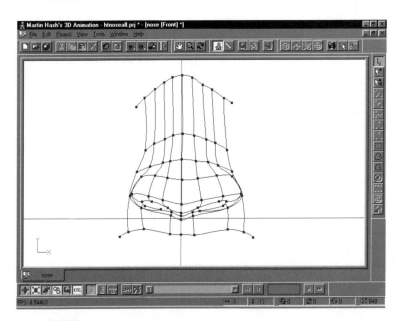

FIGURE **7.16** *Nose splines, front view.*

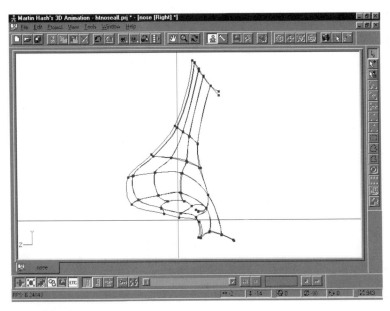

FIGURE **7.17** *Nose splines, right view.*

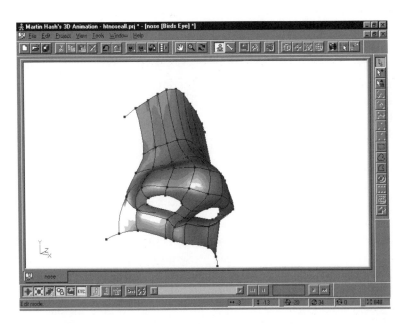

FIGURE **7.18** *The completed nose.*

MODELING CHARACTERS

When it comes to modeling a character, the first questions you want to ask yourself are the same questions any good actor asks when preparing for a role: "Where did I come from?" "Where am I going?" and "How did I get here?" Yes, it's been said many times before in this book, but it warrants repeating.

Nothing is more crucial in the development of a character than its biography. To properly model the character so that it has personality, you need to know where it has been and what it's done. You need to get inside its head and explore the intricacies of its personality. You can't know too much about the character.

In the following segments you will be modeling a ghost character that was provided by the art director on the project. Even though you have sketches of the character, you need to understand its personality to model it properly. This allows you to determine if the features in the design sketch really are appropriate for the character. You certainly wouldn't want a character with a friendly personality to be modeled with a frown on his or her face. That's an obvious case, so how about one that's less obvious, like a ghost?

What if the ghost was a fat man when he was alive? Would a thin ghost make any sense? Certainly not — if he died fat, his ghost would be fat. For this reason you need to take a close look at the character's biography to get a better understanding of his personality. In fact, let's look at the ghost character's biography.

ALBERTO'S BIOGRAPHY

When he was with the living, Alberto owned a small Italian restaurant in Manhattan, and was highly regarded by his patrons for his fantastic meatballs. (He took the recipe to his grave, so don't ask.) He was a large man, thanks to his custom of tossing one meatball into his mouth before each plate was allowed to pass into the dining area to a patron. This eventually killed him, tragically on the day he was to receive his wish of receiving a four-star rating. As a matter of fact, it was from the very plate that was to go to the food critic. Well, that's life for you, and Murphy's Law too.

So he was chef while he was alive, but what about the afterlife? Alberto didn't find himself in a utopian heaven, nor a fiery hell — but in ghostly limbo. While in limbo, he haunted other four-star restaurants, ate their food, gorged himself on Italian, Mexican, French, and Chinese. He figured what the heck, a ghost can't gain weight. Of course, he doesn't have much of a taste for Indian, but he will down a couple of plates of Bhaja in a pinch.

He doesn't usually leave after just one plate, however. He'll give it his best to eat every last scrap of food in the place. He'll steal food from customer's plates during the day, and spend the night in the kitchen cooking various dishes and gobbling them down. When morning approaches he'll abandon cooking and simply guzzle whole cans of tomato sauce or devour a side of beef uncooked.

Now that you have an idea of who the character is, take a look at the art director's concept sketch, and then get on to modeling.

MODELING ALBERTO—THE GHOST CHARACTER

Take a look at Figure 7.19, which shows the art director's concept sketch of Alberto. He's pretty rotund, isn't he? How about that huge, like-a-plow mouth that is perfect for shoveling in the food? Don't forget that sly grin. Doesn't he look content, in fact, downright delirious? And as luck would have it, the nose you just modeled, with a few modifications, is Alberto's nose so you don't need to build a new one. Try tweaking the nose to match the art director's sketch.

This is a good time to play with the splines from both the front and side views, then turn on shaded mode and see the effects of your modifications. Try to match the look of the nose in the sketch. Take a look at Figure 7.20 to see how these modifications of the nose might look. The main alteration is that the bridge of the nose has been pinched to make room for the eyes.

FIGURE **7.19** *Art director's concept sketch for Alberto.*

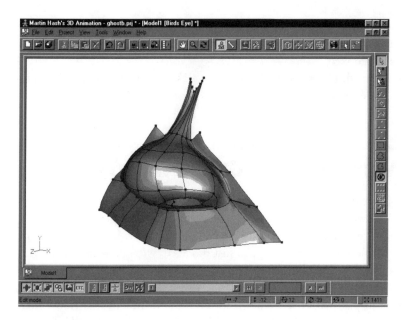

FIGURE **7.20** *The nose modified to match the artist's sketch.*

Once this is done, you can move on to adding the next area of greatest detail — the mouth. Note: you will be building this character without hooks and without spline bias adjustment. Doing so will give you a better understanding of why hooks are necessary, and a greater appreciation for them.

MODELING ALBERTO'S MOUTH FOR EXPRESSION

Before you begin laying down splines, think about how the mouth and cheek area will be animated. You're probably going to want Alberto to be capable of expressing a wide variety of emotions, and since this is a rather cartoonish figure, these emotions likely will be quite exaggerated (Wow, look at all the food!). The mouth will have to assume a great number of shapes ranging from a small circle for "oh" and "ooh" sounds, a wide slit for smiles and long-e sounds, to wide open for that barrel of ribs in the back, probably stretched beyond what a realistic human could manage.

Some mouth shapes, to be used for lip-synch, require teeth and a tongue to portray expressions accurately, so you have to use some judgment as to whether you want to include these in the modeling or not. We'll be modeling a set of teeth and a tongue in the next chapter, so we won't go into this detail with Alberto. Later you might wish to add the teeth on your own so Alberto won't be left to gum his leg of lamb.

Now you have to decide how many CPs will make up the perimeter of the mouth. This is partly dictated by the shapes you'll want it to assume (eating, gulping, slurping) and partly by the splines coming off of the nose. Since the nose has eight splines coming off the bottom, the top lip will have at least eight splines (unless you were using hooks — but in this example you are not). Figure 7.21 shows some of the shapes the mouth will assume.

You can see that, in some way, the number and placement of CPs around the mouth will determine the character of Alberto. In Figure 7.21 you can see that the bottom lip is capable of stretching out flat, forming a V, and forming the bottom half of a circle for "ooh" sounds. If he were to have fewer CPs around the mouth, say two on the bottom, he could stretch it flat, but would have trouble forming a V or a circle. Conversely, with the number of CPs you'll give him, his mouth cannot ripple when he burps the way the barfly Barnie from *The Simpsons* does. We would need many more CPs for that. But that's okay — with Alberto it all goes in and never comes back out.

If you have any trouble visualizing how many CPs a mouth should contain, you could make a simple spline-loop and play with its shape while varying its CP count. Add a horizontal spline as shown in Figure 7.22 to allow you to give more shape to the mid-lip and cheeks.

Continue the outer cheek spline in a loop that connects with the opposite side as you see in Figure 7.23. This will be the base of the lower lip.

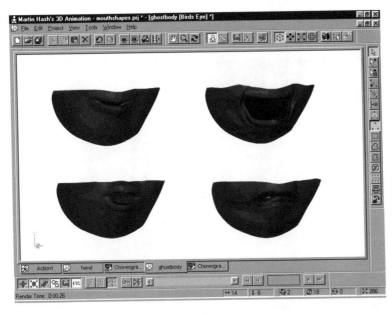

FIGURE **7.21** *Some mouth shapes Alberto will be required to make.*

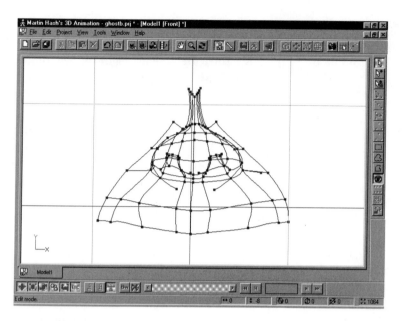

FIGURE **7.22** *Spline for the upper lip.*

Next, fill this shape as you see in Figures 7.24 and 7.25.

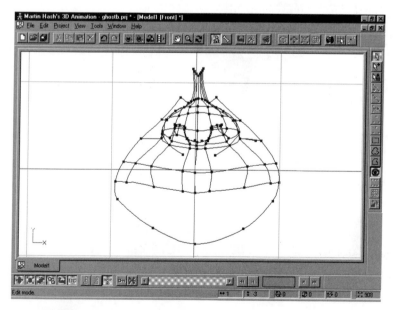

FIGURE **7.23** *The base of the lower lip.*

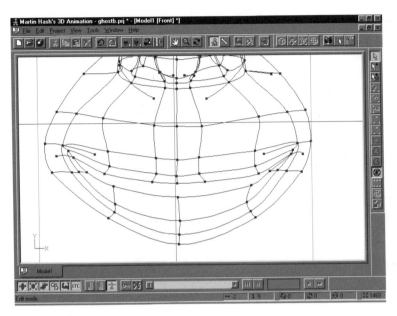

FIGURE **7.24** *The patched mouth shapes, front view.*

Now build the eyebrows as in Figures 7.26 and 7.27. Notice that these four splines of the brow are continuations of the nose and cheek splines.

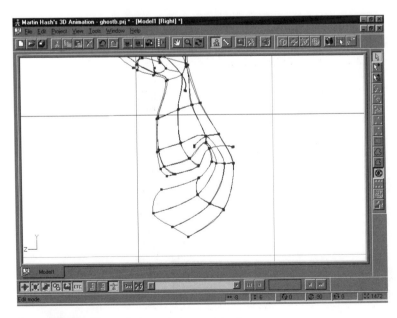

FIGURE **7.25** *The patched mouth shapes, right view.*

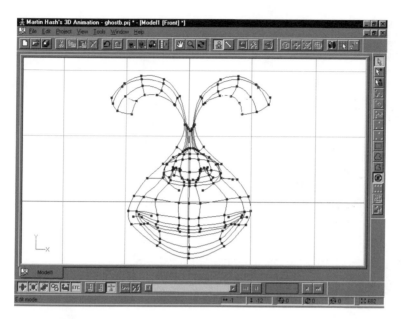

FIGURE **7.26** *Eyebrows, front view.*

Now you should have something that resembles the image in Figure 7.28. To continue, connect the bridge of the nose as shown in Figure 7.29.

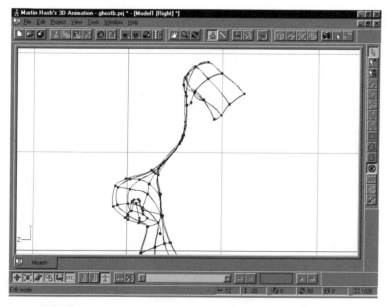

FIGURE **7.27** *Eyebrows, Right view.*

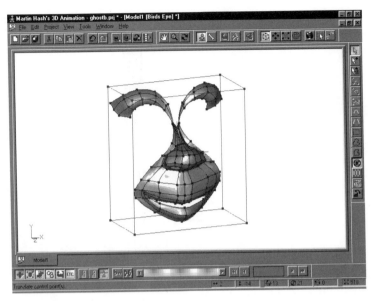

FIGURE **7.28** *Alberto's face, so far*

Completing the front of the face is a simple matter of creating splines that radiate out from the eyes and brows and loop around under the mouth to create the chin (or chins, if you prefer). Refer to Figures 7.30 and 7.31 to see how to do this.

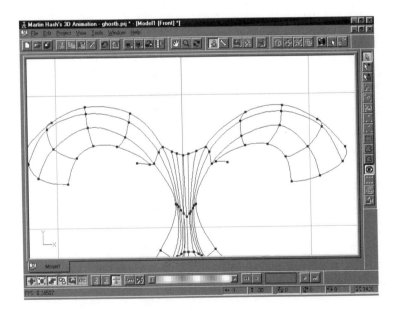

FIGURE **7.29** *Bridge of the nose connected.*

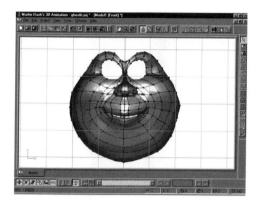

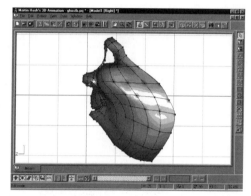

FIGURE **7.30** *Radiating splines completing the face, front view.*

FIGURE **7.31** *Radiating splines completing the face, right view.*

To complete the head, select the lower portion of the outer spline of the face except the lowest CP, as shown in Figure 7.32.

Next, in the top view, extrude this three times, each time scaling and shaping the new spline to get what is shown in Figures 7.33 and 7.34. In the right view, create a spline for the very back of the head as seen in Figure 7.35 (Ghosty).

Figure 7.35 shows what the back of the head looks like at this point. Connect the horizontal splines on one side of the gap to those on the other.

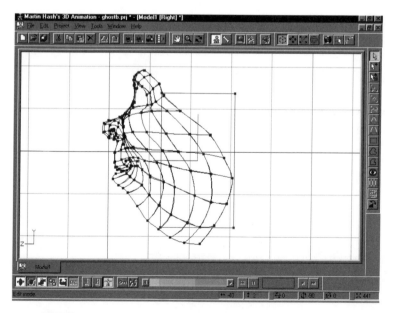

FIGURE **7.32** *Select a portion of the face.*

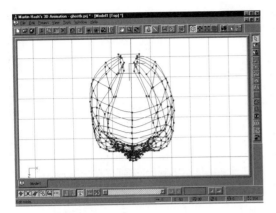

FIGURE **7.33** *The face spline extruded three times, front view.*

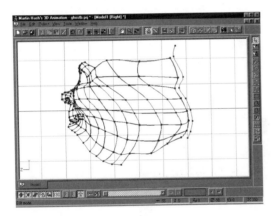

FIGURE **7.34** *The face spline extruded three times, right view.*

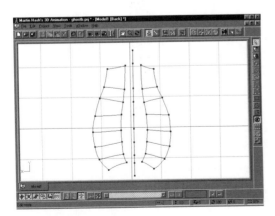

FIGURE **7.35** *Back of Alberto's head.*

Since the top of the head is not a continuous spline, you could either extrude it, then break and reattach to create continuity, or you could perform two extrusions, once on the back of the head and once on the brow, then connect these.

Either way, you will wind up with a continuous spline loop at the top of the head and two 4-point dangling-spline patches at the temples, as seen in Figure 7.36.

Now extrude the top spline a number of times and shape to create the nightcap sort of form you see in the sketch. Figures 7.37 and 7.38 show this form completed.

Leave the head as it is for now. You can add details such as the eyes and eyelids later. A portrait painter doesn't paint skin wrinkles and reflections in the irises until the whole composition is roughly laid in because if the head needs to be moved a quarter of an inch to the left for compositional reasons, the painter will be glad he or she didn't. You should do the same, and save the details for later in the modeling process where possible.

MODELING ALBERTO'S BODY

Alberto has a cartoon body, which is basically a cylinder with two tubes attached at the sides. The main problems to be solved are attaching the arms to the body and, since you

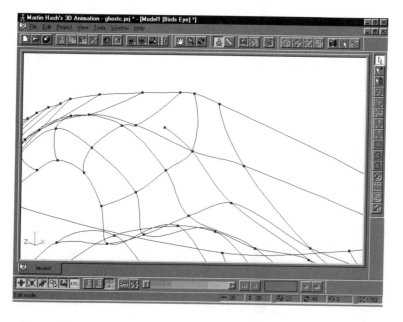

FIGURE **7.36** *A continuous spline and 4-point dangling-spline patch.*

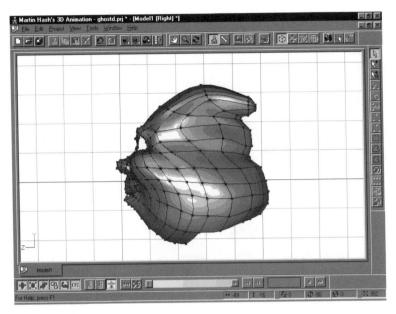

FIGURE **7.37** *The top of the head, right view.*

aren't using hooks, attaching the hands to the wrists. Let's begin modeling all that ecto-plasmic blubber with the arms.

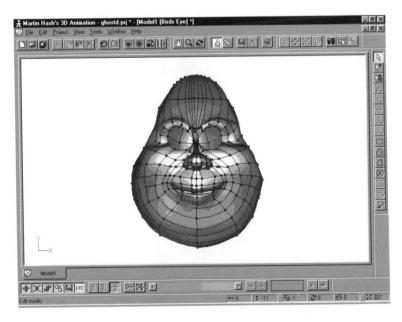

FIGURE **7.38** *The top of the head, front view.*

First, create the arms by lathing a five-CP spline with a lathe setting of 8 in the **Options>Tools>Modeling menu**. Then rotate this and shape it as shown in Figures 7.39 and 7.40.

Connect the two arms with splines across the chest as shown in Figure 7.41.

Next, connect the head to the chest as shown in Figure 7.42.

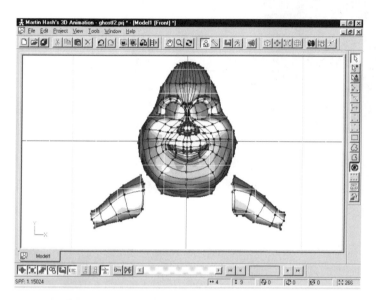

FIGURE **7.39** *Alberto's arms, front view.*

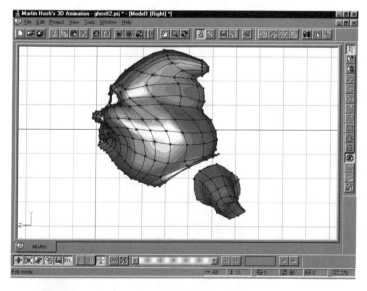

FIGURE **7.40** *Alberto's arms, right view.*

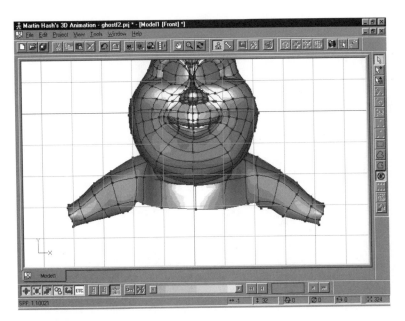

FIGURE **7.41** *Two splines across the chest.*

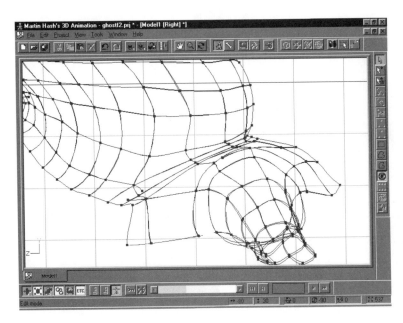

FIGURE **7.42** *Connect the head to the chest.*

Now extend the chest down as shown Figure 7.43.

Figure 7.44 shows in more detail how the arm is connected to the body.

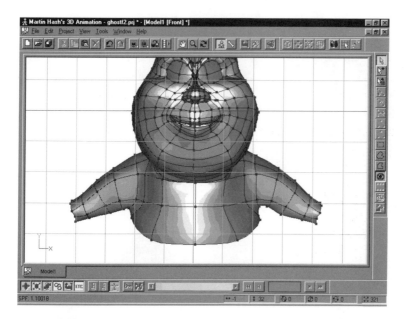

FIGURE **7.43** *Extend the chest down.*

Extrude the bottom spline, which should be a continuous spline loop, to create the body. I strongly recommend shaping each extrusion before making the next. This way

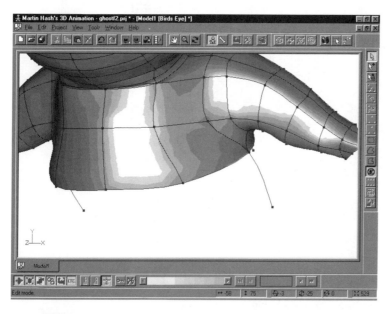

FIGURE **7.44** *Detail of the arm connection.*

you can tell where the next loop should be situated and how it will be shaped. Figures 7.45 and 7.46 show this work completed. Keep it round and full, which is the perfect description of Alberto.

To close up the hole at the end of the tail, extrude the last spline-loop twice; first scaling down about 70 percent, then to near zero. Don't scale to less than zero, which will

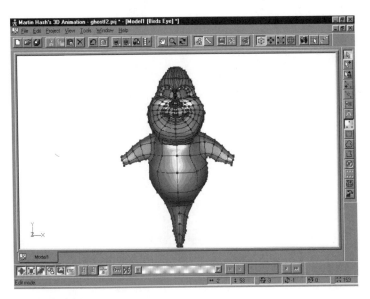

FIGURE **7.45** *The body extruded and shaped, front view.*

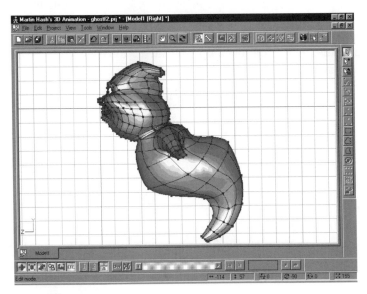

FIGURE **7.46** *The body extruded and shaped, right view.*

crimp the tail. To check this, simply hide all but the last loop and zoom in close in the front view. Take a look at Figure 7.47, which shows how the tip of the tail should appear.

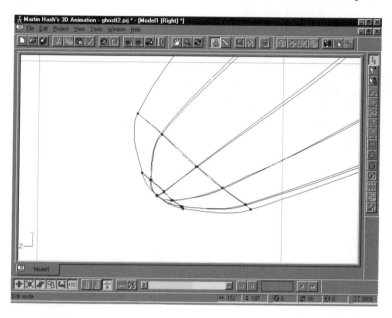

FIGURE **7.47** *Close up the hole in the tail.*

Now you're really getting somewhere. You should have a model that resembles the object in Figure 7.48. Now would be a good time to perform a bit of surgery on our egos with the blade of criticism. The three splines running down Alberto's back on the model are a bit harsh and narrow, however. Let's fix these.

Turn on **Shaded/Wireframe mode** and touch up your mesh. You'll find that regardless of how experienced you are at organic modeling, you'll still end up tweaking you're model to make it perfect. It would be nice if every point in your finished models were where you first placed it, but that isn't always the case, so tweaking is a way of life.

Once you've tweaked to your satisfaction, move on to the hands.

MODELING ALBERTO'S HANDS

The style that best describes Alberto is *cartoonish*. This is fortunate as far as his hands are concerned because wrist contains eight splines, which limits the detail you'll be able to give them. This in turn isn't such a good thing for the joints of the fingers, as you'll see. A greater amount of detail than you are allowed here would be necessary to give these joints a natural smoothness.

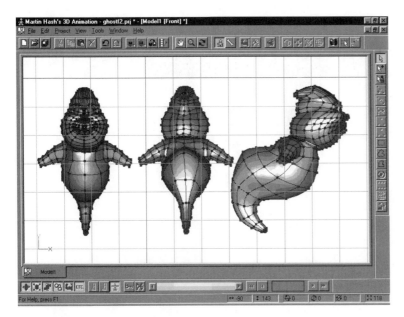

FIGURE **7.48** *Alberto in progress.*

Begin the hand with the fingers. First, lathe a seven-CP spline with a setting of 4 in the Options>Tools>Modeling menu. Then rotate this into position as shown in Figure 7.49.

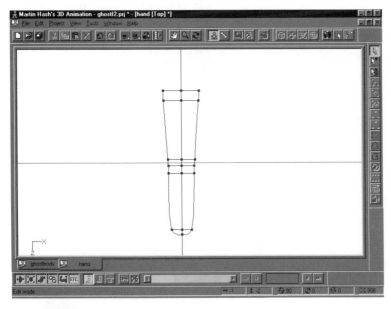

FIGURE **7.49** *A lathed finger.*

Copy this twice to create three fingers, and copy the end of one of these to create the thumb. This is shown in Figure 7.50.

Next you need to hide all but the end spline-loops of the three fingers. In the front view, draw a spline around these three loops and connect it up as shown in Figure 7.51.

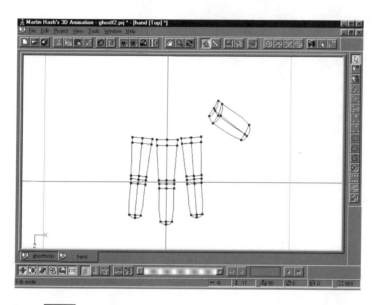

FIGURE **7.50** *Three fingers and a thumb.*

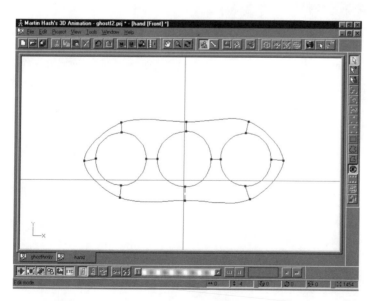

FIGURE **7.51** *A spline around the ends of the fingers.*

Notice that there are four patches of six CPs. These won't render, so you need to lay in four splines connecting the top CPs of the fingers as shown in Figure 7.52.

Now extrude this outer loop back six times as shown in Figure 7.53 to create the body of the hand.

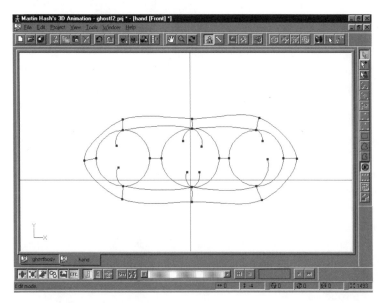

FIGURE **7.52** *Connect the top CPs to create four CP patches.*

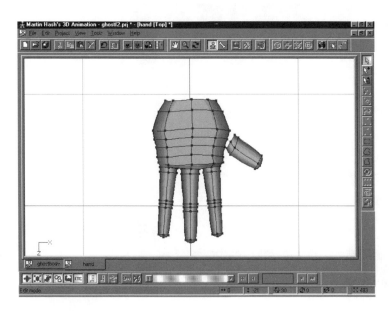

FIGURE **7.53** *Extrude the outer loop to create the hand.*

Now hide all but the end of the thumb and the edge of the hand where the thumb will be attached. Of course, a problem immediately seen in Figure 7.54 is that the thumb has four CPs, but the hole created in the hand will have eight CPs.

This isn't such a huge problem. Simply delete that thumb and lathe a new one with a lathe setting of 8, and rotate it into position. Again select the end of the thumb and the splines of the hand. Figure 7.55 shows that this will work.

Now break and delete the two splines on the hand that cross the thumb spline as shown in Figure 7.56.

This is the general method of attaching an appendage to a body. The CD-ROM includes a creature model that contains many appendages attached to a body in the same manner. This model can be found in *Chapter07/Alberto/Creature.mdl*. Take a look to see what this technique can do.

Now you need to attach the thumb to the palm by attaching the thumb loop to the palm as shown in Figure 7.57.

The simple hand is completed. Building a hand with so few splines is a bit of a pain, if not slightly painful to look at. The biggest problem is the area between the fingers, because there are no splines to adjust these curves. Later in the Steele (action hero) tutorial in Chapter 8 we'll build a more complex hand that allows for more adjustment in those areas.

Since the wrist and arm are both eight-CP cylinders, simply save the hand model and load it into the ghost model, rotate, scale, and translate it into position and attach (attach here means patch up the two outer spline loops).

Let's add some finishing touches to Alberto.

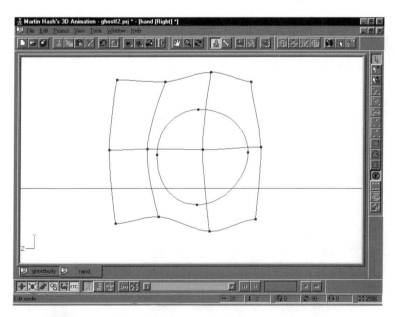

FIGURE **7.54** *A four-CP thumb and an eight-CP hole.*

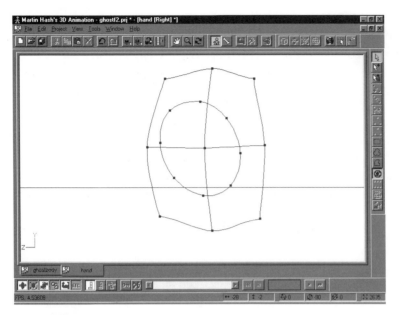

FIGURE **7.55** *A new eight-CP thumb.*

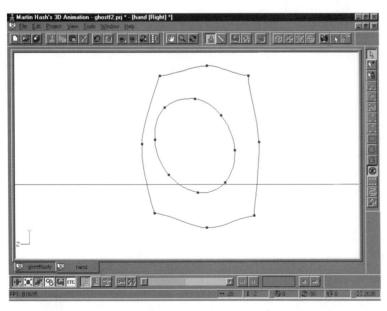

FIGURE **7.56** *Break and delete two splines to create a hole.*

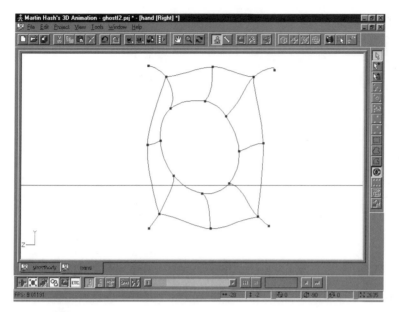

FIGURE **7.57** *Attach the thumb loop.*

COMPLETING ALBERTO

You don't need to do very much more to Alberto. Keeping him simple is in keeping with his style. Of course, once you're done, you may wish to give him complex texturing (food drippings, lard splotches, and wine stains).

First, finish up the eyes. Hide everything but the front of the face. (Group the face and press H to hide.) Add three spline loops and attach these to the existing eyeholes as shown in Figure 7.58.

Form the upper portion of these loops into a closed pair of eyelids as shown Figure 7.59. This work is made much lighter by turning on **Shaded/Wireframe mode** and sculpting at an angle.

You need to exercise these lids so they will be capable of opening and closing simply by rotating them. Select the lids, go into rotate mode (turn on the rotation manipulator by pressing **R**), set the pivot point to where the center of the eyeballs will be, and rotate the eyes open as shown in Figure 7.60.

Nudge the CPs into shape and rotate them closed. You might want to do this with the eyeballs in place to check for intersection with the eyes. Either way you'll want lids that will look good both closed and folded up into the head. There are other techniques that allow for lids folding up like a fan through the use of bones and constraints, but that is beyond the scope of this tutorial.

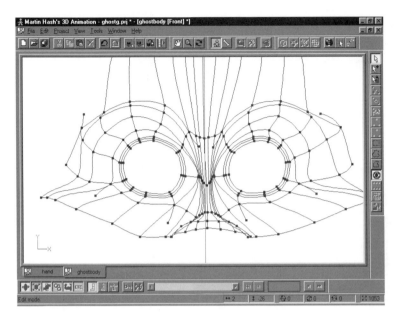

FIGURE **7.58** *Three spline loops added to the eyes.*

To create the inner surface of the eye, select the innermost rims and extrude them into the head as shown in Figure 7.61. Group this surface and give it a unique name such as "Inner Eye."

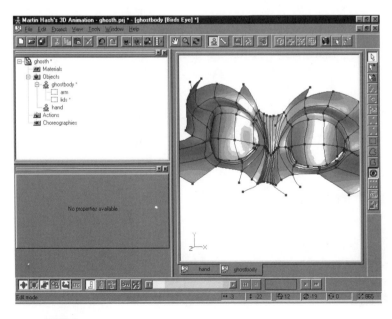

FIGURE **7.59** *Form the eyelid.*

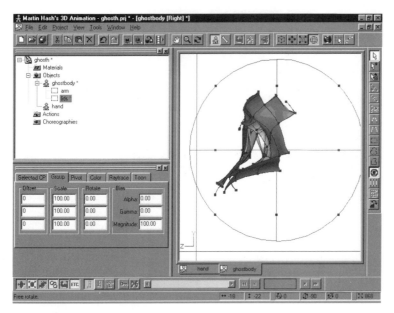

FIGURE **7.60** *Rotate the eyelid open.*

Now either create a sphere for the eyeballs or import *SPHERE.MDL* from of the Hash CD in the *data>models>primitives directory*. Position these into the sockets and make any final adjustments to the eyelids they may need.

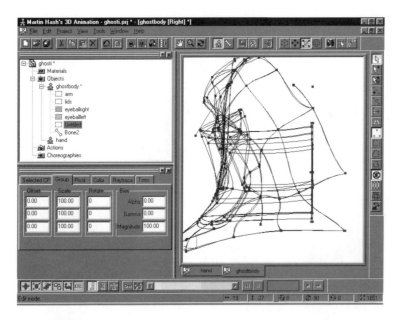

FIGURE **7.61** *The inner surface of the eye.*

Create the inner mouth the same way you created the inner surface of the eyes, by selecting the innermost ring and extruding it into the head. Now extrude again and scale it down to create the throat as shown in Figure 7.62. Give this inner surface a unique group name such as "Throat."

For now, that's as far as we'll take Alberto's geometry. As you can see, he's really starting to show some personality. Now it's time to take a look at surfacing Alberto, which will complete his personality.

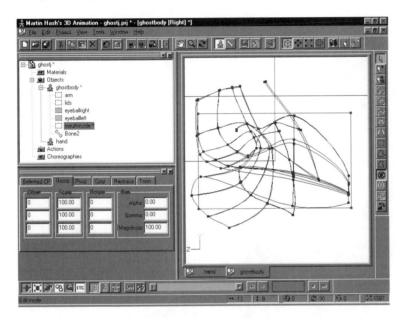

FIGURE **7.62** *The inner surface of the mouth.*

SURFACING ALBERTO

Surfacing is a wide and complex subject, which we'll explore in more detail in the next chapter. For now, the only surfacing you'll perform on Alberto is to apply eye decals. Select the eye groups and press **H** to hide everything else. Import the decal *irisghost.tga* from the CD in the directory *Chapter07/Alberto/ irisghost.tga*. Double click the decal icon in the project workspace and position the decal over the left eye. Once you are satisfied with its placement, apply the decal. Simply move the decal over the right eye and apply again. If you have any questions about how to apply decals, refer to the Hash user manual.

Again, we'll get more deeply into surfacing in the next chapter. In the meantime, take a look at Figure 7.63 and consider what sort of surfacing you might like to apply. Consider how he would be animated. Walk his walk. Talk his talk. Use your imagination.

The basic character is finished, using splines. This was a relatively basic model, but you were able to give Alberto personality by using splines properly. Of course, you may have higher expectations for character models than the likes of Alberto. But don't worry, we'll be diving into a rather complex character in the next chapter.

FIGURE **7.63** *Alberto, fully dressed.*

Robby

It's Alive

Bill Fleming

Sgt. Spore

Bill Fleming

Alien Bat

Bill Fleming

Komodosaurus

Bill Fleming

Sea Turtles

Bill Fleming

Jurassic Pac!

Bill Fleming

PastaMan!

Bill Fleming

Munch

Bill Fleming

Steele

Robert Ward

Knuckles

Shane Olson

Chubbs

Bill Fleming

Now That's a Burger

Bill Fleming

Tree Frog

Bill Fleming

Another World

Bill Fleming

MOVING UP TO COMPLEX CHARACTERS

What about more complex characters? The techniques are all basically the same: you lay down points, tweak, connect, adjust, and you're done. Of course, this is done on a larger scale. That's probably oversimplifying the issue — actually, it's really not that bad, it just requires a bit more work.

Why don't you take a break, and then we'll move on to forging some Steele. That is, we'll be creating a super action hero. I'll see you in the next chapter.

CHAPTER
8
Forging Steele— Creating an Action Hero

© 1998 Robert Ward

It's time to have a bit of fun. We'll be creating a character that is situated about a third of the way toward realism on a scale from cartoon to photorealistic. His name is Steele, and like many modern heroes, everything about him is a little off kilter. Take a look at Figure 8.1 and you'll see what I mean. It's Steele as he'll be when he's fleshed out.

He seems a bit angry, doesn't he? Well, before we even open a new model window and start plugging away, let's think about who this guy is and why he seems so intense. Now is the perfect time to take a look at Steele's biography.

STEELE'S BIOGRAPHY

What drives Steele? He's a man who believes that a shadow government is the true power — a corrupt power — behind the public government and he's upset about it. He sees himself as a blast furnace removing the impurities from the pig iron of society, which usually materialize in the form of corrupt authority. This isn't an idea he simply picked up from the television — there's a bit of history behind it.

He was born Kurzy Andrews in 1945 to a wealthy industrial family in Pittsburgh. In 1962, the year his father announced his candidacy for the presidency, sixteen workers,

FIGURE **8.1** *Steele — The action hero.*

including his younger brother Addison, were killed in one of the mills. His father never believed it, but Kurzy was convinced of local FBI involvement. He insisted it was an attempt to discredit his father. A successful attempt at that — the media swallowed up the idea that the deaths were not accidental, and over the following decade fed the public stories of unsafe conditions in Andrews' mills. They printed stories of negligence in maintaining equipment, an abusive attitude toward employees, and one writer, a Pulitzer Prize winner, even implied that Kurzy's father had the sixteen killed for profit in an insurance scam without bothering to explain how such a scam would work. Either way, Kurzy's father was pushed over the edge and committed suicide in 1975, pushing Kurzy, in turn, over the edge. Within a year he liquidated his holdings in the family business, set his mother up in Florida, changed his name, and vanished.

But he didn't vanish completely. Pentagon security has been overheard discussing the costumed figure they have chased through the hallways. They say he flashes like a blade of steel when he passes under the lights, only to vanish in the shadows. You can be sure there is much discussion about Steele that will never be overheard, and wonder how large are the files kept on his movements. They are probably frustratingly small.

These files would obviously mention his obsession for uncovering conspiracy, and if they know his original identity, would probably mention that his obsession grows out of his need to give meaning to two otherwise meaningless deaths. For those involved in what Steele believes to be the Big Conspiracy, this is a blessing. It creates ambiguity in Steele's beliefs, an opening into which they can shovel whatever information they wish.

And Steele knows this, which is why he can't help but pull on every single thread that presents itself because, who knows, one may be connected to the big toe of the Big Conspiracy. So every report of black helicopters terrorizing cows, mysterious hums heard

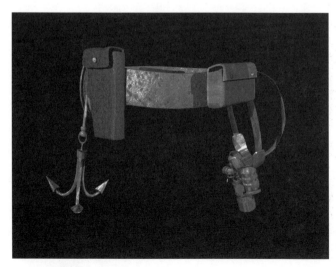

FIGURE **8.2** *Steele's utility belt.*

in the south, FBI library surveillance programs, or assassination attempts has him flying across the country to investigate, terrorize those involved, and bribe, coerce, or pummel people for information.

That's the basic background workup. What about that costume? The superhero costume is a convention, really. The intent is basically intimidation, showing off muscles and giving an otherworldly appearance and identification. The superhero wants his/her foe to know immediately who he/she is. Some guy in a T-shirt threatening to pummel you isn't quite as effective or noteworthy as Batman threatening to pummel you.

Steele usually wears an equipment utility belt because his outfit is skintight. His belt houses a variety of equipment such as handcuffs, bugs, bug detectors, portable lie detectors, cameras, blowguns, climbing spikes, claws, stun guns, grappling hooks, and whatever else might come in handy when detecting a conspiracy while avoiding detection.

For those who watch the popular show *X Files*, we could have summed it up this way: Steele is basically Fox Mulder with more toys, more muscles, and more anger. Now that you have a very detailed description of the character and his personality, you can effectively model the character.

THE ANATOMY OF A SUPERHERO

If you have a fairly detailed understanding of anatomical structures already, you're ahead of the game. If not, remember that the study of anatomy is a lifelong pursuit, and an edifying one. The more you learn, the more this knowledge will improve your thinking in modeling any type of character or creature.

Muscular information on Steele will be kept fairly low, but we'll refer to the muscles we do model by name. Figures 8.3, 8.4, and 8.5 are included for easy reference so you have an understanding of the muscles.

Of course, we all know that we have a body, two arms, two legs, and a head. Most of us know that we have muscles such as the *biceps* and *triceps*. Fewer of us know we have a *trapezious* (rear neck muscle), and probably fewer still a *gastrocnemius* (calf muscle). Just as a child slowly evolves its strange knowledge of anatomy (which includes such oddities as arms growing from the head) to a fuller understanding that includes a neck and torso, we can add to our knowledge over time to include the gastrocnemius and a thousand other structures.

Again, for Steele we'll keep things fairly simple. We'll learn the principle of building muscles, and later you can apply these ideas in any manner you'd like.

So why don't you simply grab an anatomy text any time you want to model a human figure and put in everything you see? Well, for two reasons actually. To understand the first, grab any fairly detailed anatomy book and consider just how many splines it would

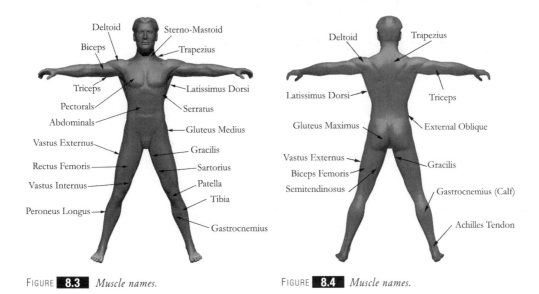

FIGURE **8.3** *Muscle names.*   FIGURE **8.4** *Muscle names.*

take to model all that detail. Second, you want to be a designer, not simply a reporter. You can pick and choose the forms you model, and you're allowed to distort these forms to express personality and character. In the physical sense, Steele is lean because he rode his mountain bike throughout his childhood, but in another sense it's an expression of the fact that he's more likely to pick a lock than pound down a door. He's an intellectual, not a total brute. On the other hand, he is a tortured fellow, which causes him to be a *bit* of a brute when it comes to punishing the unjust. So we'll give him a stern, muscular face from all that teeth-clenching as he thinks about the political conspiracies that always seem to allude him, and set his head a bit further forward over the body than normal to express his brutality.

Figure 8.6 is the art director's concept sketch of Steele. Examine it, consider the story and style, and we'll begin.

Examine these sketches, consider the story line, and the character of Steele, and walk his purposeful but strange walk — then we'll begin creating.

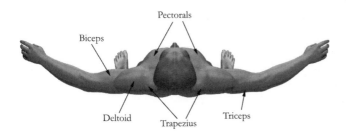

FIGURE **8.5** *Muscle names.*

FIGURE **8.6** *Concept sketch of Steele's body.*

MODELING THE FACE

Steele's face is stern, aggressive, and brutal, yet intelligent. Keep his character in mind through every step of the modeling process.

We'll use templates for the first part of the tutorial — one for the front, and one for the right. These can be found under *Steele/fronttmp.tga* and *Steele/righttmp.tga*. Load these into the modeling viewport and set them to *front* and *right*, respectively.

As you did with the ghost Alberto, begin with an outline of the nose in the right view. Since the technique here will be very similar, I've jumped ahead a few steps. Take a look at Figures 8.7 and 8.8. What's different here? Well, there are no horizontal connecting

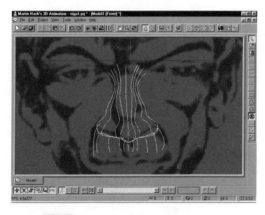

FIGURE **8.7** *Nose splines, front view.*

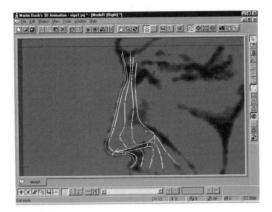

FIGURE **8.8** *Nose splines, right view.*

splines because there are times when patching the splines will slow you down, and if you find you need to adjust the horizontal spline count, detaching and reattaching splines is unnecessary work. You may wish to do this, or patch as you work. It is a personal choice.

Either way, once you have the nose and patches, extend the splines off the side of the nose around the contour of the brow ridge, over the cheekbone, and back into the nose as shown in Figures 8.9 and 8.10.

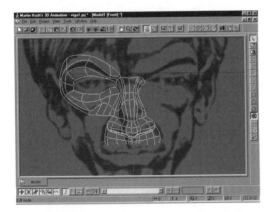

FIGURE **8.9** *The brow ridge and cheek, front view.*

You can repeat this process for the left side or copy the right, flip it on the X-axis, and attach it to the left. If you use the later method it will be much easier to match the CPs in the right view. In any event, Figure 8.11 shows how this looks.

Continue the cheek splines down to the sides of the mouth as shown in Figures 8.12 and 8.13.

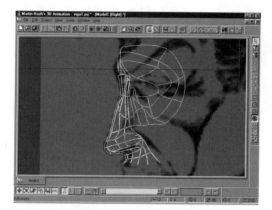

FIGURE **8.10** *The brow ridge and cheek, right view.*

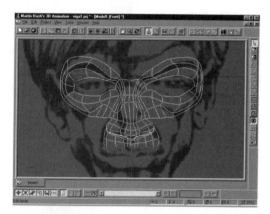

FIGURE **8.11** *Brow ridge and cheek copied to the right.*

Note that one of the splines in a hook close to the nose was terminated to lessen the number of splines running over the cheek. This can be seen in Figure 8.14.

Now continue expanding the brow area as shown in Figures 8.15 and 8.16. Again these loop around the brow and back into the cheek.

When tweaking Steele's features, keep his visual *style* in mind. It's easy to slip into attempting to force everything to the norm of human proportion. On the other hand, you don't want the eyes to have two eye-widths of space between them by accident (they should be one eye-width apart). Be purposeful. When you're satisfied with your tweaking, move on to the mouth.

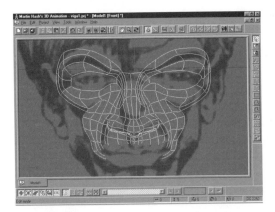

FIGURE **8.12** *Cheek splines extended, front view.*

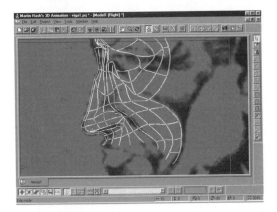

FIGURE **8.13** *Cheek splines extended, right view.*

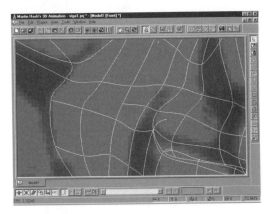

FIGURE **8.14** *A hook on the cheek.*

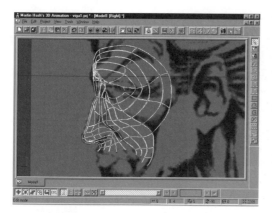

FIGURE **8.15** *Expanding the brow out further, front view.*

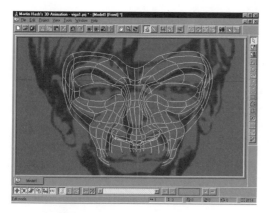

FIGURE **8.16** *Expanding the brow out further, right view.*

MODELING THE MOUTH

You may have noticed from the design sketch that Steele's mouth is abnormal — the embodiment of grim determination. It's not a human mouth stretched into an expression of grim determination, but rather a mouth permanently disfigured by it.

In general, the upper lip of a human being is shaped like a squashed M and the lower lip is shaped like a squashed W. Look at your own lips and notice how the lower one receives the upper. As always, your own face is an excellent reference of the general shape of things.

Begin Steele's lips as shown in Figure 8.17.

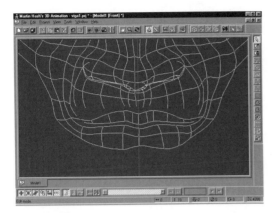

FIGURE **8.17** *Begin forming the lips.*

Notice the three vertical splines directly above the lips. The outer two are gently curved outward, and the center spline will be pulled back slightly into the face to create a groove, called the *philtrum*.

Above the lip is usually a strip of light skin that isn't quite lip, and isn't quite skin. It can catch quite a bit of light so don't leave it to image maps, model it in. Figure 8.18 shows this contour.

Now connect the splines running down from the nose to the upper lip. Notice also that the lowest spline on the upper lip has been left dangling until now. Connect this as shown in Figure 8.19.

You can now create one long, continuous spline encircling the whole face as shown in Figures 8.20 and 8.21.

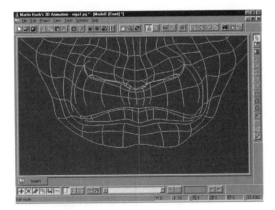

FIGURE **8.18** *Strip of light skin modeled in.*

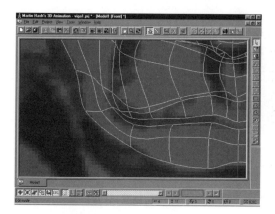

FIGURE **8.19** *Nose connected to the lip.*

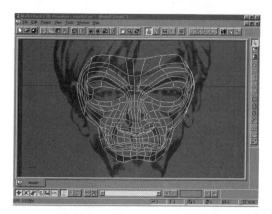

FIGURE **8.20** *Spline encircling the face, front view.*

Add two additional loops to recreate what you see in Figures 8.22 and 8.23.

Notice that each loop performs many functions. With three splines you've defined the chin, jaw, temples, and the beginnings of his mask. Of course, in this design it's not really a mask because it doesn't mask anything but his hair, but we'll call it a mask anyway. Why the mask? Well, Steele is a bit embarrassed about his hair loss. Besides, criminals are rarely intimidated by a superhero with a botched hair replacement job.

Now turn off the rotoscope templates. They served their purpose up to this point, helping to block in the shapes of his face, but there isn't much more useful information available from the sketches templates at this point, so they will just get in the way.

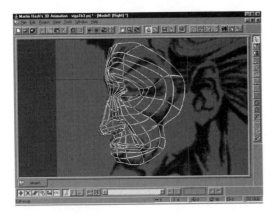

FIGURE **8.21** *Spline encircling the face, right view.*

Building the first loop around the face created one dangling-spline patch as shown in Figure 8.24.

Do a test render on this area. Pretty unsightly, isn't it? When creating such a juncture, you are presented with the possibility of dangling any one of those five splines. Each option creases differently, so you might want to try breaking apart this area and reattaching it to get a feel for how each will crease. At any rate, Figure 8.25 shows this option.

Here's a minor snag — take a look at the rim of his mask in Figure 8.26.

At the moment the rim works fine at the forehead, but these same splines are then used to form the jaw. This is no good because the rim needs to continue down around the jaw. If you simply move the ridge up one spline the problem is solved. Well, sort of, anyway. You'll still have to draw some of the splines under the jaw together to give the illusion

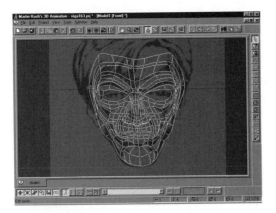

FIGURE **8.22** *Two additional spline loops, front view.*

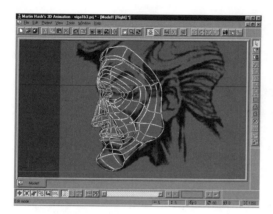

FIGURE **8.23** *Two additional spline loops, right view.*

that the ridge loops under to the other side. It is best to catch and fix such problems as they arise or you'll be pulling your hair out trying to fix them later.

Finish up a few details of the face before moving onto the head. First, extrude the nostrils into the nose as you did in the ghost tutorial. Then add a continuous spline loop in the mouth as the beginnings of its inner surface. The corners of this loop are connected as shown in Figure 8.27.

Group this new ring and name it "inner mouth." Extrude this into the head a number of times, each time adding the new spline to the group. To see how this appears, take a look at Figure 8.28.

FIGURE **8.24** *Dangling-spline patch.*

FIGURE **8.25** *Dangling-spline patch rearranged.*

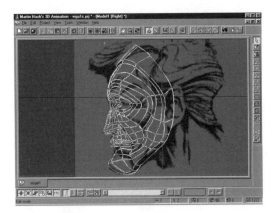

FIGURE **8.26** *Rim of the mask.*

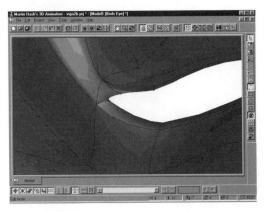

FIGURE **8.27** *Spline loop for the inner mouth.*

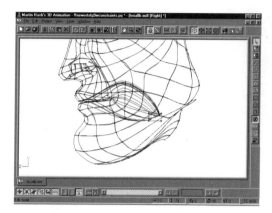

FIGURE **8.28** *Creating the inner mouth.*

To create the eyes (not the actual sphere, but the lids within the orbits), simply create three continuous rings and connect them to the existing hole as shown in Figure 8.29.

Group the innermost splines and name the group something meaningful such as "inner eye," and extrude them into the head. This makes a ledge around the eyes when you place them in their sockets.

Before moving on to building the cranium, turn on **shaded/ wireframe mode** and do a little sculpting and tweaking. Figure 8.30 shows what you have so far.

Aim for smoothness where it's called for, and creases and bulges where they are called for. This is a general principle that can be followed in any modeling job. Perfect smoothness is fine, but not everything is a baby's bottom.

Once you're satisfied, move on to the cranium.

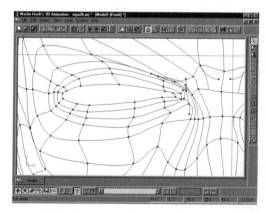

FIGURE **8.29** *Create the eyes.*

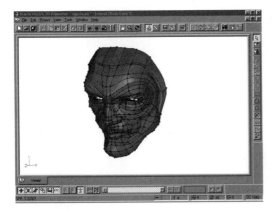

FIGURE **8.30** *Sculpt and tweak the figure.*

MODELING THE CRANIUM

After the preceding words on smoothness, something can be said for the smoothness of the cranium, especially when covered with a rubber mask. A cranium can be as smooth and rounded as a VW Bug. The cranium is the closest thing to a sphere you'll find on the body.

Build Steele's cranium by extruding the top portion of the mask and shaping this to leave an opening for the ears. Again, I recommend shaping each new spline after an extrusion before moving on to the next. After all, how will you know how many extrusions you will need or how they will be shaped if you first extrude them all, then shape them?

Figures 8.31, 8.32, 8.33, and 8.34 show these new splines from the right, front, top, and back views, respectively.

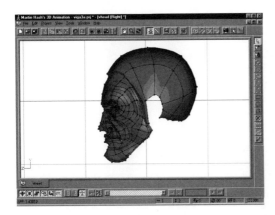

FIGURE **8.31** *The cranium extruded from a portion of the face, right view.*

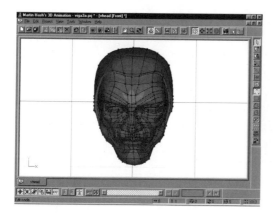

FIGURE **8.32** *Cranium, front view.*

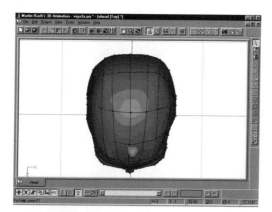

FIGURE **8.33** *Cranium, top view.*

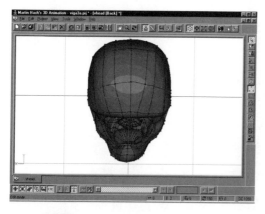

FIGURE **8.34** *Cranium, back view.*

Connect the base of the skull to the jawbone on each side and you will have a series of splines (not continuous in this case), from which you extrude the beginnings of the neck. On the first extrusion, break the new loop where the splines terminate and reattach to create a continuous spline as shown in Figure 8.35.

The ear holes should be continuous spline loops also, so break these apart and reattach the holes to create them. Figure 8.36 shows what this looks like.

Select this loop (an easy way to do this is to select one section of the spline, then press the **comma key**) and extrude into the head a bit.

Now you have Steele's face, cranium, the mask built into our mesh, and two holes that are now crying out to be filled with ears.

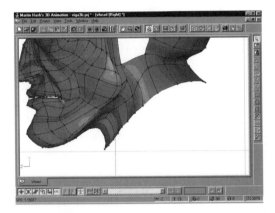

FIGURE **8.35**   *Break and reattach splines to create a continuous spline.*

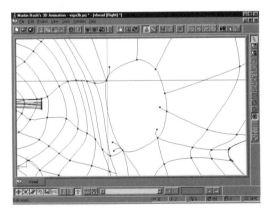

FIGURE **8.36**   *Creating continuous splines for the ear holes. Break and reattach splines to create a continuous spline.*

MODELING THE EAR

Some consider the ear to be one of the most difficult forms to model. The main difficulty is not in the modeling, but rather in the understanding what exactly it is you're looking at.

The ear is not simply a lathed form with a bunch of stuff in the middle. There is, as a matter of fact, a bunch of stuff in there but as most things in the known universe this stuff has been named. Take a look at Figure 8.37 (*Earlabeled.tga*) and familiarize yourself with the names and shapes. The names themselves aren't as important as the shapes, of course, but they'll help a lot in discussing them.

The Y shape near the top and the stem extending off of it is called the *antihelix*. It runs almost, but not quite, parallel with the *helix,* which is the outer rim of the ear and the shape we're probably all most familiar with. The antihelix flows into the *antitragus*, then the *tragus*, both of which are like ledges overhanging the deeply recessed *interagic notch* (the thing you stick a Q-Tip into). That's a lot of scientific words for one paragraph! Let's see if we can tone things down a bit.

Take a moment to familiarize yourself with these elements, then get on with creating the ear. First outline the helix and lobe with three splines as shown in Figure 8.38, and connect them.

Outline the antihelix and its Y shape, again with three splines as shown in Figure 8.39. Remember, ears are as individual as fingerprints, but you can take a look at your own ear for a good general reference.

The middle spline of this Y shape will be pulled out later to give it some bulginess. Connect the upper portion of the ear as shown in Figure 8.40.

Figure 8.41 shows how to fill in the lobe and lower section. The inner spline around the interagic notch will be pulled in toward the head later to give it depth.

Fill in the notch as shown in Figure 8.42.

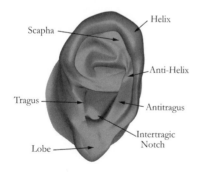

FIGURE **8.37** *The shapes of the ear.*

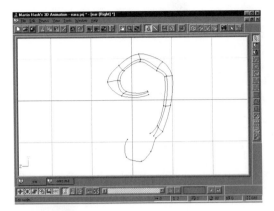

FIGURE **8.38** *Outline the helix.*

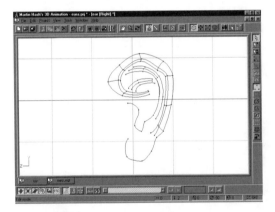

FIGURE **8.39** *Outline the antihelix.*

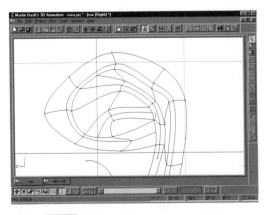

FIGURE **8.40** *Connect the upper portion of the ear.*

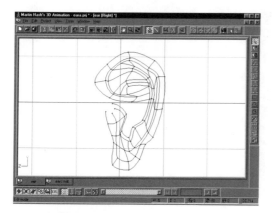

FIGURE **8.41** *Fill in the lower section of the ear.*

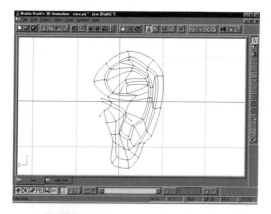

FIGURE **8.42** *Fill in the notch.*

Select the outer two splines of the helix and pull them out (in the front view, move them towards the right). Figure 8.43 shows the CPs to select.

Do the same for the raised portions of the antihelix as shown in Figure 8.44.

Grab the inner spline of the interagic notch and pull it back into the ear as shown in Figure 8.45.

Figure 8.46 shows what you have so far. Some of the bulges look a bit flat, so don't be afraid to adjust the bias and magnitude on them. It's unlikely much muscle motion will be applied to the ear, unless you plan to create Dumbo's twin.

Grab part of the outer contour of the ear and extrude as shown in Figure 8.47, and pull these back toward the head.

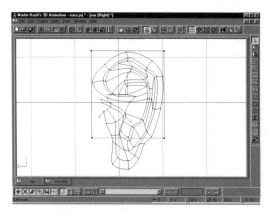

FIGURE **8.43** *Pull out the helix.*

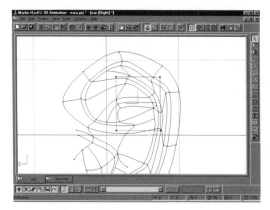

FIGURE **8.44** *Pull out the antihelix.*

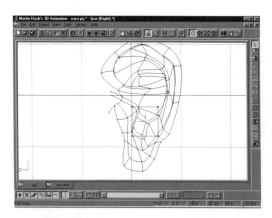

FIGURE **8.45** *Pull the notch into the ear.*

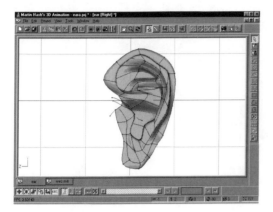

FIGURE **8.46** *The ear under construction.*

Finally, build a flap of skin off of the outer section of the ear. You'll be placing this into the ear holes to give the impression that it's part of the cranium. A number of ears are included on the CD-ROM that you can load to see the wide variety of ear types that can be built using methods similar to these. You can find these ear types in *Chapter8/Steele/Ears.*

Figure 8.48 shows what the completed ear should resemble.

This is a bit of a generic ear. The art director has suggested a somewhat more angular ear, so turn on **shaded/wireframe mode** and modify your model to resemble the sketch more closely. Figure 8.49 shows how this might be done.

When completed, save the model, not the project, as *steele.mdl* (or something similarly meaningful). Since Steele hasn't had his teeth knocked out yet, or his tongue cut off by secret agents, we need to model those.

FIGURE **8.47** *Extrude the back of the ear.*

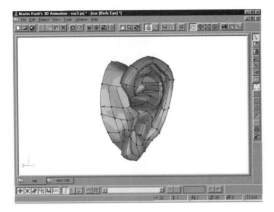

FIGURE **8.48** *The completed ear.*

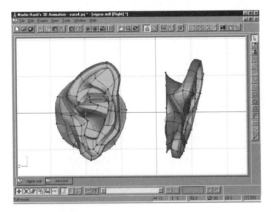

FIGURE **8.49** *The ear reshaped to resemble Steele's ear.*

MODELING THE TEETH AND TONGUE

Steele likes to bare his teeth and snarl a lot, so give him teeth and gums that really stand out and put the fear of Steele into his foes.

Beginning with the two front top teeth, draw an outline as shown in Figure 8.50.

Lathe this with a setting of 4 in the >options>modeling panel and shape the resulting form so it looks like Figure 8.51.

You're interpreting stylized photorealism here, which includes modeling some of the chaos of life. In this case it means each tooth must be created individually. To achieve this, don't be afraid to use bias and magnitude liberally. Figure 8.52 shows the first front tooth.

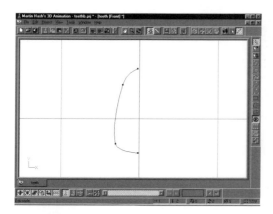

FIGURE **8.50** *Draw the outline of a tooth.*

Copy and paste this to create the second of the pair and adjust it a bit so it's unique. Then continue with this process to model the rest of the teeth, first shaping the copy, then rotating and translating it into its place in the row. This is a prime time to get out that mirror and grin at yourself, for adequate source material. Take a look at Figure 8.53, which shows the completed top row of teeth.

Now move on to the gums. In the right view, create a seven-CP spline as shown in Figure 8.54.

Select the bottom five CPs and extrude them in the top view in such a way that there are two copies above each tooth. Each of these copies is rotated to match the orientation of the tooth it's over. Once you complete one side, reselect the center copy and repeat the process on the other side. The result should look something like Figure 8.55.

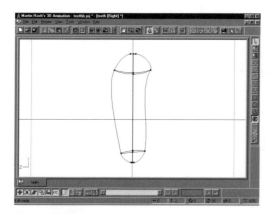

FIGURE **8.51** *Lathe the tooth.*

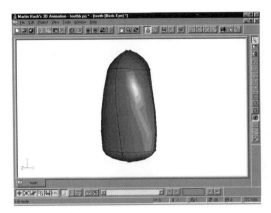

FIGURE **8.52** *The first front tooth.*

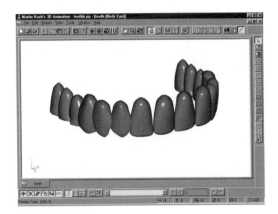

FIGURE **8.53** *The complete top row of teeth.*

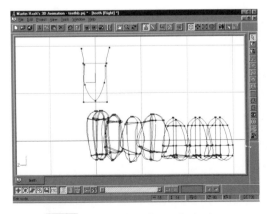

FIGURE **8.54** *Seven-point spline to begin the gums.*

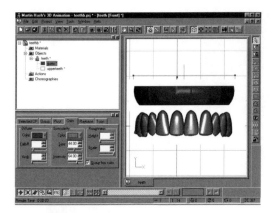

FIGURE **8.55** *Extrude the gum shape.*

Now use bias and magnitude to create the curves you see in Figure 8.56 on the lowest spline. Repeat this all around the gums.

Finally, adjust the bias and magnitude on the first spline from the bottom between each of those spline pairs to create slight bulges. Figure 8.57 shows the completed form. Before you move the gums into position slightly intersecting the teeth, name the group "gums color" and the teeth group "teeth color."

It would be convenient if you could simply copy this row of teeth and flip it to create the bottom row, but you're interpreting the phrase "stylized photorealism," not "demented and totally inaccurate realism." You can, however, follow the same procedure. Figure 8.58 shows this work completed.

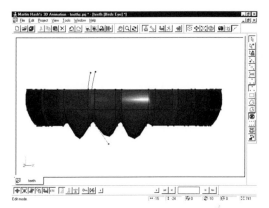

FIGURE **8.56** *Create curves using bias and magnitude.*

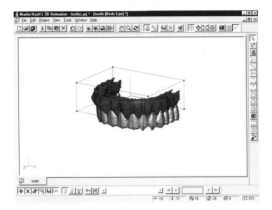

FIGURE **8.57**   *Create bulges with bias and magnitude.*

Now it's time to save the teeth. Before you save the teeth, be sure you have the following groups:

- Teethcolor
- Gumscolor
- Upperteeth
- Lowerteeth

The first two groups isolate the teeth and gums for surfacing, and the second two for animation. (The upper teeth would be part of the skull, and the lower part of the jaw.)

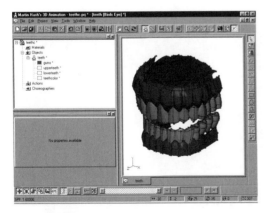

FIGURE **8.58**   *The completed teeth.*

Another detail you might wish to add is the roof of the mouth. You can do this by extruding the inside spline of the gums and scaling to near zero on the Z-axis. You can do the same for the lower teeth, maybe even scale to less than zero to create a mirror of the shape as shown in Figure 8.59.

To create the tongue, simply lathe a spline 4× and shape it using bias and magnitude as shown in Figure 8.60.

Now move on and start on Steele's body, beginning with the arms and torso.

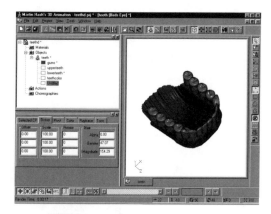

FIGURE **8.59** *Creating the roof of the mouth.*

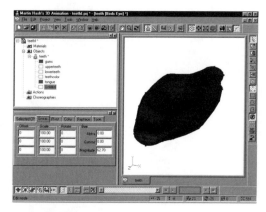

FIGURE **8.60** *Creating the tongue.*

MODELING THE ARMS AND UPPER TORSO

Remember that we're keeping things simple. Well, what could be easier than a lathed spline? We've all lathed candles and vases before, so let's go ahead and do that first; then we'll get into why we're doing it.

Begin by lathing a general shape eight times. Then rotate it in the right view as shown in Figure 8.61.

Take this form and sculpt away to create arms. Do it this way for two reasons: speed, and to test out the various techniques of construction. When you build the leg, you'll use a different technique, mainly to explore the different techniques of construction. When you built the ear, you used another technique, which was spline by spline, and you did the same with the face. You could also have lathed a form and sculpted it into an ear. Just like Steele — the more tricks you have in your belt the more likely you are to find the best one for the job at hand. *You* choose the technique best suited to the way you like to work, and best suited for the object in question.

Figure 8.61 shows the beginnings of the shapes you'll want, which include:

- Biceps
- Triceps
- Deltoids
- Two opposing masses of the forearm

Let's be content with these for now. There are, of course, many more muscles in the arm that can, and in many circumstances should, be modeled. Once you finish these tutorials, hopefully you'll have the urge to pull out the anatomy references and figure out how to lay in the brachialis (bicep and tricep muscles) and extensors (forearm muscles).

Figures 8.62 and 8.63 show the top and back of the arm. You have two options for sculpting here: hide all but the splines you're shaping, or turn on **shaded-wireframe mode**. It's useful to know how to model without shaded mode, but don't consider it a crutch.

Extrude the arm into the chest to create the pectorals. Why not just attach the arm to a lathed torso as you did with the ghost? Simply because a human torso is not a sphere with tubes attached smoothly to the sides, but bone and muscle grafted together in staggered

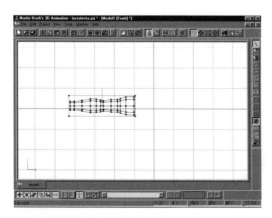

FIGURE **8.61** *Lathe a general arm shape.*

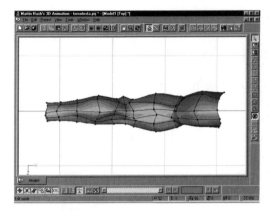

FIGURE **8.62** *Top of the arm.*

patterns. The deltoids, for instance, can be considered both part of the arms, and part of the torso, as can the pectorals. If this is so, the arm attaches to the torso at the clavicle and spine at the front and back, and at the trapezius and rib cage on the top and bottom.

Now it's time for a word about animation. The shoulder will require either some pretty complex bone relationships or quite a lot of muscle-mode tweaking in order for it to have a full range of motion *without* bulging and crimping in unnatural ways. Always keep animation in mind when modeling. The problem here is that you're modeling a somewhat realistic shoulder, the whole of which doesn't rotate around one pivot point. The muscles and tendons, after all, don't attach at one central location.

Grab all the CPs at the end of the arm closest to the body and extrude once. Then shape the new spline loop as shown in Figure 8.64.

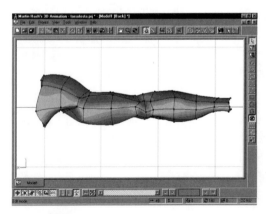

FIGURE **8.63** *Back of the arm.*

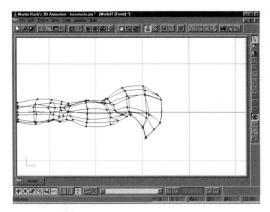

FIGURE **8.64** *Extrude and shape the end of the arm.*

Extrude again and shape as shown in Figure 8.65.

Next, you going to need another spline on the pectoral to give it some shape, so add a spline with a hook as shown in Figure 8.66.

Extrude the edge two more times and shape the pectoral muscle and rib cage as shown in Figure 8.67.

You won't be able to work from the right very easily, so again, you may either hide all but the splines you're working on or turn on **shaded/wireframe mode**. Make sure the rib cage isn't too narrow, and begin to shape the triangularis muscle, although you won't really be able to shape this until you add additional splines. These will probably come off the neck later. Figure 8.68 shows how the back of the figure is formed at this point.

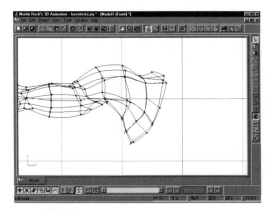

FIGURE **8.65** *Extrude again.*

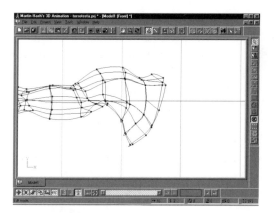

FIGURE **8.66** *Shaping the pectoral.*

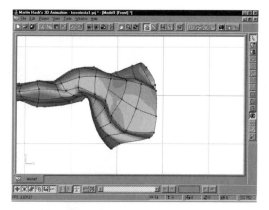

FIGURE **8.67** *Form the pectoral mass.*

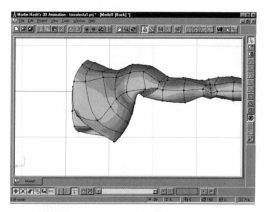

FIGURE **8.68** *The back of the figure.*

Once you are satisfied with your work, select the whole thing, copy and paste it, and flip the copy on the X-axis. Position the copy as shown in Figure 8.69.

Create a spline between these two halves in both the front and back, and connect them as shown in Figures 8.70 and 8.71.

It's pretty obvious that the base of the upper torso is *not* a continuous spline loop, which is what you want when forming the abdominal muscles.

Select this bottom loop and hide everything else. In the top view build a new spline loop around it as shown in Figure 8.72, and connect it.

Shape this ring as shown in Figure 8.73. This will be the base of the rib cage in the front.

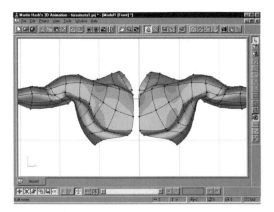

FIGURE **8.69** *Create a copy of the arm.*

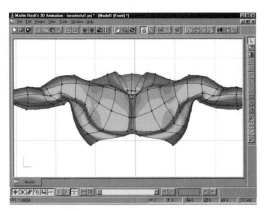

FIGURE **8.70** *Connect the two halves with a spline.*

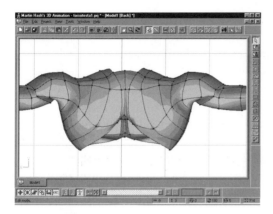

FIGURE **8.71** *Connect the two halves with a spline.*

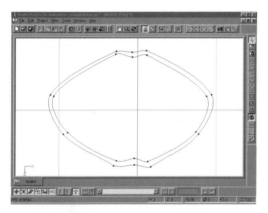

FIGURE **8.72** *Build a new loop under the chest.*

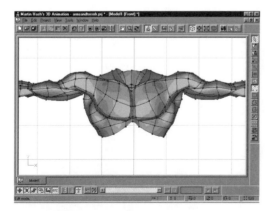

FIGURE **8.73** *Shape the new loop.*

Steele's arms and upper torso are built, and you've created a lathed object that looks more like an arm than a candlestick or vase. Move on to the legs using another technique; then you can connect the two halves like sections of a bee.

MODELING THE LEGS

Steele has fairly powerful legs, but not nearly as bulky as the Incredible Hulk's are. However, they do show some definition, so you will be modeling various bulges.

Again, you'll be using a slightly different technique for building the leg. Start with a simple four-spline cylinder shape, then add splines to outline the muscles and use bias and magnitude adjustments to form the bulges.

Start by creating a contour spline as shown in Figure 8.74.

Then set the lathe to 4x and lathe the spline. Rotate this around the Y-axis so the four splines are on the outside of the leg. Also, since the muscles of the leg are generally lower on the inside, pull the CPs down on the right side of the mesh as shown in Figure 8.75.

In the right view, vaguely sculpt the form of the leg. Don't bulge the calf muscles out, however, because these will be defined with bias adjustment. See Figure 8.76.

Let's take a moment to discuss bulges before starting to lay in the contours of the muscles. To create a bulge, you need two vertical splines of three CPs to define the outer shape. You then adjust bias and magnitude to define its bulginess. Take a look at Figure 8.77. The left shows the spline setup, and the right shows this with bias adjustments. (These examples have nothing to do with the Steele character model.)

Now you have a bulge. What if you need two bulges next to each other? Do you need three vertical splines? Remember: When curvature becomes convex on one side of a CP, it

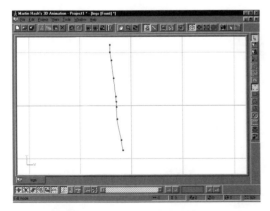

FIGURE **8.74** *Create a contour spline for the leg.*

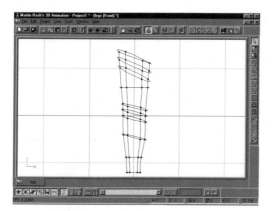

FIGURE **8.75** *Adjust the lathed form.*

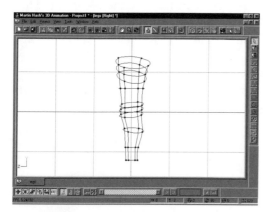

FIGURE **8.76** *Vaguely sculpt the form of the leg.*

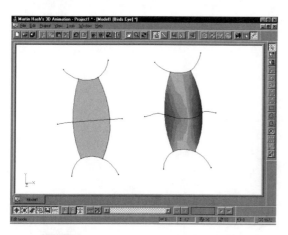

FIGURE **8.77** *A bulge.*

becomes concave on the opposite side. Take a look at the object on the left side of Figure 8.78.

You attempted to create two bulges with three splines, but instead you created a sort of *wave*. Keep this in mind, even though it's not what you want here. Look at the right side of Figure 8.78 (bulge2) where you created two bulges with four splines. This works because the area between the two middle splines becomes concave while the area between the two outer pairs becomes convex, or bulgy. This is what you want — think of the area between the two as a point of rest.

How does magnitude relate to this type of bulge? To put it simply, magnitude will define how far the bulge extends from the object. Take a look at some bulges with increasing magnitude applied, as shown in Figure 8.79.

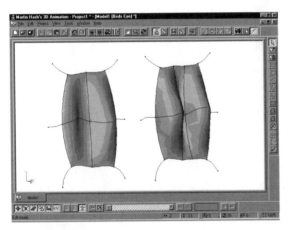

FIGURE **8.78** *Two bulges side by side.*

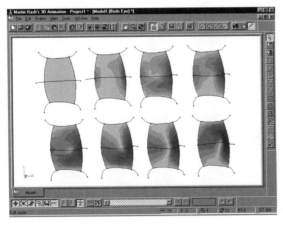

FIGURE **8.79** *Bulges with increasing magnitude.*

Pretty impressive stuff when considering that no additional splines were added to achieve the definition of the bulges.

Begin placing the outer contours of the muscles. First, hide all but the two front splines. In the front view, add four splines in the middle as shown in Figure 8.80.

Notice that the two in the center are the bulges, and the outer two are the point-of-rest splines. Now hide all but the back of the leg and add two splines as shown in Figure 8.81.

Now you can begin adjusting the bias and magnitude on the muscle splines to create bulges. Take a look at Figure 8.82 to see what this begins to look like.

The bulge above the knee is the rectus femoris, and below the knee is the tibia. The muscle to the left on the upper leg is the vastus externus, and will share a point-of-rest

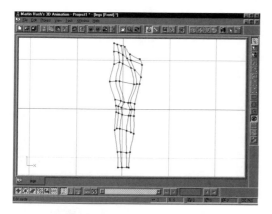

FIGURE 8.80 *Add four splines to the front of the leg.*

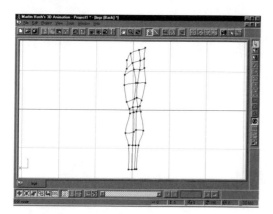

FIGURE 8.81 *Add two splines to the back of the leg.*

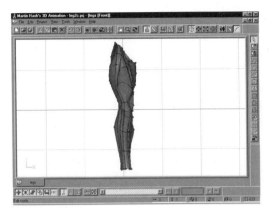

FIGURE 8.82   *Adjust bias and magnitude on the muscle shapes.*

spline with the rectus femoris. The muscle on the right is the adductor longus. Again, there are many more muscles visible on the surface of a well-developed leg, and I strongly recommend pulling out that anatomy reference, learning where they are and what they do, and modeling them. It's only then that you can begin to design realistic characters rather than simply report what you see. But note: Be sure to place all your splines before beginning bias adjustments. Adding splines becomes a very trying venture after bias has been increased, and you'll develop migraines very quickly as you are forced to readjust everything as you add splines.

Figures 8.83, 8.84, and 8.85 show the leg after bias and magnitude adjustments have been applied all around. If you wish, you can load the file *Chapter8\Steele\legsa.mdl* from

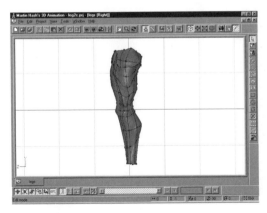

FIGURE 8.83   *The bias adjusted leg.*

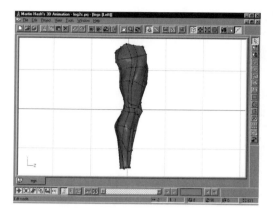

FIGURE **8.84** *The bias adjusted leg.*

the CD and inspect how the bias and magnitude have been altered by selecting a spline and checking the numbers in the properties panel.

Figure 8.86 shows four views of the leg in rendered mode to clarify what you're after. These are pretty bold muscles, but since Steele is a somewhat lean guy (never forget that they aren't just legs, but a particular *character's* legs), you may want to tone them down a bit later. As a mater of fact, as a general procedure you might lay in bold forms first and tone down, rather than bulk up later.

Now move on to the feet, which simply will be extruded off the end of the leg. Again, every time you extrude, deselect the points and sculpt them before continuing.

Figure 8.87 shows the foot in the left view extruded off the leg and sculpted into shape. There is, of course, a hole in the tip. This can be patched easily as shown in Figure 8.88.

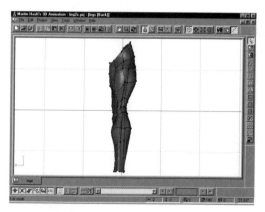

FIGURE **8.85** *The bias adjusted leg.*

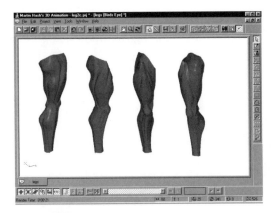

FIGURE **8.86** *Four views of the leg.*

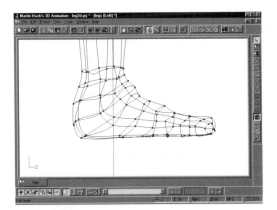

FIGURE **8.87** *The foot extruded from the leg and shaped, left view.*

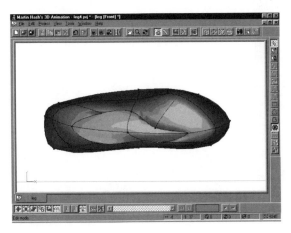

FIGURE **8.88** *Patch the hole at the tip of the foot.*

Now take a look at Figures 8.89, 8.90, and 8.91, which show the foot from the front, right, and back views for reference. Note the formation of the big toe indicated with a slight bulge.

Now you have one full leg. Copy this, paste it, and flip it on the X-axis. Then position the copy as shown in Figure 8.92.

Connect these with the groin, stomach, and buttocks. Select the spline loop at the top of one of the legs and copy/paste it between the two legs. Then turn on scale mode and scale this to near zero on the X-axis, effectively flattening it. Now delete the CPs at the top of the spline since they won't be used.

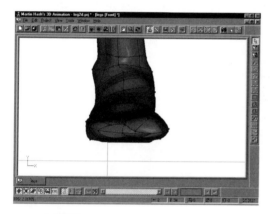

FIGURE 8.89   *Foot, front view.*

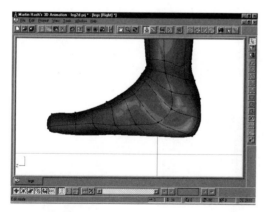

FIGURE 8.90   *Foot, right view.*

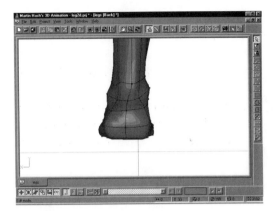

FIGURE **8.91** *Foot, back view.*

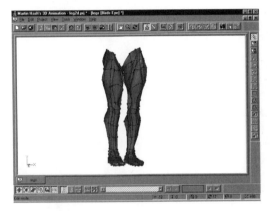

FIGURE **8.92** *Create a mirror of the leg.*

This, with the addition of a pair of splines on either side, allows you to patch between the legs. Figures 8.93 and 8.94 show how this is done. Notice that the two splines on either side of the center terminate with hooks. You may decide to continue these around to the buttocks later; leave them as is for now.

Figure 8.95 shows the legs as they stand (no pun intended). Remember, you are a designer, not a reporter, so yours may not look exactly like these.

That wasn't too bad. Let's move on to the hands.

MODELING THE HANDS

Human hands are almost little characters in their own right when you consider their complexity. They play a huge part in character expression as a whole. Try acting out various

FIGURE **8.93** *Legs connected, front view.*

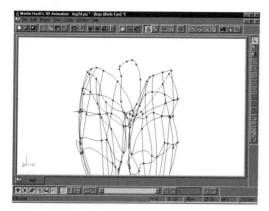

FIGURE **8.94** *Legs connected, rear view.*

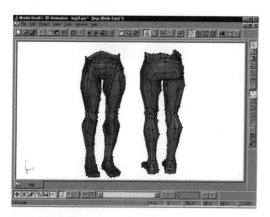

FIGURE **8.95** *The legs.*

emotions with your hands as though they were puppets. Keep an eye on the folding, creasing, and bulging going on. You need to put enough detail into the hand meshes to allow for some fancy muscle animation later on.

Let's begin by creating the contour of a finger as shown in Figure 8.96.

Set lathe to 8 in the >options>modeling panel, lathe the spline, and rotate it in the right view so it is oriented as shown in Figure 8.97.

Next, shape the splines as shown in Figure 8.98.

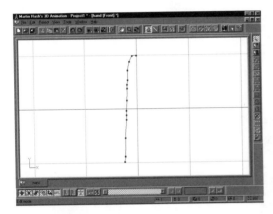

FIGURE **8.96** *Create the contour of a finger.*

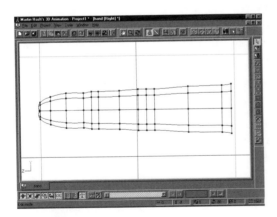

FIGURE **8.97** *Lathe and orient the finger.*

Splines

Hide the bottom of the finger and adjust the splines to look like Figure 8.99.

Hide the top and shape the finger pads in the bottom view to look like Figure 8.100.

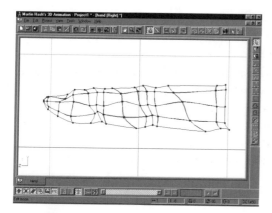

FIGURE **8.98** *Shape the Splines.*

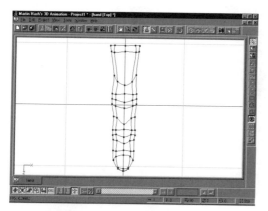

FIGURE **8.99** *Shape the top of the finger.*

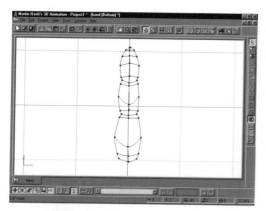

FIGURE **8.100** *Shape the finger pads.*

Remember that you have an excellent reference at the end of your arm. Figure 8.101 shows what you have so far.

Now select all the fingers and name the group something meaningful such as "finger." This is important because once you add the fingernail, you don't want to have to figure out which CPs belong to the finger and which belong to the nail.

To create the fingernail, select the CPs you see selected in Figure 8.102.

Then copy these and paste them a bit above the finger. Hide all but the fingernail and shape it in the top view as shown in Figure 8.103.

Now select the whole fingernail, extrude it, and scale the extrusion down a bit. Figure 8.104 shows you how this appears.

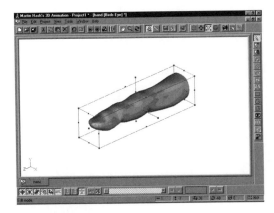

FIGURE **8.101** *The finger.*

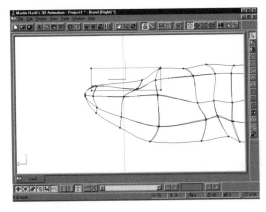

FIGURE **8.102** *Select CPs for the fingernail.*

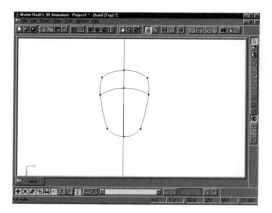

FIGURE **8.103** *Shape the fingernail.*

Next, select the whole fingernail and name the group. Now unhide your finger and position the nail as shown in Figure 8.105. Look at your own finger to see how the nail emerges.

You'll use this finger to form the other three, so save it as *finger.mdl*, then import it three times. Do this instead of copying and pasting it to maintain the group names. You'll notice the project workspace now contains the groups finger1, finger2, finger3, etc. Scale these and position them where they would lay on the hand. The middle finger is the largest and the furthest forward, and the pinky is the smallest and longest.

Now tweak each finger into shape. You should use your own hand or a photo as reference; however, here are a few useful hints to keep in mind as you work.

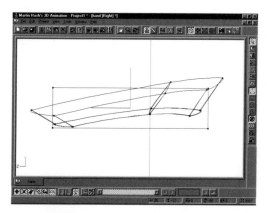

FIGURE **8.104** *Extrude the fingernail to give it depth.*

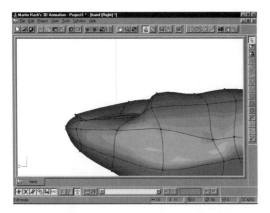

FIGURE **8.105** *Position the fingernail in the finger.*

- The fingers generally arch in toward the middle finger.
- The segments of the fingers as seen from the top are of different lengths.
- The pads of a finger as seen from the palm side of the hand are all of the same length. Look at your own fingers and you'll see that not all the creases are directly under the joints because of this.
- The lengths of the index and ring fingers end at the midpoint of the last section of the middle finger.
- The pinky ends at the joint of the last section of the ring finger.

Figure 8.106 shows how these fingers are sculpted. You must keep in mind the character of the subject as you work on such things. Steele's hands must be used for delicate

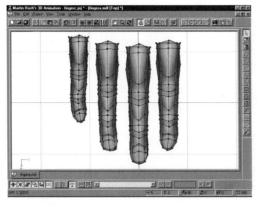

FIGURE **8.106** *The sculpted fingers.*

work such as picking locks and assembling small explosive devices, but they must also be used for beating people to a jelly. Thus, they're thin, but they're a bit gnarled. What you *don't* want to end up with are four sausages that have simply been scaled relative to each other. These were kept somewhat separated from each other to ease selection when shaping, but they should now be moved in close to each other.

Now hide all but the spline rings at the end of each finger closest to the hand. In the front view, encircle these with a spline as shown in Figure 8.107. Note the number and placement of CPs.

In the side view select the topmost CPs and pull them back a bit. If you look at your own hand, you'll see that the spaces between the fingers slope outward from top to bottom. This is what we have just created, as shown in Figure 8.108.

In the front view, connect the inner rings to the outer rings as shown in Figure 8.109.

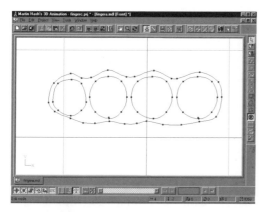

FIGURE **8.107** *Encircle the ends of the fingers with a spline loop.*

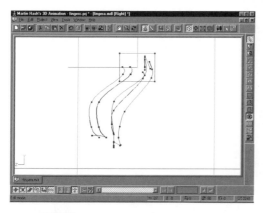

FIGURE **8.108** *Pull back the top CPs.*

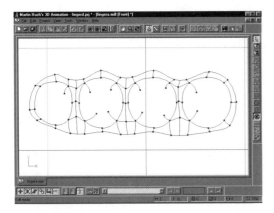

FIGURE 8.109 *Connect the inner rings to the outer rings.*

Figure 8.110 shows the completed finger-hand juncture.

To create the thumb, copy one of the fingers from the second knuckle to the top (ten CPs long), rotate it into position, and shape it as shown in Figure 8.111. Again, use your own thumb as reference. Also be sure to pick out the nail CPs and name their group.

Now select the spline surrounding the fingers and extrude it back into the wrist. (You could lessen the spline count through the use of hooks, but in this case use all those splines to form tendons with bias adjustments.) Attach the thumb to the hand in a manner similar to what you used in the ghost hand exercise. See Figure 8.112.

Take a look at Figures 8.113 and 8.114, which show the thumb/palm juncture in greater detail.

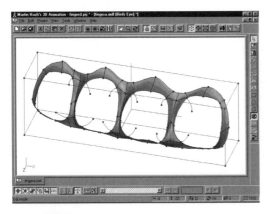

FIGURE 8.110 *The completed finger-hand juncture.*

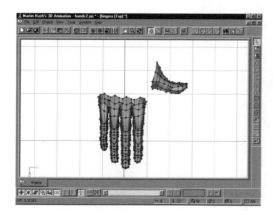

FIGURE **8.111** *Create the thumb.*

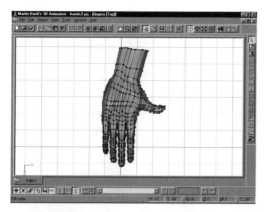

FIGURE **8.112** *Extrude the spline loop to create the body of the hand.*

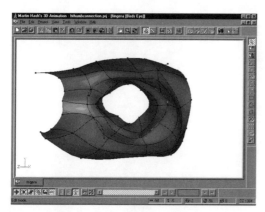

FIGURE **8.113** *The thumb/palm juncture.*

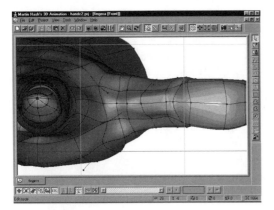

FIGURE **8.114** *The thump/palm juncture.*

Now with **shaded/wireframe mode** on, sculpt the palm side of the hand as shown in Figure 8.115.

Now that you're done with the hand, save the model. Something you might consider is rotating the hand and boning it here; that way you can import it into the main model twice and both copies will already contain bones. Then you would flip the mesh and scale the bones 100 percent (effectively mirroring them). This tutorial does not cover this however.

You now have all the major elements of Steele: the head, the arms and torso, the legs, and the hands. The hands simply will be placed within the sleeve (we create the sleeve by extruding the end of the arm and scaling it down a bit to give it some depth). The torso, however, must be connected to the legs with the use of splines.

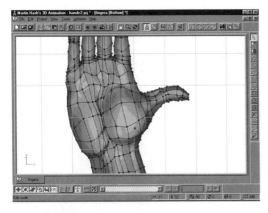

FIGURE **8.115** *Sculpt the palm.*

CONNECTING ALL THE PIECES

As previously mentioned, the two major sections will be connected like the sections of a bee. The stuff that goes in the middle is just what you'd expect — the abdominals and the lower back.

Open a new project and model window and import *arms.mdl* and *legs.mdl*, then scale and adjust these to their relative proportions. Figure 8.116 shows these two forms positioned, but they still need to be tweaked quite a bit.

Now select the spline loop under the chest and extrude it down three times and shape the new area as shown in Figures 8.117 and 8.118.

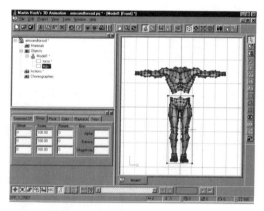

FIGURE **8.116** *Position and scale the two sections of the body.*

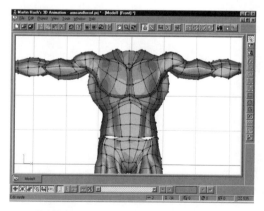

FIGURE **8.117** *Extrude the chest into the midsection.*

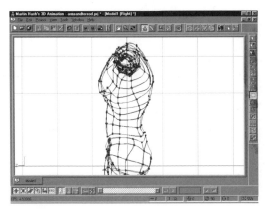

FIGURE **8.118** *Extrude the chest into the midsection.*

Now hide all but the midsection you see in Figure 8.119 and begin to connect them.

Since you can see there aren't enough splines on the top section, use hooks. Continue the new splines into the stomach beyond the waist before hooking as shown in Figure 8.120. Hooks are pretty robust, but doing this avoids any tearing at the joint.

Figures 8.121 and 8.122 show the two sections stitched together.

Hide all but the front of the stomach area, and form the abdominal muscles using bias and magnitude. First, pull out the CPs for the first row of abdominals as shown in Figure 8.123, increase the magnitude, and widen the peak of the curves on both the horizontal and vertical splines.

For the second row of abdominals, adjust bias as shown in Figure 8.124.

Finally, adjust the stomach as shown in Figure 8.125.

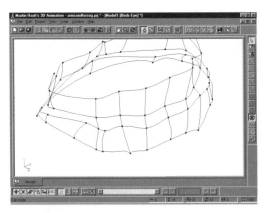

FIGURE **8.119** *Connect the midsection to the hips.*

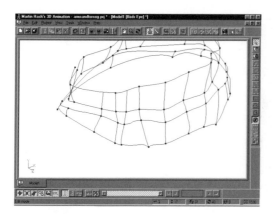

FIGURE **8.120** *Place hooks beyond the waist.*

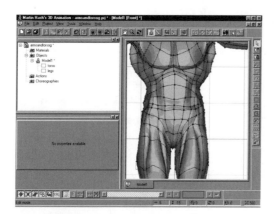

FIGURE **8.121** *The two sections stitched together.*

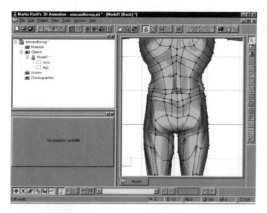

FIGURE **8.122** *The two sections stitched together.*

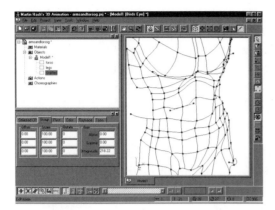

FIGURE **8.123** *Create the first row of abdominals with bias.*

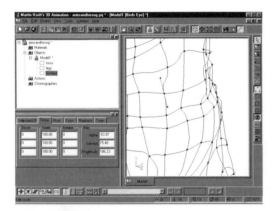

FIGURE **8.124** *Create the second row of abdominals with bias.*

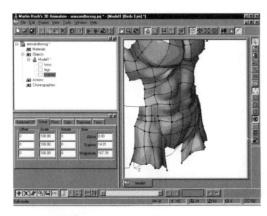

FIGURE **8.125** *Adjust the stomach.*

You may have noticed that there are two hooks on the stomach and two on the buttocks. Break these four hooks and connect them by inserting splines. This will allow you to give more shape to the groin and buttocks areas as shown in Figure 8.126.

Sculpt the back of the torso and add any necessary splines as shown in Figure 8.127.

Now attach the head. Import the *steele.mdl* project, scale it relative to the body, and position it over the torso. Then extrude the neck down from the head, and in the process, break some of the splines and reattach them to new spline as hooks. This is shown in Figure 8.128.

Attach the neck to the shoulder. Notice that the Adam's apple and sterno mastoids (the muscles running from behind the ear down to the pit of the neck) have been indicated with slight bulges.

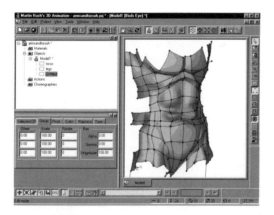

FIGURE **8.126** *Break the four hooks and connect the front to the back.*

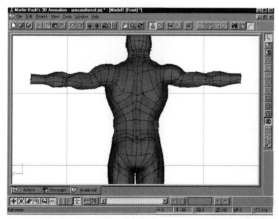

FIGURE **8.127** *Sculpt the back and add necessary splines.*

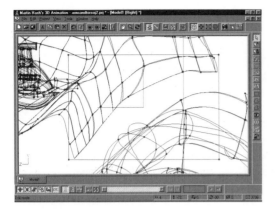

FIGURE **8.128** *Lessen the spline count on the neck with hooks.*

Figures 8.129, 8.130, and 8.131 show these connections from three views. Notice that some of these splines have been continued through the trapezius muscle to terminate near the shoulders. These splines give you the opportunity to shape the trapezius more accurately.

Now import the hands and position them as previously discussed.

⇨ HINT

This method is helpful for setting these up for eventual animation. By placing the wrists within the sleeves, you've greatly eased the task of rotating the forearm (supination and pronation). To do this you would bone the wrist separately from the forearm so it can rotate *within* the sleeve, and the rest of the forearm can mimic this rotation to a lesser degree. Unfortunately, further discussion of this is beyond the scope of the tutorial.

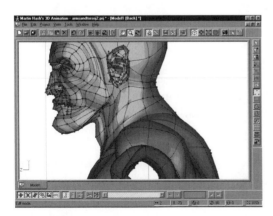

FIGURE **8.129** *The neck connected to the shoulders.*

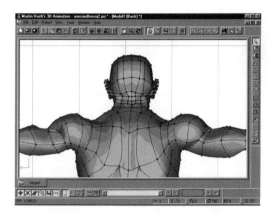

FIGURE **8.130** *The neck connected to the shoulders.*

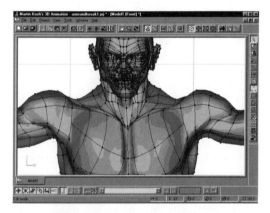

FIGURE **8.131** *The neck connected to the shoulders.*

SURFACING STEELE

For the most part, we'll be using the techniques described in Chapter 9, which you should read before continuing. The exception is the face, which we will flatten.

The first step, as you read in Chapter 9, is to create groups, or "split up" your model. Of course, we aren't actually breaking any splines, but creating groups.

CREATING GROUPS

Open the project *Steeltexgroup.prj* to see the numerous groups that were created for Steele. Also notice that two actions were created:

- **Faceflatten.** The face is flattened to allow it to be mapped with one decal without stretching at the sides.
- **Bodytexture.** The feet have been rotated down a bit so the tops can be surfaced with the same decal that will be applied to the front of the suit.

Notice that the name of all the groups that have been created for the purpose of decaling begin with a T, which stands for texture. Naming your surfaces this way will make it much easier to keep track of which surfaces need image maps.

The topics of taking snapshots and painting textures are covered in Chapter 9, so move onto applying the decals after they have been created.

APPLYING THE MAPS

The process of applying the decals is as follows:

1. Hide all but the group you will be decaling.
2. Open the wireframe bitmap (the template you used as a template for painting over).
3. Scale and position the decal over the mesh (holding down the **Shift key** while scaling will constrain the aspect ratio).
4. Apply the decal.
5. Replace the wireframe bitmap with the actual texture map.

The benefit of first applying the template to the mesh instead of the texture is that it allows wonderfully exact positioning. Simply line up the decal until the wireframe appears to vanish into the mesh.

To apply more than one decal at the same position, say to add bump and diffuse maps, simply copy each of the four position values in the properties panel of the first decal and paste them into the properties panel of the second decal, then apply.

Before you begin applying all those decals you've created, you might want to add one last bit of mesh to the model for eyelashes. We can do this by extruding the tops and bottoms of each eye twice, as shown in Figure 8.132.

Create two new mapping groups, upper lashes and lower lashes, for this new geometry. Snapshots of these would be taken from the top view, and then cookie-cut maps painted to create the individual lashes.

The way cookie-cut maps work in AM is this: The RGB values give the patches their color, and the alpha channel acts as the cutter. Keep in mind that no antialiasing in the alpha channel is taken into consideration. A pixel is either on or off, so make your cookie-cut maps at least twice as large as you normally would.

Here are a couple tips on applying the decals to Steele:

- Since the feet were rotated in the Bodytexture action, you should apply the sole decals in the modeling window in the bottom viewport. (In general, find a position for decaling that gives you the flattest surface possible.)
- If you want to apply the same decal to the right and left sides of a mesh, you can mirror, or flip the decal horizontally by swapping the left and right decal position values in the properties panel. This is exactly what was done to map the sides of Steele's costume, and both inner leg surfaces.

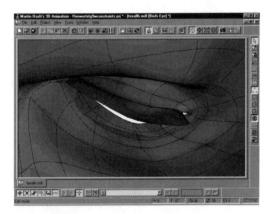

FIGURE **8.132** *Extrude the eyelashes.*

The last touch for Steele is to load the file *Chapter9\Steele\Utilitybelt.mdl* and position it at his waist. And that's it! Take a look at Figure 8.133 to see what Steele looks like when fully surfaced.

You're done modeling the superhero! As you can see, it takes a bit more work to create complex characters but it really isn't terribly difficult. It just takes a commitment to see it through. Now it's your turn to see what you can do. Go back and see if you can add muscle detail to Steele. Beef him up a bit, give him a little more character. Basically, have some fun.

CONCLUSION

There is certainly much more to learn in regard to characters, such as animation and bones, but that will have to be for another book. If you do plan on boning and animating Steele, keep in mind that he's a fairly complex mesh and you'll need to use a few constraint tricks and some muscle animation to keep him from crimping and bulging up in areas. This isn't a problem, of course, because you've become accustomed to hard work.

FIGURE **8.133** *Steele with his surfacing applied.*

A final word: You should use the ideas presented in this chapter, and indeed the whole book, as a springboard to creating your own characters and creatures. Don't be afraid to experiment with new techniques and working procedures, and by all means improve upon those you've learned here. The sky is truly the limit. Say, there's an idea; why don't you make Steele a cape?

Just remember, there is no limit to what you can do if you just put your mind to it — and maybe a couple of splines, too.

PART

V

Surfacing Your Creatures

Now that you've spent countless hours perfecting the ultimate 3D character, what's next? It's time to bring that character to life with surfacing. This is no simple task, but it doesn't have to be as daunting as it appears. Traditional views held that creating seamlessly surfaced creatures and characters without the use of UV mapping was impossible, or at least improbable. Well, that couldn't be further from the truth.

Creating seamless surfacing is just a matter of understanding the surfacing tools and where they are best used. This part covers everything you need to know about seamlessly surfacing your characters. It also covers some very useful techniques for creating details on your character's surfaces that add tremendous credibility to its photorealism.

Photorealistic Creature Surfacing

by Geoffrey Smith

There are 3D graphics, and then there are photorealistic 3D graphics. Both have their respective place in the world of art and commerce. But if you're reading this book you're probably interested in learning how to create photorealistic 3D characters. One striking feature that really separates a unique, photorealistic 3D model from a mediocre one is the use of high-quality surface maps.

3D models don't need to be photorealistic to be worthwhile, but some thought does need to be given to the surface of the model if it's going to stand out as a photorealistic 3D object or character.

How often have you seen an otherwise very cool looking CG model that just doesn't seem quite finished because the surfacing is poorly done? Probably all too often. In most cases the reason for this is that its surface seems unrealistic and intangible. The surface consists simply of a primary color, which looks like some kind of smooth, unworldly plastic and if there is any texture to the surface, it's probably a noticeably repeating pattern. Such is the nature of default 3D shaders. If you want to create stunning, realistic images you can't rely on default shaders. Why? Because they simply do not have the detail and chaos that's required to mimic the details of real world surfaces.

Unfortunately, it seems that many 3D artists don't take full advantage of the surfacing capabilities hiding inside their 3D applications. In most cases, this is because artists simply don't know how to access those capabilities or they don't realize the importance of an object's surface. It's as if the creator of a character or object sees surfacing as a secondary, nonimportant task, and gives very little or no thought as to what the surface of their creation might be. Sure, surfacing can be difficult and rather daunting, but why go through all the effort to create a really stunning model, only to undermine it with poor surfacing?

This chapter will shed some light on the thought process and actual activity involved in creating photorealistic image maps for your 3D creatures. To illustrate this process, we'll use the fabulous creature represented in Figure 9.1.

This is Chubbs in all of his photorealistic glory. Not your average 3D model thrown together with cylinders and spheres, to be sure. Chubbs was a very cool model to begin with, but once the image maps were added, he became more than just a cool 3D model; he became Chubbs, a character with life and personality.

As with just about any creative process, there are a few important steps to follow when you set out on the path to creating photorealistic image maps. These steps are outlined briefly here, and discussed in greater depth later in this chapter.

THE SIX STEPS TO CREATING PHOTOREALISTIC IMAGE MAPS

1. Defining the character's biography and environment, which determines the look of the character.
2. Splitting the model into separate sections for surfacing.
3. Rendering out views of the model to be used as templates for surfacing.

4. Working with painting programs and painting the image maps. These include color, bump, specular, diffusion, and/or transparency maps.
5. Creating seamless image maps.
6. Creating test renders and tweaking problem areas.

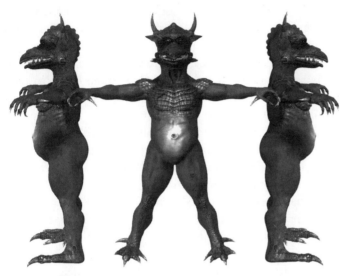

FIGURE **9.1** *Chubbs in all of his final glory.*

Then sit back and enjoy your creation. Let's start with the first step to creating some awesome creature image maps.

THE CHARACTER'S BIOGRAPHY

When it comes to surfacing a photorealistic character, the first questions you want to ask yourself are the same questions any good actor asks when preparing for a role: "Where did I come from?" "Where am I going?" and "How did I get here?"

Basically, before you can apply the skin to your character, you need to know where that skin has been. Before surfacing the 3D character, Chubbs, I received a very thorough description of him from his creator.

CHUBBS' BIOGRAPHY

Chubbs, who acquired his name for obvious reasons, is a one-inch-tall alien that lives thousands of feet beneath the earth's crust. He spends much of his time riding around on his faithful steed, a Madagascar Hissing Cockroach shown in Figure 9.2. They are quite the menacing duo!

Chubbs is the last of a long line of warriors who were bred for violence. When he was but a wee lad, Chubby promised his venerable dying father that he would strive to unite and protect the last remnants of his vanishing race from extinction.

As you can see by Chubbs' heavy build, he requires vast food stores in order to keep his figure. The only problem is that his main food source, the nymph beetle, is also the main food source of the Jartung Dogth. The Jartung Dogth happens to be a fiercely competitive, six-legged, underground weasel, who would like nothing better than to see the end of Chubbs' family bloodline and to annihilate the last of the small Chubby tribe. Considering that Chubbs is only an inch tall, while the Jartung Dogth is well over eight inches in length, you can see Chubbs has his work cut out for him.

Take a look at Figure 9.3. You can see that Chubbs is ornamented with many horns, which serve him well in protecting those vulnerable areas like his spine. Now take a look at those hazardous horns, which protrude from his arms, head, hands, and feet. These serve him well as formidable weapons, which he uses to dismember his enemies.

Take a look at his shoulders, chest, and elbows as shown in Figure 9.4. You can see that he has very thick skin like a rhino's, which serves to protect his vital organs and weak joints such as his elbows. Now take a look at the skin covering his belly. Notice how it's softer, more like a human's skin, which makes him vulnerable in this area. It's always a good idea to include some area of vulnerability on your characters since their predators need some way of penetrating their defenses.

Although Chubbs can be fierce, he's also a very wise warrior with considerable cunning. He's certainly not a mindless brute. In fact, he is often immersed in moments of

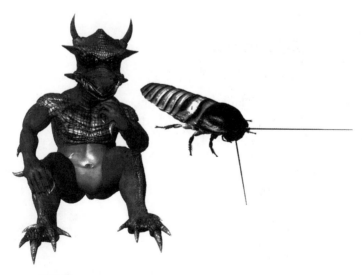

FIGURE **9.2** *Chubbs and his faithful steed.*

FIGURE **9.3** *Chubbs' formidable horns.*

deep contemplation. After all, wouldn't you be if the weight of your species' survival balanced on your shoulders?

When he's not responsibly involved in the mixed roles of provider and protector for his people, Chubbs can be found playing a unique version of chess whereby the two players sit astride an ornamented Raven's beak, and use diamonds as playing pieces, something that no doubt makes J. P. Morgan roll over in his grave.

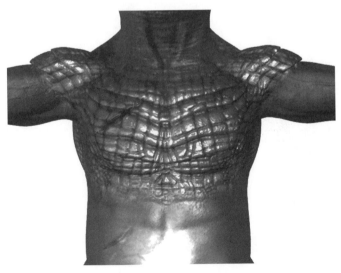

FIGURE **9.4** *Chubbs' upper chest and top view of his arm.*

FIGURE **9.5** *Chubbs' camouflaged skin coloration.*

Chubbs struggles much of the time buried deep within the strata of the earth, so nature has kindly provided Chubbs with a very useful camouflage, shown in Figure 9.5. Notice that his body colors are earth tones: tan, reddish-brown, and rust, which allow him to blend into his environment. He also proudly bears the remains of many battle scars, both new and old, which adorn his tough little body.

Take a look at his head in Figure 9.6. Notice how he has a soft and pitted nose, somewhat like a cow's. This affords him the potential to appear gentle and humorous.

FIGURE **9.6** *Chubbs' rendered head.*

We certainly don't want Chubbs to be limited to mere aggression and anger. In fact, he's been known to be quite the joker at times. Notice how his face is rather wrinkled and porous, displaying Chubbs' struggle, the striation of years. His gums are wrinkled much the way a human's are, but a bit more exaggerated, which is the result of the many facial expressions he has made over the years.

He has soft ears that enable him to register even the slightest out-of-place sound in the underground caverns. When you're only an inch tall you need plenty of warning when danger approaches. Don't forget the powerful horns on Chubbs' head, which have been worked thoroughly and show plenty of battle scars. These are not the newly sprouted horns of a youth, but the battered, old horns of a veteran warrior who has known few moments of peace on this earth.

Given a description of this depth, surfacing Chubbs becomes not a chore to be undertaken but rather a creative adventure! You're able to help create the reality of something that certainly does not exist. At the same time, you can help to bring about a reality that others can enjoy.

At this point, Chubbs becomes something more than a mere 3D character; he becomes a living, breathing incarnation with a distinct personality. This gives you a profile that you can use to create the appropriate skin, wrinkles, scars, bruises, scales, and other surface attributes that are the result of Chubbs' experiences and life. The challenge now is to carry that reality to others when they view Chubbs.

After your imagination has had a chance to run amok and come back to earth, it's time to get the raw material that is the Chubbs model in Figure 9.7, to match up with your imagination's vision of what Chubbs should look like when you're done with him.

FIGURE **9.7** *Chubbs in the raw — no image maps here.*

Once you're clear on the type of environment the creature inhabits, what his biological predisposition is, and what his behavior is like, you can begin planning which types of surfaces are most appropriate for this type of creature. The first step in this process is to gather source material.

GATHERING SOURCE MATERIAL

Source material is the foundation of quality creature surfacing. It provides a starting point for the surfacing. You could rely on your imagination to surface the character, but if you want it to be truly photorealistic you'll need to mimic the creature surfaces of real-world animals.

Since you know that Chubbs is a warrior, some type of armor plating might be helpful to cover the vital areas like his chest, shoulders, eyes, spine, elbows, and knees. But this plating should also look organic, as if a creature could grow this type of skin, rather than looking like he's wearing a suit of armor. Something akin to the underbelly of an alligator might be the appropriate reference for his plating since it's flexible and tough. See Figure 9.8 for an alligator reference image.

As you can see, this image serves as a great reference for creating the scales on Chubbs' skin. In this case, the color is not the primary concern, but rather the detail of the scales. Chubbs' colors won't match any crocodile or alligator so you need to find other source material for this attribute.

The next step is either to head out to the library or start surfing the Internet for imagery. The local library provides a huge selection of high-quality images for free.

FIGURE **9.8** *The alligator reference image.*

Although the Internet can offer a lot of images, it's just too slow and the quality of images is rarely adequate for source material. Besides, how many dead links can you find before you become completely homicidal?

In the interests of sparing my sanity, I headed to the library and picked up several *National Geographic* magazines, which had some great alligator photos. I also grabbed a bunch of books on insects and mammals; since Chubbs lives among and eats mainly insects, but has many of the physical attributes of a mammal, I figured that these might come in handy.

Photographic references and scans are really necessary when it comes to creating photorealistic image maps. That sounds obvious, but you'd be surprised at how many people neglect to take the time to research photographic, visual cues for reference. Even when it comes to recreating the look of human skin for a model, many folks will not ever bother to grab a mirror or simply to look at their own hands as a reference. You may think that you know what the surface of something looks like, but when it comes to artistically recreating that surface, it is surprising how little you know or remember about what is actually there in reality. In fact, consider an example using a unique character named Scratch, shown in Figure 9.9.

Figure 9.9 provides a nice close-up of Scratch's back. Most people would have remembered the skin tone of hands and most likely the wrinkles on the knuckles, but would anyone be able to recreate the minute creases and cracks in the skin without source material? Probably not, since no one typically catalogs the tiny details in memory. Surely no one would have remembered to add the tiny hair follicles that are visible on the back of the fingers.

FIGURE **9.9** *The importance of using source material.*

As you can see, it's of paramount importance that you utilize source material if you plan to make your creature surfacing photorealistic.

➡ **TIP**

Always use reference photos to point you in the right direction. There is nothing like mother nature when it comes to creating endlessly interesting visual resources, so be sure to utilize her fine artwork and gather some photographed resource images.

Let's return to the discussion on Chubbs' surfaces. Since Chubbs' nose is a bit like a cow's, take a look at what a cow's nose really looks like, in Figure 9.10.

Notice how the light is captured in specific areas, while it puddles in others. This makes the nose appear wet. Now take a look at the irregularities on the surface. How would it feel to the touch? Probably rather sticky since I've never seen a cow that wasn't licking its nose.

The nose is a small, isolated feature that can possibly be done without source material, but for the wrinkles on Chubbs' skin you'll definitely to need the assistance of Mother Nature. In nature, the closest thing to what Chubbs requires for that tough, leathery skin is the skin of the black rhinoceros. Take a look at Figure 9.11.

Notice how the rhino skin wrinkles at specific joints, the thickness of it, and how it slightly hangs from his bones in certain areas. Did you notice the way the particular areas erupt in small, almost scaly, bumps and how the light plays across the surface? All of these

FIGURE **9.10** *Take a look at a cow's nose.*

FIGURE **9.11** *The skin of the black rhinoceros.*

things can be emulated with the magic of image maps. Let's give all these wonderful surfaces to Chubbs.

Once you've accumulated all of the photographic reference material you can carry, you're ready to begin painting the image maps. But first you must prepare the model for the application of these image maps. This requires defining a few surfaces on the model.

DEFINING SECTIONS OF THE MODEL FOR SURFACING

These days, most of the better 3D applications allow the users to select specific sections of their model so they can be isolated and named separately. If your 3D application does not allow you to isolate and name specific sections, most likely it will at least allow you to plop an image map onto a specific area of your model — not quite as exacting, but some very desirable results can still be achieved this way.

Once a section of the model has been isolated, it can have an image map applied to just that section. For Chubbs, 12 different sections of his body were isolated and named for surfacing. Figure 9.12 shows each of these isolated sections represented as different colors.

The reason for breaking the model up into different sections is to avoid the stretching that can occur when a flat, 2D image map tries to wrap itself around a 3D surface. One way to combat this stretching problem is to find the parts of the model that are somewhat

FIGURE **9.12** *Isolated sections of Chubbs' surface.*

flat and map your images onto those surfaces. For instance, take a look at the front of Chubbs in Figure 9.13.

You can see that a good deal Chubbs' front section has been isolated for the application of image maps. If you were simply to plop an image map onto the entire model of Chubbs without selecting specific sections, the map would try to cover his entire body as

FIGURE **9.13** *The front of Chubbs — no image maps.*

best it could. It would end up wrapping all the way around to his back. The result would look like he'd been shrink-wrapped in pixels (each pixel would try to stretch around, or project through, the model) as shown in Figure 9.14.

NOTE   Some 3D programs allow the user to flatten the model's geometry in order to use this pancake of flattened geometry as a template for the image maps. It is preferable to see what the model actually looks like while you're painting its image maps; that way it's the actual model that influences how you choose to paint it. You also get a better idea of what the final result will look like.

As you can see, this is a very undesirable way to surface a creature, particularly if you want it to be photorealistic.

To better understand how image maps connect to the surface of the model, imagine that you had a can of spray paint and painted the model from the front. Without turning the model or the can of spray paint, where would the paint hit? Well, it would hit any portion of the model that was parallel to the paint can. Wherever the spray paint hit would be the section of the model that you want to isolate, minus a little bit of the outer edge as you saw in Figure 9.14.

Now that you understand the importance of defining surfaces, how do you determine where the stretching would occur? That's a great question. It's actually rather simple. Let's take a look at how we do it.

FIGURE **9.14** *Chubbs, shrink-wrapped in pixels — not the most desirable look.*

REMOVING SURFACE STRETCHING AREAS ON YOUR MODEL

Nothing undermines the credibility of your model faster than surface stretching. It's an unfortunate problem, present in nearly every 3D creature that has been modeled using polygons or splines. It's actually fairly easy to avoid surface stretching.

The first step in removing the stretching areas on your model is to eyeball the surfaces when you create your initial selections. Basically, you guess where the stretching might occur and redefine the surfaces to remove the potential stretching problem. This isn't an exact science but it will get you about 90 percent of the way towards removing all stretching. You simply need to locate the areas on the model that are irregular in shape and define surface areas that are relatively flat. Look at Chubbs' arm to see how the surfaces were defined to remove surface stretching. Take a look at Figure 9.15.

Several surfaces are defined with unique colors. Each of these colors represents a different surface definition. For example, the color indicated in Figure 9.15(A) represents the top selection of the arm and the color indicated in Figure 9.15(B) represents the front selection of the arm. Take a look at Figure 9.15(C) and you'll see that the color indicated represents the finger selection of the arm, and the color in Figure 9.15(D) represents the bottom selection of the arm.

As you can see, the different selections are relatively flat, which will prevent surface stretching. Of course, to be completely accurate with our surface definition you need to render some test images to identify the areas where surface stretching occurs.

Once you have eyeballed the potential surface stretching areas you are ready to test your selections to see if there are any remaining areas where stretching exists, which is done by using a test pattern image map to surface your model. The test pattern is a repeating

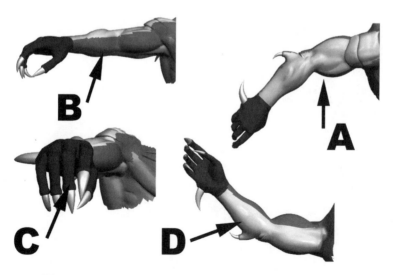

FIGURE **9.15** *The colored selections for Chubbs' arms.*

image map, which will show stretching in problem areas on your model. I prefer to use a simple repeating grid pattern as shown in Figure 9.16.

Here we have a simple repeating grid. This is the ideal image map for testing potential stretching areas since any shape other than a square means it's being stretched. To test your model for surface stretching you'll need to planar map the text image map to each surface of your model, along the appropriate axis as shown in Figure 9.17.

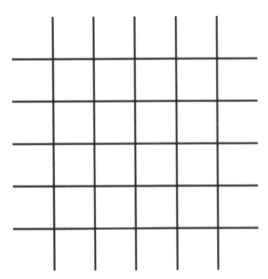

FIGURE **9.16** *A surface stretching test pattern image map.*

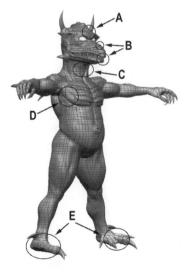

FIGURE **9.17** *Mapping your model with the surface stretching test image map.*

Here we have Chubbs' surfaces with the test image map. You can see that the grid pattern is relatively consistent, with a few exceptions that are indicated by the circled selections. These areas represent stretching zones on the surfaces, which are usually identified by missing lines or thicker lines. The great thing about the grid pattern is that it's easily distorted, which makes spotting the stretching areas a great deal easier. Take a look at each of the circled selections to identify the stretching problem.

(A) This area represents the forehead. It's currently planar mapped from the Y-axis which is causing stretching as the forehead slopes toward the eyes. This problem can be resolved by making the front of the forehead a separate surface that is mapped along the Z-axis.

(B) Here you have the tip of the nose, which is showing signs of stretching with really dark lines. The nose is currently mapped from the side, along the X-axis. You need to map the tip of the nose from the front along the Z-axis to remove the stretching.

(C) You can see that the neck shows severe stretching because the vertical lines are missing and the horizontal lines are very thick in the middle of the neck. This surface is currently mapped from the X-axis. Select the polygons on the front of the neck and map them from the front, along the Z-axis.

(D) Here is a tricky problem area. The side of the chest has a rather sharp taper to the shoulder, which is causing the image map to stretch. The chest is currently mapped from the front, along the Z-axis. Select the polygons on the side of the chest and map them from the X-axis to remove the stretching.

(E) This is the final stretching problem. There are many signs of image map stretching on the feet because the toes are rounded, yet they are planar mapped along only the Y-axis. Select the sides of the feet and toes, then map them along the X-axis. This will fix the stretching problem.

Now that you have identified the stretching areas on the surfaces, you need to determine which polygons are causing the problem so you can give them a new surface definition.

You must render a wireframe version of the model, in the same pose you just rendered to identify the stretching spots. Next, open the surface stretching render in a painting program, such as Photoshop, and load the wireframe render as a new layer. Now that both images are on different layers, you need to make the top layer (wireframe) semitransparent so you can see both layers as shown in Figure 9.18.

You've combined the surface stretching test render and wireframe render to determine the problem polygons. The only thing left to do now is to redefine the surfaces for the problem discussed earlier and render another test image. Look at the new surface stretching test render shown in Figure 9.19.

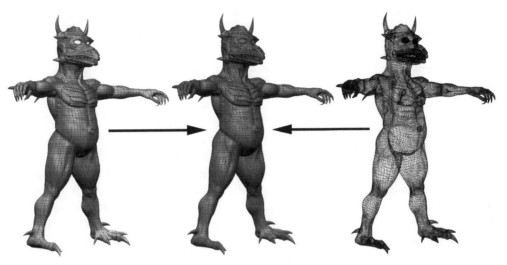

FIGURE **9.18**   *Identifying the polygons where surface stretching occurs.*

That's much better. You can see that the stretching on the forehead, nose, and side of the chest is now removed. The surfaces of the Chubbs model are now properly defined for image map surfacing.

Now that you've selected and named each of the sections to prevent image map stretching, you're ready to render out a bunch of different views, each of which will be used as templates for painting the surfaces. In fact, let's take a look at how you create painting templates.

FIGURE **9.19**   *The result of redefining the surfaces to remove problem stretching areas.*

RENDERING YOUR PAINTING TEMPLATES

Like the second step, this step is fairly technical but necessary for achieving photorealistic image maps surfacing. Without these rendered templates it is pretty much impossible to get certain details to line up properly; for instance, say you wanted to line up something like the color map for your character's red lipstick with the actual character's 3D lips. Guesswork isn't going to cut it, so you'll need to have an actual picture of the surface to which you want to apply these details.

When creating renders for use as templates, never use the camera or the perspective view for the actual render because these views will distort your model with perspective.

Just compare the difference as shown in Figure 9.20. Figure 9.20(A) shows Chubbs viewed through the camera with a normal lens, and Figure 9.20(B) shows Chubbs viewed through the camera's lens zoomed in very close (or tight), but then physically pulled back very far away from the model. This action tends to help flatten out the perspective view of Chubbs but doesn't completely eliminate the perspective. Both Figures 9.20(A) and (B) constitute perspective views, which are undesirable. On the other hand, Figure 9.20(C) shows an orthographic view of Chubbs, which is the best representation of what the software actually sees when it tries to apply an image map to the surface of your model. An orthographic view is basically a two-dimensional representation of the image, which lacks the distortion of perspective. Figure 9.20(C) was screen captured from the modeling program since it displays an orthographic view of the model.

The best thing to do, if your 3D application allows it, is to render from one of the orthographic windows such as the front (X, Y), side (Z, Y), or top (X, Z) views. If the 3D

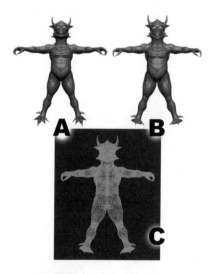

FIGURE **9.20** *Perspective and orthographic views of Chubbs.*

application you're using doesn't allow you to render from one of the orthographic views, zoom in very tightly (at least a setting of 100–200) on your object (as opposed to zooming out), and then pull the camera back until you get a good view of your model. This will flatten out your 3D object, removing the perspective.

Even with this template, you'll still need to do a screen grab of the wire mesh from one of the orthographic views just to be sure that you have a solid orthographic template. Use this orthographic view as the main template image for painting the image maps. Why create a rendered view? In many cases the orthographic view tends to flatten the details of the surface, which can make painting a little difficult. Use the rendered view to get a feeling for the depth of the models surface details. Of course, you need to resize the rendered perspective view to conform to the orthographic view's dimensions.

With the painting templates completed you are ready to begin painting the image maps.

WORKING WITH PAINTING PROGRAMS

Finally, you're actually ready to begin the image map painting process for Chubbs. This is where you actually get a chance see your illustrious visions of Chubbs' surfacing begin to take shape. It's where you start applying the impact of Chubbs' environment to his surfaces, and where Chubbs is truly transformed from a cool 3D model into a photorealistic creature with a visible history.

To begin, simply load your largest prerendered template into the painting program of your choice. It's best to start with your largest template (that is, the one that covers the most surface area of your model) because this will dictate the color, bumpiness, and specularity of all that maps that connect with it. Also, since this map is the largest, it will define the size of the maps that follow. If you can, try to keep all of your maps the same scale. This will make touch ups much less confusing later on. Nothing is worse than having irregular sizes of image maps, which cause some portions of the model's surface to blur due to image map resizing.

So how do we keep the image maps to the same scale? It's actually rather simple. You just need to take a few measurements. The first thing you need to do is render a size template, which is merely a front view of the model that shows the different surface selections as shown in Figure 9.21.

Make sure that the image you render represents the size of the actual image maps you will be creating. It's a good idea to make creature image maps at least 2,500 pixels tall so they are large enough for close-ups. Figure 9.21 was rendered at 2,500 pixels tall to ensure an accurate size template.

Take a few measurements of the different surfaces on the image map. The first step is to open the Information Window in your painting program. Then use the selection tool to place a box around the individual surfaces. The Information window will then show

FIGURE **9.21** *Sizing your image maps to scale.*

the height and width of the selection in pixels. The width is the significant measurement here; it represents the width you will need to make the image map for the specific selection. Look at a few measurements taken from Figure 9.21.

(A) Front surface 2400 pixels
(B) Hand surface 280 pixels
(C) Arm top surface 776 pixels
(D) Arm bottom surface 624 pixels

As you can see, it's very simple to create image maps that are to scale when you start with a size template. Your final step is to open the image map templates you created earlier and resize them (proportionately) to the proper scale.

You see, it wasn't difficult at all to create image maps to scale. OK, before we go any further with painting image maps, let's take a look at how to choose a painting program.

CHOOSING THE RIGHT PAINTING PROGRAM

Since you'll be painting the maps with digital tools rather than real brushes and paints, perhaps you should consider what digital painting tools you'll need. Everyone has their own favorite software packages and platforms to work with. Some even hold their software packages up as deities. But that may be getting a little too extreme; whatever software package lets you do the high quality job you want to do, with the least amount of hassle as possible, is the one you should stick with and learn thoroughly.

I prefer Adobe Photoshop for painting image maps. I like Photoshop's uncluttered, intuitive interface along with its vast painting and image manipulation capabilities. There are many paint programs out there that will do many of the same things that Photoshop can do, but one capability is crucial when you're creating image maps, and that's the use of layers. Layers let you lay multiple images one on top the other. You can control the transparency of each layer so you can see the layers below, move layers around, merge selected layers, and even perform operations on more than one layer at a time if you choose.

Some of my favorite, and most often used tools in Photoshop are the smudge, clone, burn/dodge, saturate/desaturate, airbrush, and selection tools. I use each and every one of these tools when creating image maps and have found the *feel* of them to be superior to anything else that's out there. I suggest that you select a program that supplies these tools since it will be difficult to create photorealistic image maps without them.

In this chapter, I'll be using Photoshop for the tutorials. If you have another program don't worry; as long as you have similar features you should be able to follow along.

You have the templates, with the proper scale, and a painting program — now you need to determine your image map needs.

DETERMINING YOUR IMAGE MAP NEEDS

Since Chubbs is a humanoid creature that lives, breathes, sweats, bleeds, eats, cries, etc., you're going to need at least four image maps for each of his preselected surfaces: color, bump, specularity, and diffusion. Take a look at each of these image maps and the role they play in creating photorealistic surfaces.

> **Color Map.** As the name specifies, this will give Chubbs all of his color informa-tion, which includes his overall skin color. Of course, a living creature's skin should never be just one solid color, because it's just unnatural. Take a look at the back of your hand in good light, disregarding any shadows. Notice how your knuckles are a slightly different color than the flesh of your arm. Look at the slight color difference where your veins protrude. These are very slight differences to be sure, but things like your lips are quite a different color than the rest of your face. If you've been up all night writing or rendering you may find that the hue that lies just beneath your eyes is a bit different from the color of your chin. For Chubbs, the color maps included all of his bruises, scars, nose color, ears, tummy color, scales, veins, and also any areas where you'd find more blood flow to his body like his feet, elbows, and hands. It's these details that make the color image map believable.

> **Bump Map.** Bump maps are great, not only because they can save you considerable time in modeling, but mainly because they allow you to create those tiny details

that would be nearly impossible to model. Bump maps are used to create the appearance of physical skin texture, wrinkles, and even muscle details. Chubbs' veins, tendons, scars, wrinkles, scales, pores, and his overall skin texture were created using bump maps. Bump maps give you the feel of the model's skin and add depth to the surfaces.

Specularity Map. Specularity maps give you the power over the way light plays across the surface of a model. With a specularity map you can tell the model where you want it to be shiny and where you want it to be dull. Skin tissue changes specularity depending on how taught and hard it is. The skin on your forehead is more specular than the skin on your stomach since it's rather taught. You'll also find that creatures with scales will be more specular since the scales are harder than skin tissue. Of course, there's always the issue of moisture. Moisture is very specular so specularity maps are used to create the appearance of moisture by making the surface shiny.

Diffusion Map. Diffusion maps are one of the most important of all the maps in creating realistic surfaces, particularly skin. They are also one of the most often overlooked maps. Diffusion maps are often used for creating an aged or dusty look to the surface. But more important, the diffusion map controls how much of an object's color can be seen. The problem is that you'll rarely find a creature with diffusion. A diffusion map would be used to darken the low points of the creases in a character's fingers, wrinkles on the forehead, and various other parts of the body. People rarely, if ever, use diffusion maps on a character, even though they're a necessary part of photorealism. One thing that most 3D artists do is set their diffusion levels to 100%. This is a big mistake since very few surfaces in the real world display 100% of their color. Skin certainly doesn't. Skin has a diffusion level of about 70 percent or lower.

There you have it, the four image maps that are required to create photorealistic creature surfaces. This chapter provides much greater detail of each of these types of image maps as you continue, starting with color mapping.

STARTING OUT WITH THE COLOR MAP

When you apply color to a 3D model it's almost like creating a painting but with one major difference: no need for shading. This can be difficult if you're used to painting or drawing images with a lot of modeling and shadowing of form. But it's important to realize that the 3D application's render engine is going to supply all of the shadows and shading for the model. If we put them into the image map they're only going to get in the way, and they probably won't match the lighting of the scene in most cases.

If you look at Figure 9.22, you'll see that some of the shadows in the crevices of Chubbs' chest armor are painted. This is because sometimes your bump maps need a little help, and also dirt would have accumulated in between the scales of Chubbs' armor. There are always exception to the rules — just don't make a habit of breaking them.

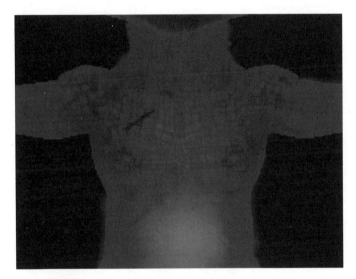

FIGURE **9.22** *A close-up of Chubbs' chest plating.*

It looks as if the scales protecting Chubbs were meticulously painted one by one, but this is not the case. To create a highly detailed area like the chest scales, all you need to do is start off by creating a small area of the scales. Then, using Photoshop's cloning tool, carefully spread these scales out across the surfaces where Chubbs needs them the most for his protection (see Figure 9.23(A)). The best way to do this is to concentrate on only one side of Chubbs at a time. In fact, this leads to the rules of painting 3D image maps. It's a bit of a tangent but it's important.

THE RULES OF PAINTING 3D IMAGE MAPS

Many folks don't like a lot of rules impeding the creative process. But following these basic rules can save you countless hours and headaches when you paint image maps.

Painting Rule #1 Select one predominant color for your character's skin. This base color will be the main color for all of the color maps. It will also be the edge color for each of the image maps; this will insure that you will not see any color difference or seams where all of the color maps connect with one another.

Painting Rule #2 Mirror Details. Mirror complex areas in order to save time. There's no point in repeating your efforts.

Painting Rule #3 Remove Symmetry. Order + Chaos = Reality. Mirror those complex areas, but avoid too much symmetry. Once you've mirrored the complex areas you need to go back and add a little irregularity.

Painting Rule #4 Avoid High Detail on Image Seams. Avoid complex, highly detailed areas at the far edges of your image maps. It can be very difficult to create seamless image maps when there is a lot of detail on the seam. Of course, you can't always avoid it but you should definitely make an effort to limit the detail on seams.

Painting Rule #5 Rely on Source Material. Refer to your resource material frequently while painting. Unless you have a photographic memory, keep those visual resources pasted right next to your monitor. There's nothing like the real world to clue you in when you're trying to paint something as realistic as possible.

Painting Rule #6 Create Frequent Test Renders. Render a test to check out each and every image map as it's created. It takes a little time, but allows you to catch a small problem before it becomes a big problem.

Painting Rule #7 Fix Problems Immediately. Fix any problem that pops up as soon as you notice it. It may seem annoying to go back and fix little problems with your image maps, but the more problems you fix, the less likely they are to spread to your other image maps and pop up in the future.

These simple rules will make photorealistic surfacing a great deal easier and more effective. If you follow these rules you'll be sure to create dazzling creature image maps.

MIRRORING DETAILS TO SAVE TIME

As previously discussed, the initial scales on Chubbs' chest were created using Photoshop's cloning tool. The chest was painted by completing one side as shown in Figure 9.23(A). The next step involved making a copy of the chest by selecting them and simply pasting them (as a new layer) to the other side of Chubbs as shown in Figure 9.23(B). With this accomplished, flip (mirror) the scales horizontally. The result of this procedure is shown in Figure 9.23(C). This new layer is merged with the original layer.

As you can see, the scales covering Chubbs are a bit too symmetrical, resulting in an unrealistic look as shown in Figure 9.23(C). The scales need to be symmetrically ordered to cover Chubbs' flesh, but this is a little too much order. This looks unrealistic because the scales have no chaos, and as you've learned in previous chapters, chaos is necessary to photorealism. Take a look at any creature that's covered in scales and you'll see that there are irregularities in the shapes of the scales. To correct the symmetry problem with Chubbs' chest scales you need to apply the second rule of image map painting: Order + Chaos = Reality.

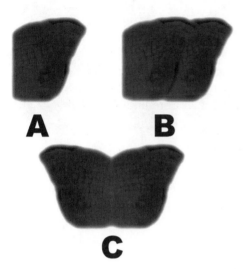

FIGURE 9.23 *Section of Chubbs' chest plating — part of the front color map.*

CREATING PHOTOREALISM WITH CHAOS

The reason the symmetry in the scales can be picked out so easily is that the human eye is extremely adept at picking out patterns. In fact, pattern recognition is the number one way that you remember visual phenomena like faces, places you've been, and even styles of handwriting. When creating image maps for 3D models, use patterns often; otherwise you'll go crazy painting in tiny, repeating details like the scales on Chubbs' chest. The only problem with using the clone tool or tileable textures is that quite often you recognize a pattern that is totally unrealistic.

One way to combat the pattern problem is to go back into the color map and add a little variety to areas that stand out as patterns. This can be accomplished fairly easily by throwing a little chaos into the image map, perhaps by breaking up the continuity with a scar or by reordering (repainting) some of the scales. Let's take a look at how the symmetry was removed in Chubbs' chest scales.

Compare images (A) and (B) in Figure 9.24. The pattern seen in Figure 24(A) was broken up using only the burn and dodge tools to introduce a little chaos to disrupt this pattern. Figure 24(B) is only slightly altered, but as you can see, it's enough to interrupt the eyes constant search for a pattern. The large scar on the left side really draws the viewer's eye, preventing him or her from focusing on the symmetry.

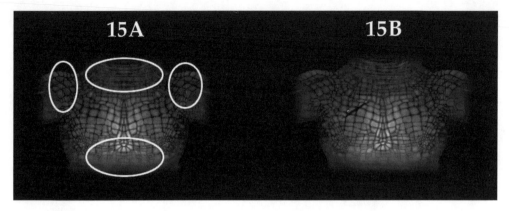

FIGURE **9.24** *Creating a little chaos.*

Keep an eye out for those unrealistic patterns popping up here and there. When you find a recognizable pattern occurring, immediately zap it with some chaos. Break up the unrealistically symmetrical with something different, like a scar, a bruise, a coffee stain — whatever it takes to break up that all-too-perfect symmetry. You'll be surprised how a small change can go a long way towards establishing photorealistic credibility.

LET'S GET UNDER CHUBBS' SKIN

This section addresses some of the necessary attributes of Chubbs' skin. You probably just want to drop that default shader onto the model and be done with it, but if you do that, that's all the creation will look like: a 3D model with a default shader. Maybe ten years ago that was enough to wow the viewer, but today 3D graphics are no longer regarded as a novelty. They're nearly commonplace, so if you want to elicit that wow reaction today you need to do the necessary work involved that warrants such a reaction. One way is to invest your time and energy into creating super realistic surfaces. One of the surfaces that receives the most attention is a creature's skin. This being the case, you need to create skin so believable the viewer can almost feel it.

When creating image maps for a character's skin, you need to imagine what it would be like to wear that skin. Basically, you have to walk in the character's shoes for a day to see what the skin is subject to on a daily basis. Take look at the image of Chubbs in Figure 9.25.

Chubbs' skin consists mainly of earth tones because he lives most of the day deep in the earth. There are a wide variety of earth tones ranging from red clays to gray-blue mud to the golden hues of sand. Many of these colors were incorporated to create the skin for Chubbs. For starters, his skin is a reddish brown, closely resembling mineral-rich dirt.

FIGURE **9.25** *Chubbs' natural, earth-tone skin coloration.*

Now take a look at the gray-blue mud color of the veins on Chubbs' belly and the pigmentation of his gums, which consist of the purplish-black color of grapes grown from the wet, soft, fertilized earth. Don't forget the bruises that crop up on his flesh, where you see the dark-blue color of cold stone.

Chubbs' skin color is certainly influenced by his environment. He has a wide variety of colors as does nature, but how do you incorporate this variety of colors and still have color maps that are compatible with one another?

You don't want to end up with Chubbs adorned with all the colors of the rainbow. You need one predominant color for Chubbs, which brings you to the next rule.

SELECT ONE PREDOMINANT COLOR FOR YOUR CHARACTER'S SKIN

To make the surfacing job easier, a single predominant color must be chosen, which will constitute the base color for the character's skin. Once this predominant color has been found, be sure to write down its RGB values. This base color will be the main color for all of the color maps for the character. It will also be the edge color, which will insure that no color difference or seams will be visible where each of the color maps connect with one another. Take a look at the Chubbs' base color, as shown in Figure 9.26.

Using a single, uninterrupted color for your character really looks rather bland doesn't it? Chubbs now looks more like an awkward, chocolate addition to your Easter basket than a living, breathing creature. But now that you have a base color for your character,

FIGURE **9.26** *Chubbs' base skin color.*

you can concentrate on some more distinctive markings that will make the surface more realistic.

You can see that a color map certainly will enhance the overall look of any creature's skin. But just how are you to go about putting together a photorealistic color map? Take a look at how Chubbs' skin color was created.

Creating a Color Map for Chubbs' Skin

1. First, it's best to visualize the creature in its natural environment. For Chubbs, this is deep within the earth so you'll want to use the same colors you'd find there.
2. Once you've selected several earth tones you must decide how these colors might appear on Chubbs' flesh.
3. Since he's adorned with a lot of scale like armor plating, a specific color needs to be chosen to differentiate Chubbs' scales from his regular flesh. I chose an ochre color (RGB=90,63,35) for this effect, as shown in Figure 9.27.
4. Although Chubbs has many human attributes (he walks erect and has somewhat human limbs and posture), I wanted to make his skin coloring a bit more like an animal. Many creatures, like frogs and lizards, have accentuated or brighter coloring on their bellies. I thought Chubbs might look nice with this attribute also. So I made Chubbs' belly a much lighter color than the rest of his body. Utilizing the airbrush tool in Photoshop, with an opacity setting that varied between 7 percent (near the edges)and 45 percent (for the center of the belly), and a creme color (RGB=170,128,110), I painted in the belly color difference as shown in Figure 9.28.

5.   Now that this large stomach area is defined, you need to consider chaos once again. Chaos occurs throughout any animal's skin coloration; some areas like the knuckles, feet, head, and hands receive more blood flow than other areas of the body, so these areas need to have different coloration than the majority of the body. It's usually a good idea to make the joints a bit darker than the rest of the body.

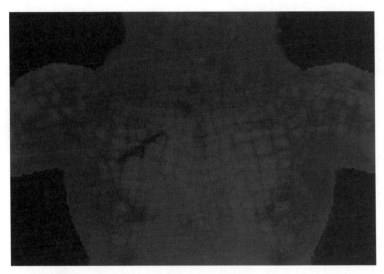

FIGURE **9.27**   *Chubbs' ochre colored chest scales.*

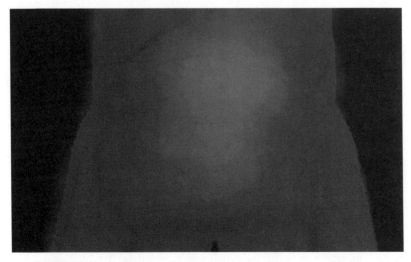

FIGURE **9.28**   *Chubbs' belly color.*

The basic skin tone coloration is defined. Of course, since Chubbs lives within a hostile environment, he's constantly getting bruised up, scarred, and dirty. Let's take a look at what goes into creating some scars for Chubbs.

CREATING SCARS

It's very important when creating photorealism that you use your imagination to put yourself into the shoes of your characters — even if they don't wear shoes. The viewer may not make all of the connections you intend, but the more you invest in the lifestyle, habits, and environmental setting of your character, the more realistic it will become.

When mentally walking the walk of Chubbs, you'll find that it's not the most pleasant walk you've ever taken. The guy is only about an inch tall and he lives thousands of feet beneath the earth's crust. It's a pretty hostile environment down there, so naturally he has some scars. The types of scars he's received have come mainly from his battles with the dreaded Jartung Dogth, but don't forget the scars resulting from his daily interactions with a plethora of dangers in his world. He's got to deal with ferocious insects, rodents, giant thorns, collapsing tunnels and perhaps a fall here and there from a precarious stance on a leaf. And don't forget that his proportions do tend to make him a little bit clumsy, so he's going to have some scars.

Scars show that Chubbs interacts with his environment and allow viewers to connect him to their world. The more visual influences of the real world you reflect on your character, the more realistic he will become to the viewer.

Creating a scar with a bump map is certainly much less painful than acquiring one in real life. Of course, good source material is important, but it's much easier to look at a medical book or even search the Internet than to acquire your own scar. .

Take a look at Figure 9.29, which shows the process of creating a bump map scar. Once again, this is simply a procedure of defining the high areas (with the dodge tool) surrounding the scar, and defining the low areas (with the burn tool) of the scar.

Figure 9.29(A) shows the flesh pattern before adding a scar. In Figure 9.29(B) the burn tool in Photoshop was used, with an exposure setting of 67 percent, to darken the scar tissue. Several passes with the burn tool may be required before the scar is dark enough. In Figure 9.29(C),the dodge tool was used to create the bump map. With the dodge tool also set to 67 percent you simply need to make a few passes around the outer edge of the scar. The result of lightening the area around the outer edge of the scar causes this area to be raised, in contrast to the dark area where the cut of the scar is low. This lighter area has been added to represent the swelling, which occurs when you get a cut in reality.

Once a bump map scar has been burned into poor Chubbs, you can add a little dried blood and reddish soreness around the wound. I know it sounds pretty sadistic, but no one has ever been locked up, that I know of, for cruelty to 3D models.

FIGURE 9.29 *The process of creating a scar.*

Creating Bloody Sores

1. You need to have the template in the bottom most layer (see Figure 9.30(A)), the bump map (with scar) in the middle layer, and the color map on top. Don't worry about the specularity map just yet, but that should be sandwiched in there somewhere as well.

2. Select the color layer and find a nice dark color to represent blood. The Red, Green, Blue values for the color I chose are 28, 11, and 9. Select a paintbrush that will fit inside the wound area of the scar. Try a little test to see how this color looks on your color map. (Be sure to do *no more than one click of the mouse* because you'll want to undo this little test later.) Make the color layer about 50 percent transparent by setting the opacity to 50 percent. You can see where the scar is on the bump map layer below (see Figure 9.39(B)).

3. Next, paint the dried blood color into the dark area of the scar onto your color map, as shown in Figure 9.31.

4. Now you just need to add a little redness around the wound. First, bring the opacity of your color map layer back up to 100 percent. Then find a good reddish-pink soreness color and a good brush to use. The RGB color values I used for this were R=61, B=33, and G=19. I used an airbrush with its pressure set to about 10 percent. Just spray the color around on the color map to see how it affects the skin tone. Once you're satisfied with the settings, undo the results of the test.

5. Once you're happy with the look of the soreness color, set the color map layer back to around 50 percent opacity so that you can see the scar below.

6. Now you need to spray paint some soreness around the wound (avoiding the dark, dried blood area). One good way to avoid messing up the dark wound area is to set the airbrush options to overlay. With the overlay setting, the paint will not affect the dark area. Once again use the airbrush tool to do this with a low pressure setting (around 10%).

7. Set the color map back to 100 percent opacity and save the results.

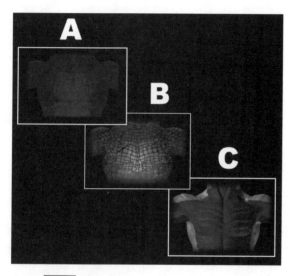

FIGURE **9.30** *More about scars.*

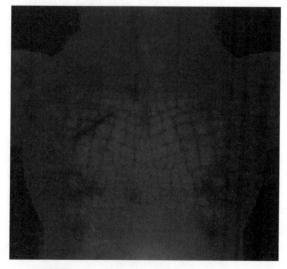

FIGURE **9.31** *Painting the scar details.*

That's just about all there is to creating a photorealistic scar for your creature. If you want it to look a little bit more like a fresh wound, rather than using a dark, dried blood color, use a redder (RGB color: 35, 16, 14), more saturated color and apply the blood as it would flow from the wound. Dig up your existing creatures and beat them up a bit with some scars and sores. It adds personality and is actually rather fun, in a sadistic sort of way.

Scars are cool, but they're not the only thing to consider when painting skin like that which is covering Chubbs. You still need to consider other attributes, which conspire to form the texture of Chubbs' skin. After all, he's been through a lot in his lifetime and his skin needs to tell us his experiences. The perfect device for creating very small, intricate textures is the bump map. Let's take a look at how a bump map is used to create subtle surfacing details.

CREATING DETAILS WITH BUMP MAPS

Bump maps are extraordinarily valuable when it comes to creating photorealistic imagery. They are ideal for creating believable skin textures, wrinkles, pockmarks, scars, muscles, and many other surface attributes that would either be too difficult to create or take too long to model.

Although bump maps don't actually change the surface of the model, they do make light react to your model's surface as if they did. The physical geometry isn't changed, as with a displacement map, but it creates the illusion that it does.

The principle behind bump maps is fairly simple: dark areas of the map equal low altitude and light areas equal high altitude, with black being the lowest and light being the highest.

Creating a bump map is relatively simple. One way to save a lot of time and trouble is merely to duplicate the color map you've already created and use it as the beginning for the bump map. To duplicate the color layer all you need to do is the following.

Duplicating the Color Map for Use as a Bump Map

1. Be sure you're in the color layer.
2. Select all (Control A).
3. Paste the color information into a new layer (Control V).

After duplicating the color layer you'll need to remove all of the color from the image. This can be accomplished easily by choosing hue/saturation (Control U) in Photoshop and turning the saturation all the way down to zero. This will cause the duplicate of the color layer to become a gray-scale image. This method allows you to keep the original color layer intact, yet turn its duplicate layer into a gray-scale image as shown in Figure 9.32.

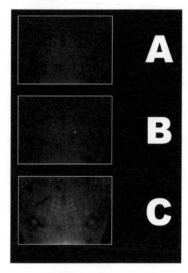

FIGURE **9.32** *Adjusting the color map for use as a bump map.*

Turning back to the now desaturated, black-and-white duplicate of the color map shown in Figure 9.32(B), you can see the areas that will be represented as high and those represented as low.

In some areas of the chest you can see that this bump map may not work too well as it is. For instance, the scales covering Chubbs' chest may need a little accentuating. By utilizing the brightness and contrast control panel in Photoshop, you can bring out the definition of the chest scales as shown in Figure 9.32(C). Typically, you'll want to set the brightness to a value of –10 to –15 and the contrast to a value of 30–50. This will sharpen the difference between the light and dark tones in the image.

That's the basics of creating a bump map. Now let's take a look at how you create specific bump details on your surfaces.

CREATING SKIN WRINKLES

Wrinkles are extremely important when creating photorealistic skin. Just take a look at the variety of wrinkles upon the faces you see the next time you're at the check-out counter of the supermarket. Wrinkles are like the road map of time. They can give you an idea of how old the character is and how often that person has smiled or frowned. It can also tell us what region they come from — dry and sunny or moist and cold. Wrinkles can show worry, confusion, anger, fear, or extreme joy — and that's just speaking of the wrinkles in the face.

Can you imagine a face without wrinkles? Even a baby's face has its share of wrinkles. The only instance that comes to mind is in the realm of 3D graphics. Not a spherical, cartoon-y, George Pal look-alike, but instances where the 3D artist is desperately trying to emulate realism, but forgot the wrinkles.

When applying wrinkles to a creature's surface, it's helpful to ask where the the skin would fold, where it would be loose, and where wrinkles would appear from repetitive bending actions like walking. Let's take a look at some of the areas where wrinkles are sure to occur in Chubbs. See Figure 9.33.

Though Chubbs is a rather portly character, he still has areas where skin will fold. The places where wrinkles would occur have been circled. Let's take a look at each of the areas where you'll find wrinkles on Chubbs.

(A) In this small area there are four sections that will need some wrinkles: the area above the nose, below the eyes, the forehead, and the area beside each eye where crow's feet might appear.

(B) The lips constitute a very expressive part of any character. The result of speech is wrinkles. You'll find that exaggerated facial expressions cause wrinkles too. Chubbs' lips have a great deal of wrinkles. He's not that much of a talker but he certainly does have an extensive library of battle expressions.

(C) The neck contains many joints, which result in an abundance of wrinkles that are a by-product of frequent head movement. Since he's such a little guy, he'll need to be looking up an awful lot; this will cause a profusion of wrinkling in his neck.

(D) Wrinkles appear in areas where joints occur. This is typically because there is an excess of skin tissue to allow the arm to straighten without stretching the skin.

(E) The fingers are one of the most wrinkle laden areas of the body, for the same reason as the larger joints. Extra skin is provided to allow freedom of movement.

(F) The knee area and the areas where the toes bend also get their share of wrinkles. Extra skin allows for freedom of movement.

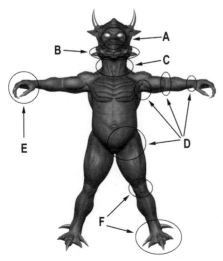

FIGURE **9.33** *The wrinkle areas for Chubbs.*

Take a close look at the wrinkles on the side of Chubbs' head. Compare the bump map in Figure 9.34 to the resulting render beside it.

You can see how the bump map has added a great deal of detail to Chubbs' head. Take a look at how wrinkles were created on Chubbs' head.

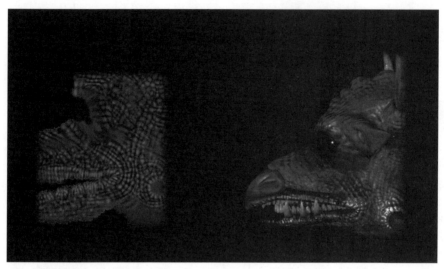

FIGURE 9.34 *The bump map and the resulting wrinkles.*

Creating Wrinkles with a Bump Map

1. In Figure 9.35, you can see the plain bump map for the skin texture of the side of Chubbs' head. This should be the top layer in Photoshop. If you give this bump layer an opacity setting of 35 percent, you can see the template of the head below it as shown in Figure 9.36, which will allow you to see where you need to paint the wrinkle bump.

2. The green potions of the template represent the side surface of the head, which is the surface where the bump map will be used. With the bump map layer semitransparent, you can see where the wrinkles will occur by looking at the template below.

3. You should be in the layer that contains the semitransparent bump map. You'll want to set the opacity setting of the bump layer to about 85 percent, so that you'll be able to see the marks you'll be making. Utilizing Photoshop's burn tool, with an exposure setting of 24 percent you can begin painting the wrinkle bump.

4. As you can see in Figure 9.37, by following the contours of Chubbs' flesh with the burn tool, you can begin creating wrinkles on his face exactly where you want them.

5. Once you've created all of the wrinkles that you need for the side of Chubbs' head with the burn tool, you may want to accentuate some of these wrinkles with the dodge tool with an exposure setting of 34 percent. You may also want to create deeper wrinkles by going over them once more with the burn tool.

6. You may want to push-and-pull some of the wrinkles a bit to achieve a more stretched look to them. This can be fairly easily achieved with Photoshop's smudge tool. With a pressure setting of 45 percent, you can pull the wrinkles at their ends in order to achieve a faded look. This faded look will help prevent the wrinkles from starting or ending too abruptly. Figure 9.38 shows the final result of the paint job. You'll notice that the smudge tool will also smudge out the noise, which existed in our original bump map surface for Chubbs' skin in Figure 9.35. In some cases this is fine, but since Chubbs has very tough skin, more monochromatic noise was added with an amount setting of 2.

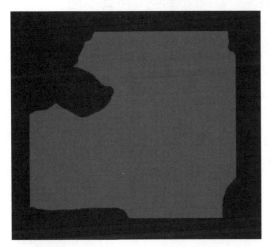

FIGURE 9.35 *The bump map without wrinkles.*

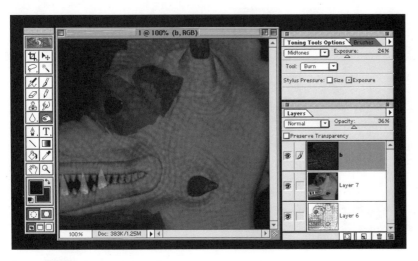

FIGURE 9.36 *Semitransparent bump map.*

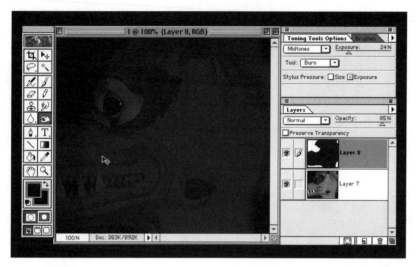

FIGURE **9.37** *Start painting in some wrinkles.*

Now that you've taken a good look at wrinkles, let's consider another integral part to creating photorealistic creatures — veins.

CREATING VEINS

Veins are also a necessary addition if we want Chubbs to look like a realistic, vigorous creature. Veins are really simple to simulate with a bump map but they pay off in realism.

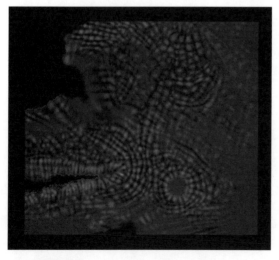

FIGURE **9.38** *The final result of the paint job.*

Take a look at Chubbs' hand in Figure 9.39. In Figure 9.39(A) you can see how the tendons are popping through the flesh, and on top of these tendons you can see veins. This effect can be achieved by thinking of these two elements as layers.

Take a look at Figure 9.39(B). The tendons are below the veins, so you paint them first by using a lighter shade of gray than the hand. Then use an even lighter shade of gray (nearly white) to represent the veins, which lie on top of these tendons. This technique is a thousand times simpler than attempting to model tendons and veins.

Once again, the bump map has come through and given you the ability to create minute, photorealistic details with a few simple operations. Now you need to consider the overall look of Chubbs' skin.

CREATING SKIN TEXTURE

Since Chubbs has somewhat leathery skin, the surface of it should appear rather rough. This effect is simple to achieve by simply adding a small amount of noise to the bump map. This will ensure that his skin has an overall texture to it and that all of his skin will have a little chaos. Take a look at Figure 9.40, which illustrates a segment of Chubbs' skin texture bump map.

As you can see, general skin texture is relatively simple to create by using fractal noise. The same effect can be used for simulating human skin. Of course, if you plan to surface a creature like a rhino, you'll need to create a chaotic pattern that has more irregularities in the size of the pores, which makes the surface appear more pitted and porous.

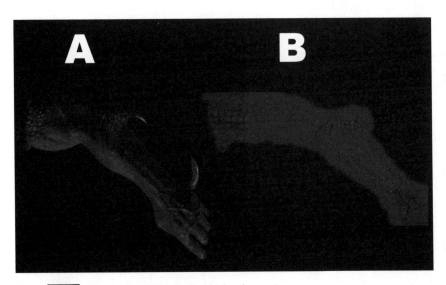

FIGURE **9.39** *Veins and wrinkles in Chubbs' hand.*

FIGURE 9.40 *Chubbs' skin texture bump map.*

Of course, you also must consider where Chubbs' skin will be shiny or dull. After all, his skin isn't just one uniform flatness like a coat of wall paint. The best way to control where the skin is shiny and where it is dull is with a specularity map.

ADDING SPECULARITY

A specularity map tells the surface which parts are shiny and which parts are dull. It's similar to a bump map in that it's usually a grayscale image, with one exception. Rather than reading light parts of the map as a high areas, it reads a light part as being shiny. The dark areas of a specularity map are read as being dull or nonshiny.

Not all areas of any creature's skin respond to light in a uniform manner. Typically the harder the surface the more specular. For example, undersea creatures typically have high specularity, but they also have parts of their bodies that have lower specularity because they are soft. In fact, take a look at the undersea creature shown in Figure 9.41.

Here we have a baby green sea turtle that shows a large variance of specularity between the hard shell and the soft skin tissue.

Consider the human face. You'll find they are shiny around the forehead and nose area because the skin tissue in these areas tightly stretches across bone and cartilage. These areas also produce more oil and sweat than say, the earlobe, which adds to their specularity.

Take a look at Chubbs. Our little friend has a wide variety of both shiny and dull areas on the surface of his skin. His scaly armor, his lips, gums and teeth, horns, scars, nose, and eyes are all shiny, while his general skin surface is rather dull.

FIGURE **9.41** *The variations in skin specularity of sea creatures.*

A fairly good rule of thumb to observe when deciding whether or not to make a particular area shiny is to consider how hard that surface is. How tightly packed together are the molecules, that compose the surface? Take, for instance, your own fingernail compared to the skin on the back of your hand. The skin is much softer and rather dull (not much light gleans off the surface), but the fingernail is pretty hard and therefore shiny. Look at our friend Scratch from the LightWave Metaform Primer. Take a look at Figure 9.42.

As you can see, the fingernails are significantly more specular than the skin tissue on the back of the hand.

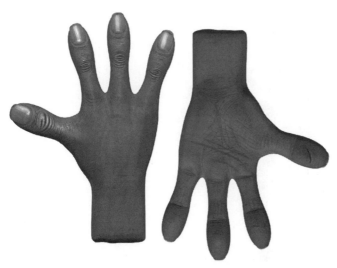

FIGURE **9.42** *The contrast in skin and fingernail specularity.*

Look at the contrast in specularity on Chubby as shown in Figure 9.43. The scales on his chest are much harder than the soft skin of his belly, so the area for the chest section is much lighter than the area for Chubbs' stomach in the specularity map.

Another instance where specularity maps can really help you achieve photorealism is in sections of the model that you want to appear as being wet — as in the mouth, nose, and scar areas of Chubbs.

Compare the difference between Figures 9.44(A) and (B). Figure 9.44(A) shows a render of the side of Chubbs' head without a specularity map, and Figure 9.44(B) shows the same view with the specularity map applied. Notice how much more complex the patterning of light is as it plays across the surface of the second image. The scales appear rather shiny and hard, while the skin surface appears dull and soft.

As you can see, specularity image maps make a big difference to the overall realism of a creature's surfacing. They can be a bit daunting at first, but once you've experimented with them for a while you'll agree they are an invaluable asset for defining your creature's surface. The more visual information that you can provide the viewer, the closer you'll be to making your creatures realistic.

Now let's move on to the most misunderstood of all image maps, the diffusion map.

DIFFUSION, THE KEY TO PHOTOREALISM

Why are diffusion maps the most misunderstood of all the map types? For one thing, they are hard to define. Also, they are hard to experiment with because you might be unsure of

FIGURE **9.43** *Comparing the specularity between Chubbs' scales and his belly.*

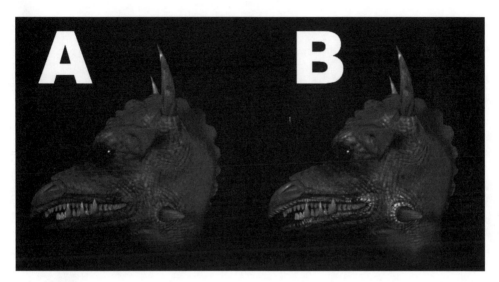

FIGURE **9.44** *The impact of specularity maps.*

how they're supposed to work. Oftentimes you'll take one of your previously made image maps and try it out in the diffusion map channel. For instance, say you took your bump map and dropped it into the diffusion map channel. The result is that your creature becomes very dark, which is undesirable. Most 3D artists ignore the diffusion map all together and crank the diffusion setting up to 100 percent. The result of this action is that there is something inevitably not quite right with the final render of the creature. It just doesn't look realistic.

So what does a diffusion map do? Well, the best way to think of a diffusion map is to consider it as the final layer of your creature's surfacing. It's the final layer that light has to pass through before reaching the viewer's eye.

Consider this: Light is the magical thing that gives any object its color. Light comes streaming down at your creature and hits the surface of its skin, but not all of the creature's color bounces back at the viewer, because the skin is diffused. Diffusion controls the amount of color that is reflected by the light. In short, it means the amount of the color that you can see.

Most objects have diffusion and they never have a value in excess of 90 percent. For example, a mirror has a 0 percent diffusion, which results in none of the mirror's color being sent back to the viewer. This makes a lot of sense since a mirror is 100 percent reflective. On the other hand, something like glossy wall paint has about 90 percent diffusion, which means nearly all of its color is visible. Finally, skin has about 70 percent diffusion. When light hits Chubbs' skin most of his color is sent back to the viewer, but 30 percent of it is lost.

Look at the impact of a diffusion map on Chubbs' skin surface. Compare Figures 9.45(A) and 9.45(B). Figure 9.45(A) shows Chubbs with no diffusion map and a global

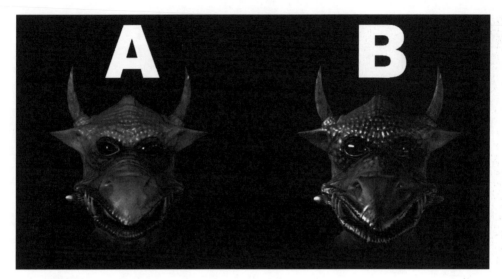

FIGURE **9.45** *The impact of diffusion maps.*

diffusion setting of 100 percent Figure 9.45(B) shows the same shot of Chubbs but with a diffusion map that varies the diffusion value over the surface, but never exceeds 70 percent.

What does a diffusion map look like? Just take a look at Figure 9.46, which is a section of the diffusion map used for Chubbs' head.

As you can see, the lower part of the skin cracks and bump are dark, which gives them a low diffusion level. This is done since little light will get into the cracks, so little surface color will be reflected. Now take a look at the light spots on the image. These represent the high points of the skin bumps, which are hard and shiny so they tend to show more of their surface color, but never more than 70 percent. For your surfaces to appear natural and realistic, you'll need to vary the diffusion values depending on the type of surface. For example, if you have dirt on your character's skin you'll need to lower the diffusion to a value of 50 percent in the areas covered by dirt since it has a rather low diffusion level. It's critical that you consider the surface carefully before you create the diffusion map.

A good rule of thumb when creating diffusion maps for skin is *never use a 100 percent diffusion setting.* Keep that in mind and you'll never go wrong with creating believable skin diffusion.

You've created the proper diffusion maps, but you still have a problem when you render the character — it comes out far too dark. This is where it is important to understand the relationship between diffusion and light.

THE RELATIONSHIP BETWEEN DIFFUSION AND LIGHT

The first thing you need to address is the intensity of natural light. Typically, a 3D artist will place a single light in the scene, which isn't nearly enough light. Reality is full of light,

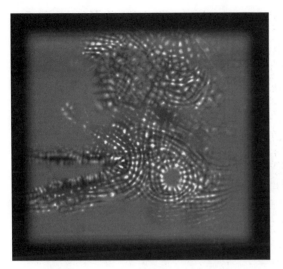

FIGURE **9.46** *With and without a diffusion map.*

which is referred to as indirect light. Indirect light is the light that reflects off objects, which lights up the scene with a great deal more light than a single direct light source. The reason your model looks too dark after you apply the diffusion maps is that you don't have enough light in the scene. Look at the difference between typical direct lighting and indirect lighting in Figure 9.47.

Figure 9.47 shows Chubbs with his diffusion maps applied. Figure 9.47(A) shows typical single-light source direct lighting, and Figure 9.47(B) shows the impact of properly

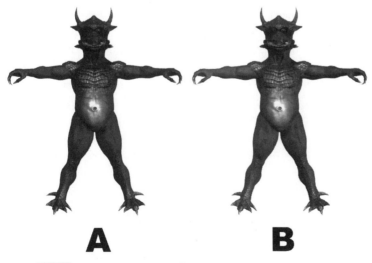

FIGURE **9.47** *Properly lighting your characters.*

lighting the character with additional indirect lights. Be sure to add enough light in your scene when you're experimenting with diffusion maps. You'll need to add lights on all sides of the character for proper lighting. A lighting setup like the one shown in Figure 9.48 is suggested.

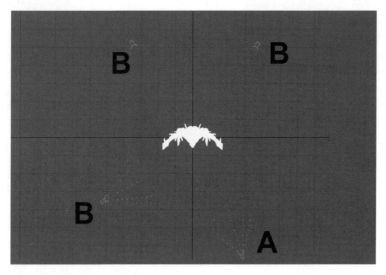

FIGURE 9.48   *The placement of indirect lights.*

The light indicated with an A is the main, direct light source with a value of 100%. The lights indicated with a B are the indirect lights with a value of around 25–30 percent. This setup will provide you with an optimal lighting scenario for testing your diffusion image maps.

For photorealistic rendering you need to apply more light in the scene. Of course, you need to make sure that the diffusion on your props have been lowered, or they will become washed out by the light. Remember, no object in reality has 100 percent diffusion. Take the time to seek out additional information about photorealistic lighting. The more you understand about lighting, the more effectively you'll be able to surface your characters.

Be sure to experiment with the your light's intensity settings when working with diffusion maps until you get that perfect, photorealistic look you're after.

Now that you've covered the types of image maps and how they are made, you're ready to take a look at how to create seamless image maps so your surfaces come together as a single, natural surface.

CREATING SEAMLESS IMAGE MAPS

One of the biggest challenges you're faced with when dealing with very large and complex image maps is to get them to line up with one another in such a way that no one can tell where one image map begins and the other ends. If either the color, bump, specularity, or diffusion pattern is even the slightest bit different, a seam will become apparent. This can really destroy the photorealistic effect that we're trying to achieve, since living creatures don't have seams.

The best way to insure against seams is to be certain that each of the edges where the maps meet one another is the same color (RGB value), and the same pattern.

Figure 9.49 shows two bump maps. The one on the left shows the bump map for a section of the front of Chubbs, and the one on the right shows the bump map for a section of his side. Since the edge of the map for the front is not a solid uniform gray value, but rather a pattern of light and dark, you need to use the clone tool in Photoshop to make the images seamless. Clone the edge of the front image map and apply it to the edge of the side map. This will insure that the bump pattern will be the same for both the front and side maps of Chubbs, and that no seam will be evident.

This same technique will work for your specularity and diffusion maps. If you want to save yourself the time of having to open up both the new image map and the one you're cloning, you can create an edge template to be used for the edges of each and every new bump, specularity, or diffusion map. These templates can simply be 100 by 200 pixel images that consist entirely of the patterns you've decided to use for the edges of the bump, specularity, and diffusion maps. Figure 9.50 shows the edge template used for Chubbs.

As you can see, the edge template can make seamless surfacing a great deal easier. One way to insure that this technique will work is to make sure that your maps are all the same scale. That is, if the map for the front of your creature, from head to toe, is 1000 pixels high, the map for the side view (from head to toe) also must be 1000 pixels high. This

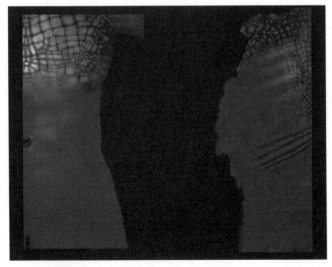

FIGURE **9.49** *Creating seamless image maps.*

FIGURE **9.50** *Chubbs' edge template.*

way the surface details will be on the same scale and have a one-to-one relationship with one another. You don't want the skin pores on the side of the leg to be twice the size of the ones on the front!

As previously discussed, to insure the color image maps all match up seamlessly you need to use the RGB values that you wrote down for the predominant color of the front color image map. Naturally there may be some variation in the skin color, particularly if you have applied the chaos of reality. To make the seams blend, simply use the cloning tool as discussed earlier.

Now that you have a handle on preventing seams, let's take a look at the quality control portion of the surfacing process.

CREATING TEST RENDERS AND TWEAKING

Being impulsive by nature, I tend to apply each new image map to the model right after I've created it. This allows for immediate inspection of the image map. So if the image map for the color of the front (even before applying any detail to it) is too dark, too light, too saturated, or too whatever, you can fix it and get it right before moving on to all the other color maps. Also, this gives an idea of what the color map will look like in the final render of the image. Another benefit of this technique is that it can push you into new directions that you may not have gone if you were dealing strictly with the color map by itself. By allowing the image to evolve, with each render being a sort of incubating period between revisions, you can achieve a much more thoroughly thought-out vision of how you want the character to look.

Once all of the maps are painted and attached to the model's surface, you're ready to begin methodically scrutinizing how these maps interact with one another. This is a point that can be both rewarding and humiliating, for it's the point where you can see where the maps succeed and where they fail. It is crucial to be as objective as possible at this point. Often, requesting someone else to lend a pair of critical, objective eyes can pay off at this stage. Everyone hates criticism but it's actually good since it pushes you to do better the next time.

Load the model into your 3D application, create several test renders from different angles, and go over it with a fine-tooth comb. Often it's helpful to render out an animation of the model doing a 360 degree rotation. This animation needn't be very long, but should be at least three or four seconds so you have enough time to see the details. Animations give you the best indication of how well light plays across the bump mapped and specularity mapped surfaces. You'll be surprised at how realistic the surfaces look when they interact with the light.

Basically, test, test, and of course, test! Unless you're part machine, you're bound to find problem areas in these stills and animations, areas where the maps don't line up quite right, the nose is too shiny, the bump maps are out of alignment, or your maps are stretching. Tackle each problem area as it becomes evident to you. You can never create too many test renders. It's paramount for creating truly seamless surfaces. I must have made at least 100 test renders of Chubbs to identify all the problem areas.

At this stage most of the bull work has been done. In most cases, a problem exists only in a relatively small portion of the image map, so open up the image map where the problem exists, fix it and rerender the results until you're completely satisfied with your work. It's worth the effort, particularly after you get the favorable feedback from the viewers.

WRAPPING IT UP

It seems like a long road to creating photorealistic image maps for a believable 3D character, and it is. But in the end, the results should more than compensate you for your labors. After a bit of practice you'll find it really doesn't take that long to create photorealistic surfaces. My first character took nearly two months to surface; now I do them in less than a week.

Start off slowly with your surfacing goals and gradually increase the surface detail as you become accustomed to the techniques. Whatever you do, don't surface a character like Chubbs until you have done a few characters with simpler surfaces. You don't want to blow out your pilot light before you've heated the house. It's Your Turn Now!

It's time for you to put the concepts in this book to good use. Start slow and gradually increase your detail until you are spitting out photorealistic creatures on a weekly basis.

Be sure to send me some renders of your creature creations — I'd love to see what you've done. Feel free to send your images to bill@komodostudio.com

So what are you waiting for? Get to work!

INDEX

WHAT'S ON THE CD

Included with this book is a companion CD that contains a variety of support materials for the tutorials on creating 3D creatures. The support materials are provided in common format that is compatible with the program being utilized for the tutorial. Below you'll find a detailed description of the contents on the companion CD.

Here's what you'll find on the CD:

Chapter 1
Figures   Color copies of the Figures for Chapter 1.

Chapter 2   A sample QuickTime file of Sgt. Spore Walking
Figures   Color copies of the Figures for Chapter 2.

Chapter 3   Model support files for the LightWave Metaform tutorial
Figures   Color copies of the Figures for Chapter 3.

Chapter 4
Figures   Color copies of the Figures for Chapter 4.
Munch   Support model and surface files for the LightWave Advanced Metaform Modeling tutorial

Chapter 5   Template files for the Patch tutorial
Figures   Color copies of the Figures for Chapter 5.
Scenes   Support MAX scene files for the Patch Modeling tutorial

Chapter 6   Template files for the Patch tutorial
Figures   Color copies of the Figures for Chapter 6.
Knuckles   Support MAX scene files for the Spline Modeling tutorial

Chapter 7
Figures   Color copies of the Figures for Chapter 7.
Alberto   Support model and surface files for the Animation Master Spline Patch tutorial
Primer   Support model files for the Animation Master Spline Patch tutorial

Chapter 8   A sample rotation animation of the Steele action hero
Figures   Color copies of the Figures for Chapter 8.
Steele   Support model files for the Advanced Animation Master Spline Patch tutorial
Steele/Maps   Support surface files for the Steele action hero

Chapter9
Figures   Color copies of the Figures for Chapter 9.

HARDWARE/SOFTWARE REQUIREMENTS

You'll need a relatively serious computer to do advanced creature modeling. Particularly since there is a lot of detail in the creatures, requiring a healthy video card and ample supply of RAM. I recommend at least a 200MHZ processor, 4MB OpenGL (8MB is best) video card and 64MB RAM (128MB is best). This requirement applies whether you are using an IBM Compatible or Macintosh computer. Below you'll find the software requirements.

Chapters 3&4: You'll need an Intel, Alpha, SGI or Mac version LightWave 5.5 for the tutorials in these chapters. You can use LightWave 5.0 but you won't be able to perform a few of the steps, such as using the Knife Tool. In place of the knife tool you'll have to use Add points.

Chapters 5&6: You'll need 3D Studio Max 1.0 or Higher to perform the tutorials in these chapters. The chapters focus on Max 2.o but the features are the same in version 1.0.

Chapters 7&8: You'll need a PC or Mac version of Animation Master or Martin Hash 3D 4.0 or higher to perform the tutorials in these chapters.

Chapter 9: You'll need a PC or Mac version of Photoshop 3.0 or higher to perform the tutorials in this chapter. You can use another painting program but you'll have to compensate for the specific references to Photoshop features.

Ask a Tough Question. Expect Solid Direction.

Help on the Horizon. Arnold Information Technology points corporations and organizations to information that get results. Access our experienced professionals who can help senior managers identify options and chart a course.

Since 1991, we've proven we can help in a range of capacities:

BUSINESS DEVELOPMENT
- Knowledge Management
- Competitive Intelligence
- Marketing & Sales
- Acquisitions & Mergers
- Patent Evaluations
- Technology Startups

INFORMATION TECHNOLOGY SERVICES
- Intranets, and Extranets
- Web-based Technologies
- Database Management
- Digital Work Flow Planning
- Information Engineering

ACTION FROM IDEAS. We helped build the service known as the Top 5% of the Internet, found at www.lycos.com. Our latest competitive intelligence tool can be explored at abcompass.com. It builds a personal daily news feed that only you receive.

A TEAM WITH STRATEGIC VISION. Our seasoned consultants can build, research, prototype, budget, plan, assess, and tackle some of the toughest jobs in information technology. Our managers have taken a leadership role in U.S. corporations and elsewhere in the world.

GET WHERE YOU WANT TO GO. TODAY. We move corporations and organizations into the future. Our work spans a variety of industries, including publishing, telecommunications, government agencies, investment banks, and startups. We welcome confidential, informal discussions of your challenges and opportunities.

CONTACT:

Stephen E. Arnold, President
Arnold Information Technology
P.O. Box 320
Harrods Creek, Kentucky 40027
Voice: 502 228-1966
E-Mail: ait@arnoldit.com
Facsimile: 502 228-0548